ORDER OF BATTLE
of the
BRITISH ARMIES IN FRANCE
(Including Lines of Communication Units)

AND

ORDER OF BATTLE OF THE
PORTUGUESE EXPEDITIONARY
FORCE.

NOVEMBER 11th, 1918.

The Naval & Military Press Ltd

Published by

The Naval & Military Press Ltd
Unit 5 Riverside, Brambleside,
Bellbrook Industrial Estate,
Uckfield, East Sussex,
TN22 1QQ England

Tel: +44 (0) 1825 749494
Fax: +44 (0) 1825 765701

www.naval-military-press.com
www.nmarchive.com

*In reprinting in facsimile from the original, any imperfections are inevitably reproduced
and the quality may fall short of modern type and cartographic standards.*

NOTES

THIS BOOK HAS BEEN REVISED IN ACCORDANCE WITH ALL INFORMATION AVAILABLE ON *NOVEMBER 11th, 1918*. REPRINTS OR AMENDMENTS WILL BE ISSUED AS MAY BE FOUND NECESSARY FROM TIME TO TIME.

THE HEADQUARTERS OF ARMY SERVICE CORPS, AND TEMPORARY ATTACHMENTS OF UNITS TO FORMATIONS FOR SHORT PERIODS, ARE NOT SHOWN IN THIS BOOK.

SECRET.   COPY No..

O.B.
―――
17

ORDER OF BATTLE
of the
BRITISH ARMIES IN FRANCE
(Including Lines of Communication Units)

AND

ORDER OF BATTLE OF THE
PORTUGUESE EXPEDITIONARY
FORCE.

NOVEMBER 11th, 1918.

GENERAL STAFF, G.H.Q.
November 11th, 1918.

Press A—11/18.

CONTENTS.

	PAGE
ORGANIZATION IN DETAIL—	
G.H.Q. TROOPS	5, 6

ARMY TROOPS—

	PAGE
1ST ARMY	7, 8, 9, 10
2ND ARMY	11, 12, 13, 14
3RD ARMY	15, 16, 17, 18
4TH ARMY	19, 20, 21, 22
5TH ARMY	23, 24, 25
R.A.F.	26, 27
TANK CORPS	28

CORPS TROOPS—

	PAGE
CAVALRY CORPS	29
I. ARMY CORPS	29
II. ARMY CORPS	29
III. ARMY CORPS	30
IV. ARMY CORPS	30
V. ARMY CORPS	30
VI. ARMY CORPS	31
VII. ARMY CORPS	31
VIII. ARMY CORPS	31
IX. ARMY CORPS	32
X. ARMY CORPS	32
XI. ARMY CORPS	32
XIII. ARMY CORPS	32
XV. ARMY CORPS	33
XVII. ARMY CORPS	33
XIX. ARMY CORPS	33
XXII. ARMY CORPS	34
AUSTRALIAN ARMY CORPS	34
CANADIAN ARMY CORPS	34
PORTUGUESE ARMY CORPS	35

DIVISIONS—

	PAGE
1ST CAVALRY	36
2ND CAVALRY	36
3RD CAVALRY	37
GUARDS DIVISION	38
1ST DIVISION	38
2ND DIVISION	39
3RD DIVISION	39
4TH DIVISION	40
5TH DIVISION	40
6TH DIVISION	41
8TH DIVISION	41
9TH (SCOTTISH) DIVISION	42
11TH DIVISION	42
12TH (EASTERN) DIVISION	43
14TH DIVISION	43
15TH (SCOTTISH) DIVISION	44

DIVISIONS—Continued.

	PAGE
16TH DIVISION	44
17TH (NORTHERN) DIVISION	45
18TH (EASTERN) DIVISION	45
19TH (WESTERN) DIVISION	46
20TH (LIGHT) DIVISION	46
21ST DIVISION	47
24TH DIVISION	47
25TH DIVISION	48
29TH DIVISION	48
30TH DIVISION	49
31ST DIVISION	49
32ND DIVISION	50
33RD DIVISION	50
34TH DIVISION	51
35TH DIVISION	51
36TH (ULSTER) DIVISION	52
37TH DIVISION	52
38TH (WELSH) DIVISION	53
39TH DIVISION	53
40TH DIVISION	54
41ST DIVISION	54
42ND (E. LANCS.) DIVISION	55
46TH (N. MIDLAND) DIVISION	55
47TH (LONDON) DIVISION	56
49TH (W. RIDING) DIVISION	56
50TH (N'UMBRIAN) DIVISION	57
51ST (HIGHLAND) DIVISION	57
52ND (LOWLAND) DIVISION	58
55TH (W. LANCS.) DIVISION	58
56TH (LONDON) DIVISION	59
57TH (W. LANCS.) DIVISION	59
58TH (LONDON) DIVISION	60
59TH (N. MIDLAND) DIVISION	60
61ST (S. MIDLAND) DIVISION	61
62ND (W. RIDING) DIVISION	61
63RD (ROYAL NAVAL) DIVISION	62
66TH (E. LANCS.) DIVISION	62
74TH (YEOMANRY) DIVISION	63
1ST AUSTRALIAN DIVISION	63
2ND AUSTRALIAN DIVISION	64
3RD AUSTRALIAN DIVISION	64
4TH AUSTRALIAN DIVISION	65
5TH AUSTRALIAN DIVISION	65
1ST CANADIAN DIVISION	66
2ND CANADIAN DIVISION	66
3RD CANADIAN DIVISION	67
4TH CANADIAN DIVISION	67
NEW ZEALAND	68
1ST PORTUGUESE DIVISION	68
2ND PORTUGUESE DIVISION	69

	PAGE
TRANSPORTATION UNITS	70
L. OF C. UNITS	71, 72, 73, 74
INDEX TO ARMIES, ARMY CORPS AND DIVISIONS	75
INDEX TO BRIGADES	76
INDEX TO UNITS	77 to end.

ORGANIZATION IN DETAIL.

G.H.Q. TROOPS.

Unit.	Attached to

Mounted Troops—
  1 Troop 17th Lancers.

Artillery—
  ANTI-AIRCRAFT ARTILLERY—
    A.A. School of Gunnery
    No. 14 Section (2—13-pr. guns)
    No. 75 Section (2—3-in. guns).

Engineers—
  Special Brigade, R.E.
    H.Q. and Depot.
    Special (Cylinder) Cos.
      "A"
      "B"
      "C"
      "D"
      "E"
      "F"
      "G"
      "H"
      "J"
      "K"
      "L"
      "M"
      "N"
      "O"
      "P"
      "Q"
    Special (Projector) Co.
      "Z"
    Special (Mortar) Cos.
      No. 1
      No. 2
      No. 3
      No. 4
  Printing Co., R.E.
  Depot Field Survey Bn.
    Experimental Sound Ranging Section.
    School for Observers.
  29th G.H.Q. Troops Co., R.E.
  Camouflage Park.
  Meteorological Section.

Signal Service—
  H.Q. "L" Signal Bn.
  Nos. 8, 10, 44, 56, 79, 82, 89 and 92 (Motor) Airline Secs.
  Nos. 7 and 8 Light Motor Set Wireless Sections.

Pigeon Service—
  Nos. 84, 119, 125, 127, 149, 150, 152, 157, 158, 160 to 170 Horse Drawn Mobile Lofts.

Infantry—
  1st R. Guernsey L.I.
  1/1st H.A.C.

G.H.Q. Troops—*continued.*

Unit.	Attached To
A.S.C.— 　No. 1 G.H.Q. Reserve M.T. Co. (68 Co., A.S.C.) 　No. 2　　"　　　　"　　(56 Co., A.S.C.) 　No. 3　　"　　　　"　　(51 Co., A.S.C.) 　No. 4　　"　　　　"　　(72 Co., A.S.C.) 　No. 5　　"　　　　"　　(400 Co., A.S.C.) 　No. 6　　"　　　　"　　(399 Co., A.S.C.) 　No. 7　　"　　　　"　　(76 Co., A.S.C.) 　No. 8　　"　　　　"　　(341 Co., A.S.C.) 　No. 9　　"　　　　"　　(79 Co., A.S.C.) 　No. 10　"　　　　"　　(587 Co., A.S.C.) 　No. 11　"　　　　"　　(588 Co., A.S.C.) 　No. 12　"　　　　"　　(45 Co., A.S.C.) 　No. 13　"　　　　"　　(959 Co., A.S.C.) 　No. 14　"　　　　"　　(960 Co., A.S.C.) 　No. 15　"　　　　"　　(1076 Co., A.S.C.) 　No. 16　"　　　　"　　(1077 Co., A.S.C.) 　No. 17　"　　　　"　　(1131 Co., A.S.C.) 　No. 18　"　　　　"　　(1132 Co., A.S.C.) 　No. 19　"　　　　"　　(1117 Co,, A.S.C.) 　No. 20　"　　　　"　　(1118 Co., A.S.C.) 　No. 21　"　　　　"　　(1128 Co., A.S.C.) 　No. 22　"　　　　"　　(1148 Co., A.S.C.) 　A.S.C. Workshop for D.G.T. (975 Co., A.S.C.) 　M.T. Inspection Unit. 　G.H.Q. Troops Train (26 Co., A.S.C.) 　G.H.Q. Troops M.T. Co. (55 Co., A.S.C.) 　103rd Aux. (Petrol) Co., Agriculture (1051 Co., A.S.C.) 　105th Aux. (Petrol) Co. (1053 Co., A.S.C.) 　Auxiliary (Omnibus) Companies— 　　1st (90 Co., A.S.C.), 2nd (91 Co., A.S.C.), 15th (405 Co., A.S.C.), 　　16th (563 Co., A.S.C.), 18th (588 Co., A.S.C.), 50th (92 　　Co., A.S.C.), 51st (339 Co., A.S.C.)	Cavalry Corps.
Reserve Parks— 　　Nos. 1 Cav. (9 Co., A.S.C.), 2 Cav. (84 Co., A.S.C.), 3 Cav. (174 　　Co., A.S.C.), 5 Cav. (670 Co., A.S.C.) 　Army Auxiliary (Horse) Companies— 　　Nos. 1 (425 Co., A.S.C.), 3 (571 Co., A.S.C.), 4 (334 Co., A.S.C.), 　　5 (129 Co., A.S.C.), 7 (30 Co., A.S.C.), 8 (88 Co., A.S.C.), 9 (125 　　Co., A.S.C.), 10 (20 Co., A.S.C.), 11 (12 Co., A.S.C.), 12 (5 Co., 　　A.S.C.), 13 (99 Co., A.S.C.), 14 (130 Co., A.S.C.), 15 (162 Co., 　　A.S.C.), 16 (327 Co., A.S.C.), 17 (310 Co., A.S.C.), 18 (165 Co., 　　A.S.C.), 19 (166 Co., A.S.C.), 20 (167 Co., A.S.C.), 21 (445 Co., 　　A.S.C.), 22 (444 Co., A.S.C.), 1st Cdn. (446 Co., A.S.C.), 2nd 　　Cdn. (680 Co., A.S.C.) 　Cavalry Divl. Aux. (Horse) Cos.— 　　Nos. 4 (577 Co., A.S.C.), 5 (578 Co., A.S.C.) **Medical—** 　Military Hospital. 　20th F. Amb. 　No. 1 Motor Amb. Convoy (418 Co., A.S.C.) 　Nos. 5, 7, 30 Sanitary Squads. **Labour Corps—** 　Area Employment Companies— 　　Nos. 765, 766, 767, 948, 949, 1043.	

ARMY TROOPS.
FIRST ARMY.

Headquarters, First Army.
    18th Cyclist Bn.

Artillery—
  ARMY FIELD ARTILLERY—
    Army Brigades, R.F.A.
      No. 18 (18—18-prs. and 6—4·5-in. howrs.)
      No. 26 (18—18-prs.)
      No. 52 (18—18-prs. and 6—4·5-in. howrs.)
      No. 77 (18—18-prs. and 6—4·5-in. howrs.)
      No. 126 (24—18-prs.)
      No. 147 (18—18-prs. and 6—4·5-in. howrs.)
      No. 175 (18—18-prs. and 6—4·5-in. howrs.)
      No. 189 (18—18-prs. and 6—4·5-in. howrs.)
      No. 242 (18—18-prs. and 6—4·5-in. howrs.)
      No. 277 (18—18-prs. and 6—4·5-in. howrs.)
      No. 282 (18—18-prs. and 6—4·5-in. howrs.)
      No. 293 (18—18-prs. and 6—4·5-in. howrs.)
      No. 311 (18—18-prs. and 6—4·5-in. howrs.)
      No. 8 Cdn. (18—18-prs. and 6—4·5-in. howrs.)

  5TH CANADIAN DIVISIONAL ARTILLERY—
    13th Bde., Canadian Field Artillery (52, 53, 55 and 51 (D) Cdn. Batts.) (18—18-prs. and 6—4·5-in. howrs.).
    14th Bde., Canadian Field Artillery (60, 61, 66 and 58 (D) Cdn. Batts.) (18—18-prs. and 6—4·5-in. howrs.).
    V/5 C. Heavy Trench Mortar Battery.
    X/5 C. Trench Mortar Battery.
    Y/5 C. Trench Mortar Battery.

  BRIGADES, R.G.A.—

Brigade	Batteries
1st (Mobile)	16 Heavy Battery (6—60-pr. guns) 21 Heavy Battery (6—60-pr. guns) 49 Siege Battery (6—6-in. howrs.) 254 Siege Battery (6—6-in. howrs.)
7th (Mixed)	115 Heavy Battery (6—60-pr. guns) 125 Heavy Battery (6—60-pr. guns) 27 Siege Battery (6—6-in. howrs.) 28 Siege Battery (6—6-in. howrs.) 198 Siege Battery (6—8-in. howrs.) 158 Siege Battery (6—9·2-in. howrs.)
8th (Howitzer—9·2-in.)	16 Siege Battery (6—6-in. howrs.) 235 Siege Battery (4—6-in. howrs.) 290 Siege Battery (4—6-in. howrs.) 90 Siege Battery (6—9·2-in. howrs.)
16th (Mobile)	23 Heavy Battery (6—60-pr. guns) 146 Heavy Battery (6—60-pr. guns) 204 Siege Battery (6—6-in. howrs.) 280 Siege Battery (6—6-in. howrs.)
19th (Howitzer—9·2-in.)	288 Siege Battery (4—6-in. howrs.) 297 Siege Battery (6—6-in. howrs.) 321 Siege Battery (4—6-in. howrs.) 46 Siege Battery (4—9·2-in. howrs.)
29th (Mobile)	12 Heavy Battery (6—60-pr. guns) 121 Heavy Battery (6—60-pr. guns) 195 Siege Battery (6—6-in. howrs.) 303 Siege Battery (6—6-in. howrs.)
30th (Howitzer—8-in.)	23 Siege Battery (4—6-in. howrs.) 241 Siege Battery (4—6-in. howrs.) 308 Siege Battery (4—6-in. howrs.) 89 Siege Battery (6—8-in. howrs.)
34th (Howitzer—9·2-in.)	112 Siege Battery (6—6-in. howrs.) 142 Siege Battery (4—6-in. howrs.) 278 Siege Battery (6—6-in. howrs.) 48 Siege Battery (6—9·2-in. howrs.)
40th (Howitzer—8-in.)	40 Siege Battery (4—6-in. howrs.) 186 Siege Battery (4—6-in. howrs.) 196 Siege Battery (4—6-in. howrs.) 256 Siege Battery (6—8-in. howrs.)

ARMY TROOPS—First Army—continued.

Artillery—continued.
BRIGADES, R.G.A.—continued.

45th (Howitzer—9·2-in.) ...
- 32 Siege Battery (6—6-in. howrs.)
- 38 Siege Battery (6—6-in. howrs.)
- 208 Siege Battery (4—6-in. howrs.)
- 62 Siege Battery (4—9·2-in. howrs.)

46th (Mobile) ...
- 133 Heavy Battery (6—60-pr. guns)
- 147 Heavy Battery (6—60-pr. guns)
- 59 Siege Battery (6—6-in. howrs.)
- 81 Siege Battery (6—6-in. howrs.)

50th (S.A.) (Howitzer—8-in.) ...
- 72 (S.A.) Siege Battery (6—6-in. howrs.)
- 74 (S.A.) Siege Battery (6—6-in. howrs.)
- 75 (S.A.) Siege Battery (6—6-in. howrs.)
- 275 Siege Battery (6—8-in. howrs.)

53rd (Mixed) ...
- 136 Heavy Battery (6—60-pr. guns)
- 1/1 Welsh Heavy Battery (6—60-pr. guns)
- 251 Siege Battery (6—6-in. howrs.)
- 252 Siege Battery (6—6-in. howrs.)
- 249 Siege Battery (6—8-in. howrs.)
- 188 Siege Battery (6—9·2-in. howrs.)

67th (Mixed) ...
- 17 Heavy Battery (6—60-pr. guns)
- 110 Heavy Battery (6—60-pr. guns)
- 149 Siege Battery (6—6-in. howrs.)
- 162 Siege Battery (6—6-in. howrs.)
- 234 Siege Battery (6—8-in. howrs.)
- 79 Siege Battery (4—9·2-in. howrs.)

78th (Howitzer—8-in.) ...
- 87 Siege Battery (4—6-in. howrs.)
- 108 Siege Battery (4—6-in. howrs.)
- 139 Siege Battery (4—6-in. howrs.)
- 36 Siege Battery (6—8-in. howrs.)

81st (Mixed) ...
- 31 Heavy Battery (6—60-pr. guns)
- 1/1 Lowland Heavy Battery (6—60-pr. guns)
- 163 Siege Battery (6—6-in. howrs.)
- 179 Siege Battery (6—6-in. howrs.)
- 239 Siege Battery (6—8-in. howrs.)
- 184 Siege Battery (6—9·2-in. howrs.)

91st (Howitzer—9·2-in.) ...
- 140 Siege Battery (6—6-in. howrs.)
- 326 Siege Battery (6—6-in. howrs.)
- 337 Siege Battery (4—6-in. howrs.)
- 96 Siege Battery (4—9·2-in. howrs.)

1st Canadian (Howitzer—9·2-in.)
- 3rd Cdn. Siege Battery (6—6-in. howrs.)
- 7th Cdn. Siege Battery (6—6-in. howrs.)
- 9th Cdn. Siege Battery (6—6-in. howrs.)
- 1st Cdn. Siege Battery (6—9·2-in. howrs.)

2nd Canadian (Mixed) ...
- 1st Cdn. Heavy Battery (6—60-pr. guns)
- 2nd Cdn. Heavy Battery (6—60-pr. guns)
- 2nd Cdn. Siege Battery (6—6-in. howrs.)
- 6th Cdn. Siege Battery (6—6-in. howrs.)
- 4th Cdn. Siege Battery (6—8-in. howrs.)
- 5th Cdn. Siege Battery (6—9·2-in. howrs.)

3rd Canadian (Howitzer—8-in.)
- 10th Cdn. Siege Battery (6—6-in. howrs.)
- 11th Cdn. Siege Battery (6—6-in. howrs.)
- 12th Cdn. Siege Battery (6—6-in. howrs.)
- 8th Cdn. Siege Battery (6—8-in. howrs.)

ARMY BRIGADES, R.G.A.
Nos. 26, 31.

SIEGE BATTERIES, R.G.A. (Unbrigaded)—
(4—6-in. guns.)
Nos. 60, 192, 393, 450, 488, 520, 521, 527, 544.
(9·2-in. and 12-in. guns on railway mountings.)
Nos. (½) 92 (1—12-in. gun), 366, 461 and 523 (2—9·2-in. guns), (½) 543 (1—12-in. gun).
(14-in. guns on railway mountings.)
Nos. (½) 471 (1—14-in. gun), (½) 515 (1—14-in. gun)
(2—12-in. howitzers.)
Nos. 65, 493.
(2—12-in. howitzers on railway mountings.)
Nos. 52, 86, 444, 514 (½).
(15-in. howitzers.)
No. 8.

ARMY TROOPS—First Army—continued.

Artillery—*continued.*
  ANTI-AIRCRAFT ARTILLERY—
    H.Q., First Army Anti-Aircraft Defence Commander—
      "C" Anti-Aircraft Battery
        - No. 20 Section (2—13-pr. guns)
        - No. 69 Section (2—13-pr. guns)
        - No. 143 Section (2—13-pr. guns)
        - No. 158 Section (2—13-pr. guns)
        - No. 202 Section (2—3-in. guns)
      "E" Canadian Anti-Aircraft Battery
        - No. 1 Cdn. Section (2—13-pr. guns)
        - No. 2 Cdn. Section (2—13-pr. guns)
        - No. 3 Cdn. Section (2—13-pr. guns)
        - No. 4 Cdn. Section (2—13-pr. guns)
        - No. 5 Cdn. Section (2—13-pr. guns)
      "K" Anti-Aircraft Battery
        - No. 9 Section (2—13-pr. guns)
        - No. 25 Section (2—13-pr. guns)
        - No. 134 Section (2—13-pr. guns)
        - No. 168 Section (2—13-pr. guns)
        - No. 226 Section (2—3-in. guns)
        - No. 230 Section (2—3-in. guns)
      "Y" Anti-Aircraft Battery
        - No. 7 Section (2—13-pr. guns)
        - No. 49 Section (2—13-pr. guns)
        - No. 79 Section (2—13-pr. guns)
        - No. 133 Section (2—13-pr. guns)
        - No. 156 Section (2—13-pr. guns)
        - No. 162 Section (2—13-pr. guns)

Engineers—
  411th and 550th (Glamorgan) Field Cos.
  Advanced R.E. Parks.
    Nos. 1 and 4.
  Army Troops Companies.
    Nos. 25, 216, 217, 282, 565, 568, 1st Cdn., 2nd Cdn., 3rd Cdn., 4th Cdn. and 5th Cdn.
  Siege Company.
    No. 1 R. Monmouth (S.R.).
  Tunnelling Companies.
    Nos. 172, 175, 176, 179, 185.
  Electrical and Mechanical Company.
    No. 350.
    No. 4 Boring Section.
  Army Workshop Co., R.E.
    No. 1.
  1st Field Survey Bn.
    "H," "L," "P," "T," "Y," "Z" Sound Ranging Sections.
    Nos. 4, 10, 11, 18, 21 Observation Groups.
  Anti-Aircraft Searchlight Sections.
    Nos. 3, 5, 9, 13, 15, 18, 22, 25, 32, 39, 42.
  A.A. Searchlight Co., Cdn. Engineers.
  Pontoon Parks (H.T.).
    No. 1.
  Transportation (Works) Co.
    No. 223.

Signal Service—
  1ST ARMY SIGNAL Co.—
    Nos. 29, 30, 52, 70 (Motor) Airline Sections.
    "BP" and "LZ" Cable Sections.
    No. 1 Light Railway Signal Company.
    No. 1 Signal Construction Company.
    Nos. 1, 2, 3, 4, 18, 31, 33 Area Signal Detachments.

Pigeon Service—
  Motor Mobile Loft—
    No. 5.
  Horse Drawn Mobile Lofts—
    Nos. 1, 7, 9, 17, 28, 32, 34, 46, 49, 123, 128, 131, 144, 159.

ARMY TROOPS—First Army—*continued.*

Pigeon Service—*continued.*
   Fixed Lofts—
     Condette.
     Bryas.
     Fosse 7, Lens.

Infantry—
   43rd (Garr.) Bn., R. Fus.—
     Nos. 1 and 2 Garrison Cos.
   44th (Garr.) Bn., R. Fus.—
     No. 1 A.A. Co.
   16th (Garr.) Bn., Yorks. L.I. ("A" Co.).
   9th Bn. B. W. Indies R.

M.G. Units—
   No. 1 (1st L.G.) Bn. Guards M.G. Regt.
   No. 3 (R.H.G.) Bn. Guards M.G. Regt.
   102nd (Lincs. and E. Riding Yeo.) Bn. M.G. Corps.
   103rd (City and 3rd Cty. of London Yeo.) Bn. M.G. Corps.

Military Police—
   Traffic Control Units—
     No. 1 Squadron.
     No. 1 Company (H.Q. and 1½ platoons).

A.S.C.—
   No. 10 Pontoon Park (M.T.) (647 Co., A.S.C.).
   1st Army Troops M.T. Co. (384 Co., A.S.C.).
   61st Aux. (Petrol) Co. (932 Co., A.S.C.).
   4th M.T. Mobile Repair Unit (657 Co., A.S.C.).
   No. 256 Co. (attached Heavy Artillery).
   No. 1 Workshop for Anti-Aircraft Guns (422 Co., A.S.C.).
   No. 3 Water Tank (M.T.) Co., (986 Co., A.S.C.).

Medical—
   Nos. 8, 13, 31, 42 Motor Ambulance Convoys (326, 566, 705, 1049 Cos., A.S.C.)
   Nos. 1, 2, 6, 7, 22, 23, 30, 33, 42, 57, 1st Cdn., 4th Cdn. Casualty Clearing Stations.
   Nos. 12, 19 and Advanced Depots of Medical Stores.
   Nos. 2, 3, 6 and 21 Mobile Laboratories.
   Nos. 1 and 6 Mobile X-Ray Units.
   No. 3 Mobile Dental Unit.
   No.   Stationary Hospital.
   Nos. 8, 10, 40, 41, 63, 1st Cdn., 2nd Cdn., 3rd Cdn., 4th Cdn. and 5th Cdn. Sanitary Sections.
   Nos. 6, 8, 34, 58, 59 Sanitary Squads.

Veterinary—
   Nos. 18, 22 and Cdn. Evacuating Stations.

Ordnance—
   No. 1 Heavy Mobile Workshop.
   No.   Medium Mobile Workshop.
   No. 30 Light Mobile Workshop.
   No. 1 Ordnance Gun Park.
   No. 1 Officers' Clothing Depot.
   Nos. 3 to 7, 12 to 16, 18, 19, 23 to 26, 57, 61, 72, 77, 78, 107, 108 Ordnance Amm. Secs.

Forestry Units—
   No. 365 Forestry Co., R.E.
   No. 2 Cdn. Forestry Co.

Labour Corps—
   LABOUR GROUP HEADQUARTERS—
     Nos. 21, 22, 23, 29, 55, 71, 88, Canadian.
   LABOUR COMPANIES—
     Nos. 2, 3, 18, 20, 37, 39, 45, 47, 50, 51, 54, 55, 80, 89, 108, 112, 127, 135, 136, 137, 152, 159, 163, 164, 169, 170, 180, 181, 182, 183, 192, 195, 704, 712, 718, 723, 733, 735, 1001.
   AREA EMPLOYMENT COMPANIES—
     Nos. 255, 256, 278, 286, 737, 755, 756, 826, 827 and 947.
   AREA EMPLOYMENT (ARTIZAN) COMPANIES—
     Nos. 928 and 929.
   AGRICULTURAL COMPANY—
     No. 1037.
   CHINESE LABOUR COMPANIES—
     Nos. 42, 43, 58, 73, 80, 84, 86, 99, 114, 118, 121, 122, 131, 147, 162, 167, 185.

Army Printing and Stationery Services—
   No. 1 Advanced Photographic Section.

ARMY TROOPS—SECOND ARMY.

Headquarters, Second Army.

Artillery—

ARMY FIELD ARTILLERY—

Army Brigades, R.F.A.

- No. 11 (18—18-prs. and 6—4·5-in. howrs.)
- No. 23 (18—18-prs. and 6—4·5-in. howrs.)
- No. 28 (18—18-prs. and 6—4·5-in. howrs.)
- No. 38 (18—18-prs. and 6—4·5-in. howrs.)
- No. 64 (18—18-prs. and 6—4·5-in. howrs.)
- No. 96 (24—18-prs.)
- No. 113 (18—18-prs. and 6—4·5-in. howrs.)
- No. 119 (18—18-prs. and 6—4·5-in. howrs.)

BRIGADES, R.G.A.—

2nd (Howitzer—9·2-in.)
- 177 Siege Battery (6—6-in. howrs.)
- 250 Siege Battery (6—6-in. howrs.)
- 352 Siege Battery (6—6-in. howrs.)
- 66 Siege Battery (6—9·2-in. howrs.)

3rd (Mixed)
- 48 Heavy Battery (6—60-pr. guns)
- 112 Heavy Battery (6—60-pr. guns)
- 88 Siege Battery (6—6-in. howrs.)
- 268 Siege Battery (6—6-in. howrs.)
- 152 Siege Battery (6—8-in. howrs.)
- 21 Siege Battery (6—9·2-in. howrs.)

4th (Mixed)
- 131 Heavy Battery (6—60-pr. guns)
- 2/1 N. Midland Heavy Battery (6—60-pr. guns)
- 223 Siege Battery (6—6-in. howrs.)
- 301 Siege Battery (6—6-in. howrs.)
- 261 Siege Battery (6—8-in. howrs.)
- 129 Siege Battery (6—9·2-in. howrs.)

6th (Mixed)
- 109 Heavy Battery (6—60-pr. guns)
- 114 Heavy Battery (6—60-pr. guns)
- 111 Siege Battery (6—6-in. howrs.)
- 245 Siege Battery (6—6-in. howrs.)
- 227 Siege Battery (6—8-in. howrs.)
- 42 Siege Battery (4—9·2-in. howrs.)

10th (Mobile)
- 150 Heavy Battery (6—60-pr. guns)
- 159 Heavy Battery (6—60-pr. guns)
- 113 Siege Battery (6—6-in. howrs.)
- 226 Siege Battery (6—6-in. howrs.)

33rd (Howitzer—8-in.)
- 31 Siege Battery (4—6-in. howrs.)
- 279 Siege Battery (6—6-in. howrs.)
- 298 Siege Battery (4—6-in. howrs.)
- 221 Siege Battery (6—8-in. howrs.)

36th (Aus.) (Mixed)
- 140 Heavy Battery (6—60-pr. guns)
- 151 Heavy Battery (6—60-pr. guns)
- 155 Siege Battery (6—6-in. howrs.)
- 353 Siege Battery (6—6-in. howrs.)
- 1st Aus. Siege Battery (6—8-in. howrs.)
- 2nd Aus. Siege Battery (6—9·2-in. howrs.)

43rd (Howitzer—9·2-in.)
- 147 Siege Battery (6—6-in. howrs.)
- 190 Siege Battery (4—6-in. howrs.)
- 351 Siege Battery (6—6-in. howrs.)
- 154 Siege Battery (6—9·2-in. howrs.)

59th (Howitzer—8-in.)
- 37 Siege Battery (6—6-in. howrs.)
- 335 Siege Battery (4—6-in. howrs.)
- 350 Siege Battery (4—6-in. howrs.)
- 30 Siege Battery (6—8-in. howrs.)

64th (Howitzer—8-in.)
- 100 Siege Battery (4—6-in. howrs.)
- 101 Siege Battery (4—6-in. howrs.)
- 102 Siege Battery (4—6-in. howrs.)
- 61 Siege Battery (6—8-in. howrs.)

65th (Howitzer—9·2 in.)
- 115 Siege Battery (4—6-in. howrs.)
- 202 Siege Battery (4—6-in. howrs.)
- 212 Siege Battery (4—6-in. howrs.)
- 118 Siege Battery (6—9·2-in. howrs.)

70th (Howitzer—9·2-in.)
- 15 Siege Battery (6—6-in. howrs.)
- 157 Siege Battery (6—6-in. howrs.)
- 217 Siege Battery (6—6-in. howrs.)
- 12 Siege Battery (6—9·2-in. howrs.

ARMY TROOPS—Second Army—continued.

Artillery—continued.

BRIGADES, R.G.A.—continued.

77th Mixed
- 9 Heavy Battery (6—60-pr. guns)
- 26 Heavy Battery (6—60-pr. guns)
- 116 Siege Battery (6—6-in. howrs.)
- 119 Siege Battery (6—6-in. howrs.)
- 286 Siege Battery (6—8-in. howrs.)
- 191 Siege Battery (6—9·2-in. howrs.)

86th (Mobile)
- 141 Heavy Battery (6—60-pr. guns)
- 1/1 Wessex Heavy Battery (6—60-pr. guns)
- 203 Siege Battery (6—6-in. howrs.)
- 324 Siege Battery (6—6-in. howrs.)

87th (Mobile)
- 154 Heavy Battery (6—60-pr. guns)
- 156 Heavy Battery (6—60-pr. guns)
- 194 Siege Battery (6—6-in. howrs.)
- 219 Siege Battery (6—6-in. howrs.)

99th (Howitzer—8-in.)
- 282 Siege Battery (4—6-in. howrs.)
- 285 Siege Battery (6—6-in. howrs.)
- 405 Siege Battery (4—6-in. howrs.)
- 151 Siege Battery (6—8-in. howrs.)

ARMY BRIGADES, R.G.A.—
Nos. 25, 72.

SIEGE BATTERIES, R.G.A. (Unbrigaded).
(*4—6-in. guns.*)
Nos. 7, 29, 187, 198, 479, 526, 528, 546.
(*2—9·2-in. guns on railway mountings.*)
Nos. 45, 53 (½).
(*2—12-in. howitzers.*)
Nos. 85, 375, No. 2 (R.M.A.).
(*2—12-in. howitzers on railway mountings.*)
Nos. 22, 63, 82, 104, 359, 381.
(*15-in. howitzers.*)
No. 4.
Bermuda R.G.A.

ANTI-AIRCRAFT ARTILLERY—

H.Q. Second Army Anti-Aircraft Defence Commander.

"H" Anti-Aircraft Battery
- No. 8 Section (2—13-pr. guns)
- No. 17 Section (2—13-pr. guns)
- No. 116 Section (2—13-pr. guns)
- No. 144 Section (2—13-pr. guns)
- No. 159 Section (2—13-pr. guns)

"J" Anti-Aircraft Battery
- No. 19 Section (2—13-pr. guns)
- No. 53 Section (2—3-in. guns)
- No. 88 Section (2—13-pr. guns)
- No. 111 Section (2—13-pr. guns)
- No. 214 Section (2—3-in. guns)

"R" Anti-Aircraft Battery
- No. 42 Section (2—13-pr. guns)
- No. 54 Section (2—13-pr. guns)
- No. 115 Section (2—13-pr. guns)
- No. 145 Section (2—13-pr. guns)
- No. 232 Section (2—3-in. guns)

"T" Anti-Aircraft Battery
- No. 35 Section (2—13-pr. guns)
- No. 43 Section (2—13-pr. guns)
- No. 56 Section (2—13-pr. guns)
- No. 76 Section (2—3-in. guns)
- No. 78 Section (2—13-pr. guns)
- No. 216 Section (2—3-in. guns)

"U" Anti-Aircraft Battery
- No. 21 Section (2—13-pr. guns)
- No. 34 Section (2—13-pr. guns)
- No. 81 Section (2—13-pr. guns)
- No. 217 Section (2—3-in. guns)

No. 171 Section (2—13-pr. guns).
No. 177 Section (2—13-pr. guns).

Engineers—

Advanced R.E. Parks.
Nos. 2, 3, and 10.
Army Troops Companies.
Nos. 20, 134, 136, 138, 141, 145, 167, 214, 235, 236, 245, 289, 554, 556, 557, 573.
Siege Company.
No. 6 R. Monmouthshire (S.R.)

ARMY TROOPS—Second Army—continued.

Engineers—continued.
    Tunnelling Companies.
        Nos. 171, 173, 184, 255, 3rd Cdn.
    Land Drainage Company.
        No. 196. (½ Co.)
    Electrical and Mechanical Companies.
        No. 354.
        No. 5 Boring Section.
    Army Workshop Companies, R.E.
        No. 2.
    4th Field Survey Bn.
        "BB," "GG," "I," "M," "S" and "W" Sound Ranging Sections.
        Nos. 1, 3, 6, 7, 12, 23 Observation Groups.
    Anti-Aircraft Searchlight Sections.
        Nos. 1, 11, 24, 28, 31, 40, 64.
    Pontoon Parks (H.T.).
        No. 7.
    Transportation (Works) Co.
        No. 220.

Signal Service—
    2ND ARMY SIGNAL CO.
        "F," "N," "WT," "WW" Cable Sections.
        Nos. 9, 18, 32 (Motor) Airline Sections.
        No. 2 Light Railway Signal Company.
        No. 2 Signal Construction Company.
        Nos. 8, 8a, 9, 10, 13, 26, 27, 28, 35, 36 Area Signal Detachments.
        No. 1 Messenger Dog Section.

Pigeon Service—
    Motor Mobile Loft.
        No. 3.
    Horse Drawn Mobile Lofts.
        Nos. 10, 18, 23, 26, 27, 29, 30, 31, 38, 40, 41, 42, 56, 57, 58, 60, 61, 62, 63, 64, 85, 87, 93 to 98, 104, 109, 118, 126, 129, 130, 133 to 135, 154.
    Fixed Lofts.
        Courtrai.   Mouscron.

Infantry—
    43rd (Garr.) Bn. R. Fus.
        Nos. 3, 4, 46 Garrison Coys.
    44th (Garr.) Bn. R. Fus.
        Nos. 2 and 3 A.A. Coys.
    11th (Garr.) Bn. Oxf. & Bucks. L.I. ("C" Co.).
    16th (Garr.) Bn. Yorks. L.I. ("B" Co.).
    3rd Bn. B. West Indies R.
    Nos. 1, 2, 3, 4, 7 Labour Cos., Middlesex Regt.

M.G. Units—
    1st Motor Brigade M.G. Corps.
    101st (Bucks. and Berks. Yeo.) Bn. M.G. Corps.
    104th (Westminster Dragoons) Bn. M.G. Corps.
    No. 39 Bn. M.G. Corps.

Military Police—
    TRAFFIC CONTROL UNITS—
        No. 3 Squadron.
        No. 3 Company.

A.S.C.—
    No. 9 Pontoon Park (M.T.) (774 Co., A.S.C.).
    2nd Army Troops (M.T. Co.) (585 Co., A.S.C.).
    9th Aux. (Steam) Co. (367 Co., A.S.C.).
    67th Aux. (Steam) Co. (934 Co., A.S.C.).
    3rd M.T. Mobile Repair Unit (584 Co., A.S.C.).
    No. 2 Water Tank Co. (718 Co., A.S.C.).
    No. 625 Co. (attached Heavy Artillery).
    No. 2 Workshop for Anti-Aircraft Guns (423 Co., A.S.C.).
    117th Aux. (Steam) Co. (1085 Co., A.S.C.).
    2nd Army 'Bus Section.

ARMY TROOPS—Second Army—continued.

Medical—
    Nos. 2, 4, 5, 14, 20 Motor Ambulance Convoys (419, 421, 323, 567, 638 Cos., A.S.C.).
    Nos. 8, 10, 11, 17, 36, 44, 62, 64, 3rd Aus., 2nd Cdn. Casualty Clearing Stations.
    Nos. 2, 11 and 2nd Cdn. Advanced Depots Medical Stores.
    Nos. 1, 4, 8, 11 Mobile Laboratories.
    No. 7 Mobile X-Ray Unit.
    No. 4 Mobile Dental Unit.
    Nos. 10 and 3 Cdn. Stationary Hospitals.
    Nos. 13, 25, 42, 45, 47, 49, 56, 71, 72, 81, 82, 119 and N. Zealand Sanitary Sections.
    Nos. 1, 9, 28, 29, 33, 37, 38, 39, 41, 42 Sanitary Squads.

Veterinary—
    Nos. 2, 7, 10 and 15 Evacuating Stations.

Ordnance—
    No. 4 Heavy Mobile Workshop.
    No.   Light Mobile Workshop.
    No. 2 Ordnance Gun Park.
    No. 4 Officers' Clothing Depot.
    Nos. 11, 56, 59, 60, 62 to 71, 73 to 75, 80 to 82, 84, 85, 88 and 89 Ordnance Amm. Secs.

Forestry Units—

Labour Corps—
    LABOUR GROUP HEADQUARTERS—
        Nos. 5, 28, 30, 31, 32, 33, 38, 43, 59, 65, 66, 75, 81, 82, 87.
    LABOUR COMPANIES—
        Nos. 4, 5, 6, 8, 10, 19, 25, 26, 31, 38, 40, 43, 46, 48, 52, 53, 58, 61, 68, 70, 73, 84, 91, 92, 93, 94, 111, 121, 126, 130, 133, 134, 139, 140, 143, 144, 147, 151, 154, 158, 172, 174, 184, 185, 188, 197, 703, 719, 728, 1002.
    AREA EMPLOYMENT COMPANIES—
        Nos. 257, 738, 742, 744, 746, 748, 749, 750, 751, 752, 753, 759, 760, 761, 763, 764, 824, 825, 911.
    AREA EMPLOYMENT (ARTIZAN) COMPANIES—
        No. 780.
    AGRICULTURAL COMPANY—
        No. 1038.
    CHINESE LABOUR COMPANIES—
        Nos. 1, 2, 3, 31, 39, 40, 45, 47, 60, 61, 67, 74, 78, 85, 101, 108, 119, 130, 139, 172.
    "A" CAPE COLOURED COMPANY.

Army Printing and Stationery Services—
    No. 2 Advanced Photographic Section.

ARMY TROOPS—THIRD ARMY.

Headquarters, Third Army—

Artillery—
  ARMY FIELD ARTILLERY—
    Army Brigades, R.H.A.
      No. 14 (18—18-prs. and 6—4·5-in. howrs.)

    Army Brigades, R.F.A.
      No. 34 (18—18-prs. and 6—4·5-in. howrs.)
      No. 72 (18—18-prs. and 6—4·5-in. howrs.)
      No. 76 (18—18-prs. and 6—4·5-in. howrs.)
      No. 93 (18—18-prs.)
      No. 155 (18—18-prs. and 6—4·5-in. howrs.)
      No. 169 (24—18-prs.)
      No. 315 (18—18-prs. and 6—4·5-in. howrs.)
      2nd N.Z. (18—18-prs. and 6—4·5in. howrs.)

  BRIGADES, R.G.A.—

5th (Howitzer—8-in.)	160 Siege Battery (6—6-in. howrs.) 200 Siege Battery (6—6-in. howrs.) 295 Siege Battery (6—6-in. howrs.) 47 Siege Battery (6—8-in. howrs.)
13th (Mobile)	22 Heavy Battery (6—60-pr. guns) 1/2 London Heavy Battery (6—60-pr. guns) 201 Siege Battery (4—6-in. howrs.) 379 Siege Battery (4—6-in. howrs.)
17th (Mixed)	135 Heavy Battery (6—60-pr. guns) 2/1 Lancs. Heavy Battery (6—60-pr. guns) 51 Siege Battery (6—6-in. howrs.) 248 Siege Battery (6—6-in. howrs.) 56 Siege Battery (6—8-in. howrs.) 13 Siege Battery (6—9·2-in. howrs.)
22nd (Howitzer—9·2-in.)	182 Siege Battery (6—6-in. howrs.) 253 Siege Battery (6—6-in. howrs.) 287 Siege Battery (6—6-in. howrs.) 265 Siege Battery (6—9·2-in. howrs.)
35th (Mobile)	111 Heavy Battery (6—60-pr. guns) 145 Heavy Battery (6—60-pr. guns) 170 Siege Battery (6—6-in. howrs.) 267 Siege Battery (6—6-in. howrs.)
89th (Howitzer—9·2-in.)	206 Siege Battery (6—6-in. howrs.) 266 Siege Battery (6—6-in. howrs.) 281 Siege Battery (6—6-in. howrs.) 133 Siege Battery (6—9·2-in. howrs.)
54th (Howitzer—8-in.)	173 Siege Battery (4—6-in. howrs.) 199 Siege Battery (6—6-in. howrs.) 207 Siege Battery (6—6-in. howrs.) 262 Siege Battery (6—8-in. howrs.)
56th (Howitzer—9·2-in.)	106 Siege Battery (4—6-in. howrs.) 144 Siege Battery (4—6-in. howrs.) 220 Siege Battery (4—6-in. howrs.) 175 Siege Battery (6—9·2-in. howrs.)
60th (Howitzer—9·2-in.)	183 Siege Battery (4—6-in. howrs.) 305 Siege Battery (4—6-in. howrs.) 342 Siege Battery (4—6-in. howrs.) 186 Siege Battery (6—9·2-in. howrs.)
62nd (Mixed)	122 Heavy Battery (6—60-pr. guns) 126 Heavy Battery (6—60-pr. guns) 224 Siege Battery (6—6-in. howrs.) 274 Siege Battery (6—6-in. howrs.) 67 Siege Battery (6—8-in. howrs.) 76 Siege Battery (6—9·2-in. howrs.)
63rd (Mobile)	38 Heavy Battery (6—60-pr. guns) 119 Heavy Battery (6—60-pr. guns) 420 Siege Battery (4—6-in. howrs.) 443 Siege Battery (4—6-in. howrs.)
66th (Howitzer—8-in.)	122 Siege Battery (6—6-in. howrs.) 306 Siege Battery (4—6-in. howrs.) 325 Siege Battery (6—6-in. howrs.) 120 Siege Battery (6—8-in. howrs.)

ARMY TROOPS—Third Army—continued.

Artillery—continued.

BRIGADES, R.G.A.—continued.

84th (Mixed) ...
- 24 Heavy Battery (6—60-pr. guns)
- 152 Heavy Battery (6—60-pr. guns)
- 276 Siege Battery (6—6-in. howrs.)
- 336 Siege Battery (6—6-in. howrs.)
- 77 Siege Battery (6—8-in. howrs.)
- 34 Siege Battery (6—9·2-in. howrs.)

88th (Howitzer—8-in.)
- 123 Siege Battery (6—6-in. howrs.)
- 258 Siege Battery (4—6-in. howrs.)
- 328 Siege Battery (4—6-in. howrs.)
- 78 Siege Battery (6—8-in. howrs.)

90th (Howitzer—9·2-in.)
- 244 Siege Battery (6—6-in. howrs.)
- 277 Siege Battery (4—6-in. howrs.)
- 299 Siege Battery (6—6-in. howrs.)
- 95 Siege Battery (6—9·2-in. howrs.)

92nd (Mobile)
- 14 Heavy Battery (6—60-pr. guns)
- 127 Heavy Battery (6—60-pr. guns)
- 129 Heavy Battery (6—60-pr. guns)
- 1/1 Kent Heavy Battery (6—60-pr. guns)

ARMY BRIGADES, R.G.A.
Nos. 32, 57 and 58.

SIEGE BATTERIES, R.G.A. (Unbrigaded).

(4—6-in. guns.)
Nos. 8, 26, 35, 58, 409, 434, 484, 500, 503, 525.

(9·2-in. and 12-in. guns on railway mountings.)
Nos. 363 and 442 (2—9·2-in. guns)
½ No. 92 (1—12-in. gun)

(14-in. guns on railway mountings.)

(2—12-in. howitzers.)
No. 431.

(2—12-in. howitzers on railway mountings.)
Nos. 83, 89, 333, 343, 495.

(15-in. howitzers.)
Nos. 3 and 10.

ANTI-AIRCRAFT ARTILLERY—

H.Q. Third Army Anti-Aircraft Defence Commander.

"L" Anti-Aircraft Battery
- No. 16 Section (2—13-pr. guns).
- No. 39 Section (2—13-pr. guns).
- No. 41 Section (2—13-pr. guns).
- No. 66 Section (2—13-pr. guns).

"M" Anti-Aircraft Battery
- No. 40 Section (2—13-pr. guns).
- No. 65 Section (2—13-pr. guns).
- No. 84 Section (2—13-pr. guns).
- No. 87 Section (2—13-pr. guns).
- No. 129 Section (2—13-pr. guns).
- No. 155 Section (2—13-pr. guns).

"N" Anti-Aircraft Battery
- No. 11 Section (2—13-pr. guns).
- No. 48 Section (2—13-pr. guns).
- No. 50 Section (2—13-pr. guns).
- No. 62 Section (2—13-pr. guns).
- No. 64 Section (2—13-pr. guns).

"O" Anti-Aircraft Battery
- No. 58 Section (2—13-pr. guns).
- No. 86 Section (2—13-pr. guns).
- No. 104 Section (2—13-pr. guns).
- No. 107 Section (2—13-pr. guns).
- No. 225 Section (2—3-in. guns).

ARMY TROOPS—Third Army—continued.

Engineers –
    547th (Kent) Field Company.
    549th (Lancs.) Field Company.
    Advanced R.E. Parks.
        Nos. 5, 7, 8.
    Army Troops Companies.
        Nos. 132, 142, 147, 149, 232, 280, 559, 577. 7th Royal Monmouth (SR).
    Siege Companies.
        No. 2 R. Anglesey (SR).
        No. 4 R. Monmouth (SR).
    Tunnelling Companies.
        Nos. 174, 177, 178, 181, 183, 252, 258, N.Z.
    Electrical and Mechanical Companies.
        No. 352.
        No. 1 Boring Section.
    Army Workshop Company, R.E.
        No. 3.
    3rd Field Survey Battalion.
        "C," "CC," "D," "F" Sound Ranging Sections.
        Nos. 15, 16, 17, 19, 20 Observation Groups.
    Anti-Aircraft Searchlight Sections.
        Nos. 2, 8, 21, 30, 45, 55, 58, 75, 76.
    Pontoon Park (H.T.).
        No. 3.
    Transportation (Works) Co.
        No. 222.

Signal Service—
    3RD ARMY SIGNAL CO.—
        Nos. 16, 19 and 100 (Motor) Airline Sections.
        "QQ" and "ZZ" Cable Sections.
        No. 3 Light Railway Signal Company.
        No. 3 Signal Construction Company.
        Nos. 17, 19, 20, 21, 22, 23, 24, 25, 29 Area Signal Detachments.

Pigeon Service—
    Horse Drawn Mobile Lofts—
        Nos. 3, 5, 21, 22, 68, 80, 82, 99, 102, 105, 106, 112, 115, 116, 120, 124, 132, 136, 141, 142, 145.
    Fixed Loft—
        Arry.

Infantry—
    43rd (Garr.) Bn. R. Fus.
        Nos. 5, 6, 45 Garrison Coys.
    44th (Garr.) Bn. R. Fus.
        Nos. 4 and 5 A.A. Coys.
    16th (Garr.) Bn., Yorks L.I. ("C" Company).
    No. 5 Labour Coy., Middlesex Regt.
    4th Bn. B. West Indies Regiment.

Military Police—
    Traffic Control Units—
        No. 4 Squadron.
        No. 4 Company.

A.S.C.—
    No. 6 Pontoon Park (M.T.) (870 Co., A.S.C.).
    3rd Army Troops M.T. Co. (871 Co., A.S.C.).
    68th Aux. (Petrol) Co. (935 Co., A.S.C.).
    66th Aux. (Petrol) Co. (933 Co., A.S.C.).
    60th Aux. (Steam) Co. (931 Co., A.S.C.).
    2nd M.T. Mobile Repair Unit (404 Co., A.S.C.).
    No. 377 Co. (attached Heavy Artillery).
    No. 3 Workshop for Anti-Aircraft Guns (726 Co., A.S.C.).

ARMY TROOPS—Third Army—*continued*.

Medical—
Nos. 6, 15, 16, 21, 27 and 30 Motor Ambulance Convoys (324, 568, 569, 639, 629, 704 Cos., A.S.C.).
Nos. 3, 4, 18, 19, 21, 29, 34, 38, 43, 45, 46, 49, 56, 59 and 3rd Cdn. Casualty Clearing Stations.
Nos. 15, 16 and 34 Advanced Depôts Medical Stores.
Nos. 10, 13, 18 and 33 Mobile Laboratories.
Nos. 5 and 8 Mobile X-Ray Units.
No. 1 Mobile Dental Unit.
No.   Stationary Hospital.
Nos. 4A, 11, 17, 20, 21, 32, 33, 35, 38, 51, 62, 70, 74 and 83 Sanitary Sections.
Nos. 10, 14, 16, 23, 24, 26, 27 Sanitary Squads.

Veterinary—
Nos. 4, 5, 6 and 17 Evacuating Stations.

Ordnance—
No. 3 Heavy Mobile Workshop.
No.   Medium Mobile Workshop.
No.   Light Mobile Workshop.
No. 3 Ordnance Gun Park.
No. 3 Officers' Clothing Depôt.
Nos. 28 to 30, 32 to 54 Ordnance Amm. Secs.

Forestry Units—
Nos. 25, 29 Canadian Forestry Cos.

Labour Corps—
LABOUR GROUP HEADQUARTERS—
Nos. 17, 26, 34, 37, 45, 46, 48, 51, 52, 57, 62, 70.

LABOUR COMPANIES—
Nos. 9, 11, 18, 23, 24, 27, 32, 35, 36, 41, 42, 60, 62, 67, 69, 75, 76, 78, 79, 101, 104, 106, 113, 115, 117, 119, 120, 125, 128, 132, 138, 142, 146, 148, 153, 155, 157, 161, 166, 167, 189, 190, 200, 700, 701, 702, 707, 710, 717, 731, 1021.

AREA EMPLOYMENT COMPANIES—
Nos. 258, 279, 280, 283, 284, 287, 288, 289, 290, 291, 293, 294, 740, 741, 747, 774.

AREA EMPLOYMENT (ARTIZAN) COMPANIES—
Nos. 834, 927.

AGRICULTURAL COMPANY—
No. 1039.

CHINESE LABOUR COMPANIES—
Nos. 7, 23, 59, 104, 126, 140, 157, 174, 188, 189, 190, 193.

NON-COMBATANT CORPS—

Army Printing and Stationery Services—
No. 3 Advanced Photographic Section.

ARMY TROOPS—FOURTH ARMY.

Headquarters, Fourth Army—

Artillery—

ARMY FIELD ARTILLERY—

Army Brigades, R.H.A.
- No. 5 (24—18-prs.)
- No. 16 (18—18-prs.)

Army Brigades, R.F.A.
- No. 5 (18—18-prs. and 6—4·5-in. howrs.)
- No. 14 (24—18-prs.)
- No. 48 (18—18-prs. and 6—4·5-in. howrs.)
- No. 65 (24—18-prs.)
- No. 84 (18—18-prs. and 6—4·5-in. howrs.)
- No. 86 (18—18-prs. and 6—4·5-in. howrs.)
- No. 104 (18—18-prs. and 6—4·5-in. howrs.)
- No. 232 (18—18-prs. and 6—4·5-in. howrs.)
- No. 298 (18—18-prs. and 6—4·5-in. howrs.)
- 3rd Aus. (18—18-prs. and 6—4·5-in. howrs.)
- 6th Aus. (18—18-prs. and 6—4·5-in. howrs.)
- 12th Aus. (18—18-prs. and 6—4·5-in. howrs.)

BRIGADES, R.G.A.

9th (Mobile)
- 128 Heavy Battery (6—60-pr. guns)
- 130 Heavy Battery (6—60-pr. guns)
- 153 Siege Battery (6—6-in. howrs.)
- 260 Siege Battery (6—6-in. howrs.)

12th (Howitzer—8-in.)
- 242 Siege Battery (4—6-in. howrs.)
- 263 Siege Battery (4—6-in. howrs.)
- 319 Siege Battery (4—6-in. howrs.)
- 70 Siege Battery (6—8-in. howrs.)

14th (Howitzer—8-in.)
- 11 Siege Battery (6—6-in. howrs.)
- 150 Siege Battery (4—6-in. howrs.)
- 296 Siege Battery (4—6-in. howrs.)
- 214 Siege Battery (6—8-in. howrs.)

21st (Mobile)
- 71 Heavy Battery (6—60-pr. guns)
- 1/2 Lancs. Heavy Battery (6—60-pr. guns)
- 24 Siege Battery (6—6-in. howrs.)
- 354 Siege Battery (6—6-in. howrs.)

23rd (Howitzer—9·2-in.)
- 41 Siege Battery (6—6-in. howrs.)
- 327 Siege Battery (4—6-in. howrs.)
- 355 Siege Battery (4—6-in. howrs.)
- 94 Siege Battery (6—9·2-in. howrs.)

27th (Mixed)
- 25 Heavy Battery (6—60-pr. guns)
- 144 Heavy Battery (6—60-pr. guns)
- 110 Siege Battery (6—6-in. howrs.)
- 216 Siege Battery (6—6-in. howrs.)
- 93 Siege Battery (6—8-in. howrs.)
- 143 Siege Battery (4—9·2-in. howrs.)

41st (Mobile)
- 1/1 Northumbrian Heavy Battery (6—60-pr. guns)
- 1/1 N. Midland Heavy Battery (6—60-pr. guns)
- 1 Siege Battery (6—6-in. howrs.)
- 6 Siege Battery (6—6-in. howrs.)

47th (Howitzer—8-in.)
- 109 Siege Battery (4—6-in. howrs.)
- 146 Siege Battery (4—6-in. howrs.)
- 309 Siege Battery (6—6-in. howrs.)
- 156 Siege Battery (6—8-in. howrs.)

51st (Mixed)
- 137 Heavy Battery (6—60-pr. guns)
- 138 Heavy Battery (6—60-pr. guns)
- 255 Siege Battery (6—6-in. howrs.)
- 283 Siege Battery (6—6-in. howrs.)
- 169 Siege Battery (6—8-in. howrs.)
- 161 Siege Battery (6—9·2-in. howrs.)

ARMY TROOPS—Fourth Army—continued.

Artillery—continued.

BRIGADES, R.G.A.—continued.

68th (Howitzer—8-in.) ...
- 114 Siege Battery (6—6-in. howrs.)
- 168 Siege Battery (6—6-in. howrs.)
- 211 Siege Battery (4—6-in. howrs.)
- 25 Siege Battery (6—8-in. howrs.)

69th (Howitzer—9·2-in.)
- 288 Siege Battery (4—6-in. howrs.)
- 291 Siege Battery (6—6-in. howrs.)
- 331 Siege Battery (4—6-in. howrs.)
- 93 Siege Battery (6—9·2-in. howrs.)

71st (Howitzer—8-in.) ...
- 9 Siege Battery (4—6-in. howrs.)
- 17 Siege Battery (6—6-in. howrs.)
- 332 Siege Battery (6—6-in. howrs.)
- 126 Siege Battery (6—8-in. howrs.)

76th (Mixed)
- 113 Heavy Battery (6—60-pr. guns)
- 132 Heavy Battery (6—60-pr. guns)
- 228 Siege Battery (6—6-in. howrs.)
- 233 Siege Battery (6—6-in. howrs.)
- 19 Siege Battery (6—8-in. howrs.)
- 91 Siege Battery (6—9·2-in. howrs.)

79th (Mixed) ...
- 142 Heavy Battery (6—60-pr. guns)
- 1/1 Essex Heavy Battery (6—60-pr. guns)
- 14 Siege Battery (6—6-in. howrs.)
- 174 Siege Battery (6—6-in. howrs.)
- 145 Siege Battery (6—8-in. howrs.)
- 185 Siege Battery (6—9·2-in. howys.)

83rd (Mixed) ...
- 116 Heavy Battery (6—60-pr. guns)
- 1/1 Highland Heavy Battery (6—60-pr. guns)
- 230 Siege Battery (6—6-in. howrs.)
- 284 Siege Battery (6—6-in. howrs.)
- 135 Siege Battery (6—8-in. howrs.)
- 69 Siege Battery (6—9·2-in. howrs.)

85th (Mobile) ...
- 120 Heavy Battery (6—60-pr. guns)
- 139 Heavy Battery (6—60-pr. guns)
- 2 Siege Battery (6—6-in. howrs.)
- 3 Siege Battery (6—6-in. howrs.)

93rd (Mixed) ...
- 85 Heavy Battery (6—60-pr. guns)
- 2/1 Lowland Heavy Battery (6—60-pr. guns)
- 231 Siege Battery (6—6-in. howrs.)
- 232 Siege Battery (6—6-in. howrs.)
- 215 Siege Battery (6—8-in. howrs.)
- 124 Siege Battery (6—9·2-in. howrs.)

98th (Howitzer—9·2-in.)
- 210 Siege Battery (4—6-in. howrs.)
- 270 Siege Battery (6—6-in. howrs.)
- 294 Siege Battery (6—6-in. howrs.)
- 121 Siege Battery (6—9·2-in. howrs.)

ARMY BRIGADES, R.G.A.
No. 73.

SIEGE BATTERIES, R.G.A. (Unbrigaded).
(4—6-in. guns.)
Nos. 50, 189, 222, 312, 449, 498, 499, 504, 545.
(2—9·2-in. guns on railway mountings.)
½ No. 546 (1—9·2-in. gun).
(2—12-in. guns on railway mountings.)
½ No. 543 (1—12-in. gun).
(14-in. guns on railway mountings.)
½ No. 471 (1—14-in. gun).
(2—12-in. howitzers.)
Nos. 80, 243, 494, No. 1 (R.M.A.).
(2—12-in. howitzers on railway mountings.)
No. 374.
(15-in. howitzers.)
No. 1.

ANTI-AIRCRAFT ARTILLERY—

H.Q. Fourth Army Anti-Aircraft Defence Commander—

"F" Anti-Aircraft Battery
- No. 6 Section (2—13-pr. guns)
- No. 44 Section (2—13-pr. guns)
- No. 57 Section (2—13-pr. guns)
- No. 110 Section (2—13-pr. guns)

ARMY TROOPS—Fourth Army—continued.

Artillery—continued.

ANTI-AIRCRAFT ARTILLERY—continued.

"G" Anti-Aircraft Battery
- No. 31 Section (2—13-pr. guns)
- No. 46 Section (2—13-pr. guns)
- No. 82 Section (2—13-pr. guns)
- No. 137 Section (2—13-pr. guns)

"P" Anti-Aircraft Battery
- No. 12 Section (2—13-pr. guns)
- No. 52 Section (2—13-pr. guns)
- No. 128 Section (2—13-pr. guns)
- No. 146 Section (2—13-pr. guns)

"Q" Anti-Aircraft Battery
- No. 15 Section (2—13-pr. guns)
- No. 67 Section (2—13-pr. guns)
- No. 71 Section (2—13-pr. guns)
- No. 109 Section (2—13-pr. guns)
- No. 236 Section (2—3-in. guns)

"Z" Anti-Aircraft Battery
- No. 37 Section (2—13-pr. guns)
- No. 127 Section (2—13-pr. guns)
- No. 148 Section (2—13-pr. guns)
- No. 205 Section (2—3-in. guns)
- No. 227 Section (2—3-in. guns)

Engineers—
  546th (Kent) Field Company.
  648th (Home Counties) Field Company.
  Advanced R.E. Parks.
    Nos. 6 and 12.
  Army Troops Companies.
    Nos. 144, 146, 213, 221, 238, 283, 288, 567, 574, 1st Aus.
  Siege Companies.
    No. 1 R. Anglesey (S.R.).
    No. 4 R. Anglesey (S.R.).
  Tunnelling Companies.
    Nos. 180, 182, 253, 254, 256, 1st Aus. and 2nd Aus.
  Electrical and Mechanical Company.
    No. 353.
    No. 3 Boring Section.
  Army Workshop Co., R.E.
    No. 4.
  5th Field Survey Bn.
    "A," "B," "G," "K," "O," "R" Sound Ranging Sections.
    Nos. 2, 13, 14 and 24 Observation Groups.
  Anti-Aircraft Searchlight Sections.
    Nos. 6, 7, 16, 17, 29, 36, 50 and 69 F. Searchlight Company.
  Transportation (Works) Co.
    No. 224.
  Barge Filtration Units (I.W.T.).
    No. 3.

Signal Service—
  4TH ARMY SIGNAL CO.
    Nos. 43, 45, 48, 53 (Motor) Airline Sections.
    "BL" Cable Section.
    No. 4 Light Railway Signal Co.
    No. 4 Signal Construction Co.
    Nos. 12, 15, 16, 30, 32, 38, 40 Area Signal Detachments.

Pigeon Service—
  Motor Mobile Lofts—
    Nos. 1, 4.
  Horse Drawn Mobile Lofts—
    Nos. 24, 88, 100, 101, 103, 107, 108, 110, 111, 114, 117, 138, 143.
  Fixed Lofts—
    Peronne, Le Quesnoy.

Infantry—
  43rd (Garr.) Bn. R. Fus.—
    No. 7 and Composite Guards Garrison Coys.
  44th (Garr.) Bn. R. Fus.—
    No. 6 A. A. Coy.
  No. 6 Garrison Guard Co.
  11th (Garr.) Bn. Oxf. and Bucks. L.I. ("B" Co.)
  16th (Garr.) Bn. Yorks. L.I. ("D" Co.)
  No. 6 Labour Co., Midd'x R.
  6th and 7th (½) Bns. B. West Indies R.

ARMY TROOPS—Fourth Army—continued.

M.G. Units—
  No. 2 (2nd L.G.) Bn. Guards M.G. Regt.
  100th (Warwicks and Notts. Yeo.) Bn. M.G. Corps.

Military Police—
  Traffic Control Units.
    No. 2 Squadron.
    No. 2 Company.

A.S.C.—
  No. 8 Pontoon Park (M.T.) (624 Co., A.S.C.).
  No. 11 Pontoon Park (M.T.) (775 Co., A.S.C.).
  4th Army Troops M.T. Co. (893 Co., A.S.C.).
  44th Aux. (Steam) Co. (62 Co., A.S.C.).
  70th Aux. (Petrol) Co. (937 Co., A.S.C.).
  75th Aux. (Petrol) Co. (939 Co., A.S.C.).
  No. 1 Water Tank Co. (646 Co., A.S.C.).
  5th Mobile Repair Unit (806 Co., A.S.C.).
  No. 770 Co. (attached Heavy Artillery).
  No. 5 Workshop for Anti-Aircraft Guns (727 Co., A.S.C.).

Medical—
  14th Cdn. Field Ambulance.
  Nos. 3, 10, 11, 24, 37, 44, Motor Ambulance Convoys (420, 359, 378, 645, 909, 1075 Cos., A.S.C.).
  Nos. 5, 12, 20, 37, 41, 47, 48, 50, 53, 55, 58, 61 Casualty Clearing Stations.
  Nos. 13, 14, 18 Advanced Depots Medical Stores.
  Nos. 12, 17, 19 and 5 Cdn. Mobile Laboratories.
  Nos. 2, 3 and 4 Mobile X-Ray Units.
  No. 2 Mobile Dental Unit.
  No.   Stationary Hospital.
  Nos. 9, 16, 23, 48, 50, 58, 59, 61, 77 ; 1, 2, 3, 4 and 5 Aus. Sanitary Sections.
  Nos. 15, 17, 45, 46, 47, 48, 49, 62 Sanitary Squads.

Veterinary—
  Nos. 9, 13 and Aus. Evacuating Stations.

Ordnance—
  No. 5 Heavy Mobile Workshop.
  No.   Medium Mobile Workshop.
  Nos.   Light Mobile Workshops.
  No. 4 Ordnance Gun Park.
  No. 5 Officers' Clothing Depot.
  Nos. 31, 58, 79, 90 to 106 Ordnance Amm. Secs.

Forestry Units—
  No. 364 Forestry Co., R.E.
  No. 35 Canadian Forestry Company.

Labour Corps—
  LABOUR GROUP HEADQUARTERS—
    Nos. 8, 12, 16, 18, 35, 47, 53, 61, 63, 67, 84, 85 and 86.
  LABOUR COMPANIES—
    Nos. 7, 12, 14, 15, 16, 21, 28, 33, 34, 44, 49, 59, 65, 72, 74, 81, 82, 83, 85, 86, 88, 90, 103, 105, 107, 110, 114, 131, 150, 156, 160, 168, 171, 173, 175, 177, 187, 191, 193, 199, 705, 706, 708, 709, 713, 714, 722, 724, 727, 729.
  AREA EMPLOYMENT COMPANIES—
    Nos. 259, 268, 281, 282, 285, 292, 743, 757, 758, 776, 778, 876, 995.
  AREA EMPLOYMENT (ARTIZAN) COMPANY—
    No. 937.
  AGRICULTURAL COMPANIES—
    Nos. 1041 and 1042.
  CHINESE LABOUR COMPANIES—
    Nos. 8, 55, 76, 79, 90, 102, 115, 116, 123, 146, 150, 164, 165, 166, 182.
  NON-COMBATANT CORPS—

Army Printing and Stationery Services—
  No. 4 Advanced Photographic Section.

ARMY TROOPS—FIFTH ARMY.

Headquarters, Fifth Army—
Artillery—
  ARMY FIELD ARTILLERY—
    Army Brigades, R.F.A.
      No. 108 (18—18-prs. and 6—4·5-in. howrs.)
      No. 150 (18—18-prs. and 6—4·5-in. howrs.)
      No. 158 (24—18-prs.)
      No. 179 (24—18-prs.)
  ARMY BRIGADES, R.G.A.—
    18th (Howitzer—9·2-in.) ...
      180 Siege Battery (6—6-in. howrs.)
      218 Siege Battery (6—6-in. howrs.)
      236 Siege Battery (4—6-in. howrs.)
      117 Siege Battery (4—9·2-in. howrs.)
    28th (Mixed) ...
      117 Heavy Battery (6—60-pr. guns)
      1/1 W. Riding Heavy Battery (6—60-pr. guns)
      141 Siege Battery (6—6-in. howrs.)
      329 Siege Battery (6—6-in. howrs.)
      213 Siege Battery (6—8-in. howrs.)
      148 Siege Battery (4—9·2-in. howrs.)
    42nd (Mobile) ...
      124 Heavy Battery (6—60-pr. guns)
      1/1 London Heavy Battery (6—60-pr. guns)
      287 Siege Battery (6—6-in. howrs.)
      323 Siege Battery (6—6-in. howrs.)
    44th (S.A.) (Howitzer—8-in.) ...
      71 (S.A.) Siege Battery (6—6-in. howrs.)
      73 (S.A.) Siege Battery (6—6-in. howrs.)
      125 (S.A.) Siege Battery (6—6-in. howrs.)
      20 Siege Battery (6—8-in. howrs.)
    46th (Mobile) ...
      108 Heavy Battery (6—60-pr. guns)
      1/1 Lancs. Heavy Battery (6—60-pr. guns)
      4 Siege Battery (6—6-in. howrs.)
      5 Siege Battery (6—6-in. howrs.)
    49th (Howitzer—8-in.) ...
      99 Siege Battery (6—6-in. howrs.)
      166 Siege Battery (4—6-in. howrs.)
      346 Siege Battery (4—6-in. howrs.)
    52nd (Howitzer—9·2-in.) ...
      164 Siege Battery (6—6-in. howrs.)
      259 Siege Battery (6—6-in. howrs.)
      264 Siege Battery (4—6-in. howrs.)
      10 Siege Battery (6—9·2-in. howrs.)
    89th (Howitzer—8-in.) ...
      68 Siege Battery (6—6-in. howrs.)
      178 Siege Battery (4—6-in. howrs.)
      225 Siege Battery (4—6-in. howrs.)
      57 Siege Battery (6—8-in. howrs.)
  ARMY BRIGADES, R.G.A.
    Nos. 11, 55.
  SIEGE BATTERIES, R.G.A. (Unbrigaded).
    (4—6-in. guns.)
      Nos. 330, 481, 521, 544.
    (2—9·2-in. guns on railway mountings.)
      Nos. 53 (½), 456 (½).
    (2—12-in. howitzers.)
      No. 349.
    (2—12-in. howitzers on railway mountings.)
      Nos. 18, 44, 64, 128, 514(½), 524.
    (15-in. howitzers.)
      No. 2.
  ANTI-AIRCRAFT ARTILLERY—
    H.Q. Fifth Army Anti-Aircraft Defence Commander—
    "A" Anti-Aircraft Battery
      No. 22 Section (2—13-pr. guns)
      No. 26 Section (2—13-pr. guns)
      No. 77 Section (2—13-pr. guns)
      No. 100 Section (2—13-pr. guns)
      No. 165 Section (2—13-pr. guns)
      No. 219 Section (2—3-in guns)
    "B" Anti-Aircraft Battery
      No. 33 Section (2—13-pr. guns)
      No. 70 Section (2—13-pr. guns)
      No. 101 Section (2—13-pr. guns)
      No. 142 Section (2—13-pr. guns)
      No. 164 Section (2—13-pr. guns)
      No. 174 Section (2—13-pr. guns)
      No. 220 Section (2—3-in. guns)
    "D" Anti-Aircraft Battery
      No. 18 Section (2—13-pr. guns)
      No. 61 Section (2—13-pr. guns)
      No. 89 Section (2—13-pr. guns)
      No. 132 Section (2—13-pr. guns)
      No. 166 Section (2—13-pr. guns)
      No. 218 Section (2—3-in. guns)

ARMY TROOPS—Fifth Army—*continued*.

Engineers—
  Advanced R.E. Parks.
    Nos. 9, 11.
  Army Troops Companies.
    Nos. 42, 133, 135, 148, 215, 230, 239, 281, 284, 290, 552, 560.
  Tunnelling Companies.
    Nos. 170, 250, 251, 257, 3rd Aus.
  Electrical and Mechanical Companies.
    No. 351.   No. 2 Boring Section.
  Army Workshop Company, R.E.
    No. 5.
  2nd Field Survey Bn.
  "DD," "J," "U" Sound Ranging Sections.
  Nos. 5, 8, 9, and 27 Observation Groups.
  Anti-Aircraft Searchlight Sections.
    Nos. 4, 14, 20, 44.
  Pontoon Park (H.T.).
    No. 2.
  Land Drainage Company.
    No. 196 (½ Co.).
  Transportation (Works) Co.
    No. 221.
Signal Service—
  5TH ARMY SIGNAL CO.
    Nos. 28, 50, 88 (Motor) Airline Sections.
    "AU," "BM," "RR" Cable Sections.
    No. 3 Messenger Dog Section.
    No. 5 Light Railway Signal Company.
    No. 5 Signal Construction Co.
    Nos. 5, 6, 7, 11, 14, 34, 37, 39 Area Signal Detachments.
Pigeon Service—
  Motor Mobile Loft—
    No. .
  Horse Drawn Mobile Lofts.
    Nos. 8, 11, 20, 33, 35, 45, 48, 51, 52, 53, 59, 67, 69, 113, 121, 139, 140, 146, 147, 148, 156.
Infantry—
  43rd (Garr.) Bn. R. Fus.
    Nos. 8 and 9 Garrison Cos.
  44th (Garr.) Bn. R. Fus.
    No. 7 A.A. Co.
  116th (Garr.) Bn. Oxf. and Bucks. L.I. ("A" and "D" Cos.).
  7th (½) Bn. British W. Indies Regt.
Military Police—
  Traffic Control Unit.
    No. 1 Company (1½ platoons).
A.S.C.—
  Fifth Army Troops M.T. Co. (385 Co., A.S.C.).
  69th Aux. (Steam) Co. (936 Co., A.S.C.).
  No. 4 Workshop for A.A. Guns (698 Co., A.S.C.).
  No. 1113 Co. (attached Heavy Artillery).
  No. 12 Pontoon Park (M.T.) (682 Co., A.S.C.).
  No. 6 Mobile Repair Unit (1112 Co., A.S.C.).
Medical—
  Nos. 12, 22, 25, 43 Motor Ambulance Convoys (559, 610, 627, 1060 Cos., A.S.C.).
  Nos. 13, 15, 32, 51, 54, 63, 1st Aus., 2nd Aus. Casualty Clearing Stations.
  Nos. 1, 31 Advanced Depot Medical Stores.
  Nos. 9, 16, 20, 39 Mobile Laboratories.
  Nos. 13 and 14 Mobile X-Ray Units.
  No. 5 Mobile Dental Unit.
  No. 39 Stationary Hospital.
  Nos. 6, 22, 34, 37, 52, 57, 66, 76, 87 Sanitary Sections.
  Nos. 35, 63 Sanitary Squads.
Veterinary—
  Nos. 1, 3, 11 Evacuating Stations.
Ordnance—
  No. 2 Heavy Mobile Workshop.
  No.   Light Mobile Workshop.
  No. 5 Ordnance Gun Park.
  No. 2 Officers' Clothing Depot.
  Nos. 1, 2, 8 to 10, 17, 20 to 22, 27, 55, 83, 86, 87, 109 Ordnance Ammunition Sections.
Forestry Units—
  No. 362 Forestry Co., R.E.

Labour Corps—
  LABOUR GROUP HEADQUARTERS—
    Nos. 24, 25, 36, 58, 68, 69, 80.
  LABOUR COMPANIES—
    Nos. 1, 17, 22, 29, 30, 56, 57, 63, 64, 66, 71, 77, 99, 100, 102, 109, 116, 118, 122, 123, 124, 141, 149, 162, 176, 178, 179, 186, 194, 198, 715, 721, 725.
  AREA EMPLOYMENT COMPANIES—
    Nos. 260, 736, 739, 762, 777, 821, 822. 823, 832, 946, 994.
  AREA EMPLOYMENT (ARTIZAN) COMPANIES—
    No. 782.
  AGRICULTURAL COMPANY—
    No. 1040.
  CHINESE LABOUR COMPANIES—
    Nos. 26, 32, 46, 83, 107, 113, 117, 161.

Army Printing & Stationery Services—
  No. 5 Advanced Photographic Section.

ROYAL AIR FORCE.

	ATTACHED TO

H.Q., R.A.F.—
    Headquarters Communication Squadron.
        No. 1 Aircraft Depot (includes 1 Port Depot).
        No. 1 Aircraft Depot (D).
        No. 1 Aircraft Depot (M).
        No. 1 Aeroplane Supply Depot.
        No. 2 Aircraft Depot (includes 1 Port Depot).
        No. 2 Aeroplane Supply Depot.
        Engine Repair Shops.
        British Aeronautical Supplies Department.

9th (G.H.Q.) BRIGADE—
    9th Wing: Nos. 18, 25, 27, 32, 49 and 62 Squadrons.
    51st Wing: Nos. 1, 43, 94, 107 and 205 Squadrons.
    54th Wing: Nos. 83, 151 and 207 Squadrons.
    82nd Wing: Nos. 58, 152 and 214 Squadrons.
    9th Aircraft Park.
    5th Air Ammunition Column.
    9th Air Ammunition Column.
    6th Reserve Lorry Park.
    20th Reserve Lorry Park.

1st BRIGADE—   *1st Army.*
    1st Wing: Nos. 5, 16, 52 Squadrons, and "L" Flight
    10th Wing: Nos. 19, 22, 40, 64, 98, 148, 203, 209 Squadrons and "I" Flight.
    1st Balloon Wing: Nos. 1, 2, 4 and 10 Companies
    1st Aircraft Park
    1st Air Ammunition Column
    1st Reserve Lorry Park
    11th Reserve Lorry Park.

2nd BRIGADE—   *2nd Army.*
    2nd Wing: Nos. 4, 7, 10, 53, 82 Squadrons and "M" Flight
    11th Wing: Nos. 29, 41, 48, 70, 74, 79, 149 and 206 Squadrons
    65th Wing: Nos. 38, 65, 108 and 204 Squadrons.
    2nd Balloon Wing: Nos. 5, 6, 7, 8 and 17 Companies
    2nd Aircraft Park
    5th Aircraft Park
    8th Aircraft Park
    2nd Reserve Lorry Park
    7th Reserve Lorry Park
    2nd Air Ammunition Column
    7th Air Ammunition Column
    No. 8 Salvage Section

3rd BRIGADE—   *3rd Army.*
    12th Wing: Nos. 12, 13, 15, 59 Squadrons and "N" Flight
    13th Wing: Nos. 56, 60, 87, 201 and 210 Squadrons
    90th Wing: Nos. 3, 11, 57 and 102 Squadrons.
    3rd Balloon Wing: Nos. 12, 16, 18 and 19 Companies
    3rd Aircraft Park
    3rd Air Ammunition Column
    3rd Reserve Lorry Park
    19th Reserve Lorry Park
    No. 6 Salvage Section
    No. 9 Salvage Section

5th BRIGADE—   *4th Army.*
    15th Wing: Nos. 6, 8, 9, 35 and 73 Squadrons, and 3rd Squadron A.F.C.
    22nd Wing: Nos. 24, 46, 80, 84, 85 and 208 Squadrons
    80th Wing: Nos. 20, 23, 92, 101, 211 and 218 Squadrons
    5th Balloon Wing: Nos. 13, 14 and 15 Companies
    4th Aircraft Park
    4th Air Ammunition Column
    4th Reserve Lorry Park
    12th Reserve Lorry Park
    No. 7 Salvage Section

ROYAL AIR FORCE—*continued.*

	Attached to

10th BRIGADE—
   80th Wing: Nos. 54, 88 and 103 Squadrons, and 2nd and 4th Squadrons A.F.C. ... ...
   81st Wing: Nos. 2, 21, 42 Squadrons and "P" Flight ...
   8th Balloon Wing: Nos. 3, 11 and 20 Companies ... ...
   10th Aircraft Park ... ...
   10th Air Ammunition Column ... ...
   9th Reserve Lorry Park ... ...
	5th Army.

INDEPENDENT FORCE.

8th BRIGADE—
   41st Wing: Nos. 55, 99, and 104 Squadrons.
   83rd Wing: Nos. 97, 100, 115, 215 and 216 Squadrons.
   88th Wing: Nos. 45 and 110 Squadrons.
   3rd Aircraft Depot.
   6th Aircraft Park.
   12th Aircraft Park.
   8th Air Ammunition Column.
   5th Reserve Lorry Park.
   10th Reserve Lorry Park.
   3rd Aeroplane Supply Depot.

TANK CORPS.

	Attached to
H.Q. Tank Corps—	
Nos. 1 and 2 Gun Carrying Companies	G.H.Q. Reserve.
Training and Reinforcement Depot	L. of C.
Tank Gunnery School	L. of C.
Tank Driving Camp and Mechanical School	L. of C.
Chief Mechanical Engineer—	
Central Workshops	L. of C.
Central Stores	L. of C.
Nos. 1, 2, 3, 4 and 5 Advanced Workshops.	
Nos. 1 and 2 Tank Field Companies.	
1st Tank Brigade—	
Nos. 7, 11 and 12 Tank Battalions	
No. 1 Tank Supply Co.	
M.T. Co. (1086 Co., A.S.C.)	
2nd Tank Brigade—	
Nos. 9, 10, 14 Tank Battalions	
No. 2 Tank Supply Co.	
M.T. Co. (1087 Co., A.S.C.)	
3rd Tank Brigade—	
Nos. 3, 6 and 15 Tank Battalions	
No. 3 Tank Supply Co.	
M.T. Co. (1088 Co., A.S.C.)	G.H.Q. Reserve.
4th Tank Brigade—	
Nos. 1, 4 and 5 Tank Battalions	
No. 4 Tank Supply Co.	
M.T. Co. (1089 Co., A.S.C.)	
5th Tank Brigade—	
Nos. 2, 8, 13 Tank Battalions	
No. 5 Tank Supply Co.	
M.T. Co. (1090 Co., A.S.C.)	
6th Tank Brigade—	
Nos. 16 and 18 Tank Battalions	
M.T. Co. (1127 Co., A.S.C.)	
Workshop for A.S.C., M.T. (711 Co., A.S.C.).	
No. 17 (Armoured Car) Battalion	Fourth Army.

CORPS TROOPS.

CAVALRY CORPS.

H.Q., Cav. Corps.
    1/1st Bedford Yeo.
    1/1st Essex Yeo.
    1/1st Leicester Yeo.
    1/1st N. Somerset Yeo.
  4th Guards Brigade:
    Headquarters.
    4th G. Gds.
    3rd C. Gds.
    2nd I. Gds.

    4th Gds. L.T.M. Bty.
Corps Signal Troops { Cav. Corps Sig. Sqn.
      Cav. Corps Wireless Squadron.
      "AD" and "GG" Cable Sections.
Cav. Corps Bridging Park, R.E.
Cav. Corps Troops M.T. Co. (392 Co., A.S.C.).
No. 12 Sanitary Section.
770th Area Employment Co.

I. ARMY CORPS.

H.Q., I. Army Corps.
Corps Cavalry.
H.Q., Corps Heavy Artillery.
V/I. Heavy Trench Mortar Battery, R.G.A.
1st Cyclist Battalion.
No. 1 Group of Sharpshooters (Lovat's Scouts).
Corps Signal Troops { "A" Corps Sig. Co.
      Nos. 5 and 85 (Motor) Airline Sections.
      "K" and "AN" Cable Sections.
"A" Corps M.T. Column { 1st Corps Troops M.T. Co. (886 Co., A.S.C.).
      15th Divl. M.T. Co. (177 Co., A.S.C.).
      16th Divl. M.T. Co. (69 Co., A.S.C.).
      58th Divl. M.T. Co. (77 Co., A.S.C.).
      Divl. M.T. Co. (Co., A.S.C.).
No. 282 Co., A.S.C. (attached Heavy Artillery).
No 15 Medium Ordnance Mobile Workshop.
Nos. 1, 6 and 57 Light Ordnance Mobile Workshops.
261st Area Employment Co.

II. ARMY CORPS.

H.Q., II. Army Corps.
Corps Cavalry.
H.Q., Corps Heavy Artillery.
V/II. Heavy Trench Mortar Battery, R.G.A.
2nd Cyclist Regt. (Yorkshire Dragoons).
Corps Signal Troops { "B" Corps Sig. Co.
      Nos. 33 and 83 (Motor) Airline Sections.
      "AP" and "J" Cable Sections.
"B" Corps M.T. Column { 2nd Corps Troops M.T. Co. (887 Co., A.S.C.).
      9th Divl. M.T. Co. (131 Co., A.S.C.).
      34th Divl. M.T. Co. (179 Co., A.S.C.).
      Divl. M.T. Co. (Co., A.S.C.).
      Divl. M.T. Co. (Co., A.S.C.).
No. 406 Co., A.S.C. (attached Heavy Artillery).
No. 5 Medium Ordnance Mobile Workshop.
Nos. 9 and 10 Light Ordnance Mobile Workshops.
262nd Area Employment Co.

III. ARMY CORPS.

H.Q., III. Army Corps.
Corps Cavalry—1/1st Northumberland Yeomanry.
H.Q., Corps Heavy Artillery.
V/III. Heavy Trench Mortar Battery, R.G.A.

Corps Signal Troops...
- "C" Corps Sig. Co.
- Nos. 6 and 76 (Motor) Airline Sections.
- "WE" and "SS" Cable Sections.

"C" Corps M.T. Column
- 3rd Corps Troops M.T. Co. (388 Co., A.S.C.).
- 55th Divl. M.T. Co. (354 Co., A.S.C.)
- 74th Divl. M.T. Co. (71 Co., A.S.C.).
- Divl. M.T. Co. (Co., A.S.C.).
- Divl. M.T. Co. (Co., A.S.C.).

No. 641 Co., A.S.C. (attached Heavy Artillery).
No. 13 Medium Ordnance Mobile Workshop.
No. 13 Light Ordnance Mobile Workshop.
263rd Area Employment Co.

IV. ARMY CORPS.

H.Q., IV. Army Corps.
Corps Cavalry.
H.Q., Corps Heavy Artillery.
V/IV. Heavy Trench Mortar Battery, R.G.A.
4th Cyclist Battalion.
No. 8 Group of Sharpshooters (Lovat's Scouts).

Corps Signal Troops
- "D" Corps Sig. Co.
- Nos. 7 and 77 (Motor) Airline Sections.
- "MM" and "P" Cable Sections.

"D" Corps M.T. Column
- 4th Corps Troops M.T. Co. (389 Co., A.S.C.).
- 5th Divl. M.T. Co. (739 Co., A.S.C.).
- 37th Divl. M.T. Co. (135 Co., A.S.C.).
- 42nd Divl. M.T. Co. (896 Co., A.S.C.).
- Divl. M.T. Co. (Co., A.S.C.).
- N. Zealand Divl. M.T. Co. (610 Co., A.S.C.).

No. 562 Co., A.S.C. (attached Heavy Artillery).
No. 16 Medium Ordnance Mobile Workshop.
Nos. 28 and 45 Light Ordnance Mobile Workshops.
264th Area Employment Co.

V. ARMY CORPS.

H.Q., V. Army Corps.
H.Q., Corps Heavy Artillery.
V/V. Heavy Trench Mortar Battery, R.G.A.
5th Cyclist Regt. (North Irish Horse).

Corps Signal Troops
- "O" Corps Sig. Co.
- Nos. 36 and 86 (Motor) Airline Sections.
- "GQ" and "OO" Cable Sections.

"O" Corps M.T. Column
- 5th Corps Troops M.T. Co. (390 Co., A.S.C.).
- 17th Divl. M.T. Co. (48 Co., A.S.C.).
- 21st Divl. M.T. Co. (273 Co., A.S.C.).
- 33rd Divl. M.T. Co. (181 Co., A.S.C.).
- 38th Divl. M.T. Co. (67 Co., A.S.C.).
- Divl. M.T. Co. (Co., A.S.C.).

No. 363 Co., A.S.C. (attached Heavy Artillery).
No. 14 Medium Ordnance Mobile Workshop.
Nos. 19 and 46 Light Ordnance Mobile Workshops.
265th Area Employment Co.

CORPS TROOPS—*continued.*

VI. ARMY CORPS.

H.Q., VI. Army Corps.
Corps Cavalry.
H.Q., Corps Heavy Artillery.
V/VI. Heavy Trench Mortar Battery, R.G.A.
6th Cyclist Battalion.
Nos. 5 and 6 Groups of Sharpshooters (Lovat's Scouts).

Corps Signal Troops
- "F" Corps Sig. Co.
- Nos. 13 and 93 (Motor) Airline Sections.
- "CC" and "O" Cable Sections.

"F" Corps M.T. Column
- 6th Corps Troops M.T. Co. (368 Co., A.S.C.).
- Guards Divl. M.T. Co. (306 Co., A.S.C.).
- 2nd Divl. M.T. Co. (61 Co., A.S.C.).
- 3rd Divl. M.T. Co. (44 Co., A.S.C.).
- 62nd Divl. M.T. Co. (719 Co., A.S.C.).

No. 565 Co., A.S.C. (attached Heavy Artillery).
No. 6 Medium Ordnance Mobile Workshop.
Nos. 25, 32 and 54 Light Ordnance Mobile Workshops.
266th Area Employment Co.

VII. ARMY CORPS.

H.Q., VII. Army Corps.
Corps Cavalry.
H.Q., Corps Heavy Artillery.
V/VII. Heavy Trench Mortar Battery, R.G.A.
7th Cyclist Battalion.

Corps Signal Troops
- "G" Corps Sig. Co.
- Nos. 20 and 80 (Motor) Airline Sections.
- "AA" and "AW" Cable Sections.

"G" Corps M.T. Column
- 7th Corps Troops M.T. Co. (382 Co., A.S.C.).
- Divl. M.T. Co. (Co., A.S.C.).
- Divl. M.T. Co. (Co., A.S.C.).
- Divl. M.T. Co. (Co., A.S.C.).
- Divl. M.T. Co. (Co., A.S.C.).

No. 283 Co., A.S.C. (attached Heavy Artillery).
No.   Medium Ordnance Mobile Workshop.
No. 3 Light Ordnance Mobile Workshop.

VIII. ARMY CORPS.

H.Q. VIII. Army Corps.
Corps Cavalry.
H.Q., Corps Heavy Artillery.
V/VIII. Heavy Trench Mortar Battery, R.G.A.
8th Cyclist Battalion.
No. 9 Group of Sharpshooters (Lovat's Scouts).

Corps Signal Troops
- "S" Corps Sig. Co.
- Nos. 64 and 94 (Motor) Airline Sections.
- "SD" and "L" Cable Sections.

"H" Corps M.T. Column
- 8th Corps Troops M.T. Co. (885 Co., A.S.C.).
- 8th Divl. M.T. Co. (74 Co., A.S.C.).
- 12th Divl. M.T. Co. (175 Co., A.S.C.).
- 49th Divl. M.T. Co. (349 Co., A.S.C.).
- 52nd Divl. M.T. Co. (89 Co., A.S.C.).
- Divl. M.T. Co. (Co., A.S.C.).
- Divl. M.T. Co. (Co., A.S.C.).
- Divl. M.T. Co. (Co., A.S.C.).

No. 886 Co., A.S.C. (attached Heavy Artillery).
No. 19 Medium Ordnance Mobile Workshop.
Nos. 4, 33, 44, Light Ordnance Mobile Workshops.
276th Area Employment Co.

CORPS TROOPS—continued.

IX. ARMY CORPS.

H.Q., IX. Army Corps.
Corps Cavalry.
H.Q., Corps Heavy Artillery.
V/IX. Heavy Trench Mortar Battery, R.G.A.
9th Cyclist Battalion.
No. 10 Group of Sharpshooters (Lovat's Scouts).

Corps Signal Troops
- "E" Corps Sig. Co.
- Nos. 11 and 81 (Motor) Airline Sections.
- "BT" and "SV" Cable Sections.

"E" Corps M.T. Column
- 9th Corps Troops M.T. Co. (716 Co., A.S.C.).
- 1st Divl. M.T. Co. (59 Co., A.S.C.).
- 6th Divl. M.T. Co. (50 Co., A.S.C.).
- 32nd Divl. M.T. Co. (352 Co., A.S.C.).
- 46th Divl. M.T. Co. (271 Co., A.S.C.).

No. 717 Co., A.S.C. (attached Heavy Artillery).
Nos. 1, 2, 7, 25 Medium Ordnance Mobile Workshops.
Nos. 17, 18, 20, 22, 29 and 53 Light Ordnance Mobile Workshops.
269th Area Employment Co.

X. ARMY CORPS.

H.Q., X. Army Corps.
Corps Cavalry.
H.Q., Corps Heavy Artillery.
V/X. Heavy Trench Mortar Battery. R.G.A.
10th Cyclist Battalion.

Corps Signal Troops
- "X" Corps Sig. Co.
- Nos. 47 and 87 (Motor) Airline Sections.
- "EE" and "LC" Cable Sections.

"X" Corps M.T. Column
- 10th Corps Troops M.T. Co. (383 Co., A.S.C.).
- 29th Divl. M.T. Co. (496 Co., A.S.C.)
- 30th Divl. M.T. Co. (261 Co., A.S.C.)
- Divl. M.T. Co. (Co., A.S.C.)

No. 594 Co., A.S.C. (attached Heavy Artillery).
No. 3 Medium Ordnance Mobile Workshop.
No. 48 Light Ordnance Mobile Workshop.
270th Area Employment Co.

XI. ARMY CORPS.

H.Q., XI. Army Corps.
Corps Cavalry, 1/1st King Edward's Horse.
H.Q., Corps Heavy Artillery.
V/XI. Heavy Trench Mortar Battery, R.G.A.
11th Cyclist Battalion.
No. 12 Group of Sharpshooters (Lovat's Scouts).

Corps Signal Troops
- "L" Corps Sig. Co.
- Nos. 27 and 101 (Motor) Airline Sections.
- "AS" and "R" Cable Sections.

"L" Corps M.T. Column
- 11th Corps Troops M.T. Co. (321 Co., A.S.C.).
- 47th Divl. M.T. Co. (277 Co., A.S.C.).
- 57th Divl. M.T. Co. (731 Co., A.S.C.).
- 59th Divl. M.T. Co. (892 Co., A.S.C.).
- Divl. M.T. Co. (Co., A.S.C.).

No. 491 Co., A.S.C. (attached Heavy Artillery).
No.   Medium Ordnance Mobile Workshop.
Nos. 31 and 56 Light Ordnance Mobile Workshops.
271st Area Employment Co.

XIII. ARMY CORPS.

H.Q., XIII. Army Corps.
Corps Cavalry.
H.Q., Corps Heavy Artillery.
V/XIII. Heavy Trench Mortar Battery, R.G.A.
13th Cyclist Battalion.
No. 11 Group of Sharpshooters (Lovat's Scouts).
No.   Group of Sharpshooters (Lovat's Scouts).

Corps Signal Troops
- "N" Corps Sig. Co.
- Nos. 35 and 95 (Motor) Airline Sections.
- "II" and "VV" Cable Sections.

"N" Corps M.T. Column
- 13th Corps Troops M.T. Co. (564 Co., A.S.C.).
- 18th Divl. M.T. Co. (63 Co., A.S.C.).
- 25th Divl. M.T. Co. (344 Co., A.S.C.).
- 50th Divl. M.T. Co. (340 Co., A.S.C.).
- 66th Divl. M.T. Co. (888 Co., A.S.C.).
- Divl. M.T. Co. (Co., A.S.C.).

No. 335 Co., A.S.C. (attached Heavy Artillery).
No. 10 Medium Ordnance Mobile Workshop.
Nos. 15, 16, 24 Light Ordnance Mobile Workshops.
272nd Area Employment Co.

CORPS TROOPS—continued.

XV. ARMY CORPS.

H.Q., XV. Army Corps.
Corps Cavalry.
H.Q., Corps Heavy Artillery.
V/XV. Heavy Trench Mortar Battery, R.G.A.
15th Cyclist Battalion.
Nos. 3 and 13 Group of Sharpshooters (Lovat's Scouts).

Corps Signal Troops
- "P" Corps Signal Co.
- Nos. 51 and 91 (Motor) Airline Sections.
- "BE" and "BF" Cable Sections.

"P" Corps M.T. Column
- 15th Corps Troops M.T. Co. (696 Co., A.S.C.).
- Divl. M.T. Co. (Co., A.S.C.).
- 14th Divl. M.T. Co. (133 Co., A.S.C.).
- 36th Divl. M.T. Co. (379 Co., A.S.C.).
- 40th Divl. M.T. Co. (608 Co., A.S.C.).
- Divl. M.T. Co. (Co., A.S.C.).

No. 604 Co., A.S.C. (attached Heavy Artillery).
No. 12 Medium Ordnance Mobile Workshop.
Nos. 14 and 21 Light Ordnance Mobile Workshops.
274th Area Employment Co.

XVII. ARMY CORPS.

H.Q., XVII. Army Corps.
Corps Cavalry.
H.Q., Corps Heavy Artillery.
V/XVII. Heavy Trench Mortar Battery, R.G.A.
17th Cyclist Battalion.
No. 2 Group of Sharpshooters (Lovat's Scouts).

Corps Signal Troops
- "R" Corps Sig. Co.
- Nos. 40 and 90 (Motor) Airline Sections.
- "BV" and "TT" Cable Sections.

"R" Corps M.T. Column
- 17th Corps Troops M.T. Co. (582 Co., A.S.C.).
- 19th Divl. M.T. Co. (257 Co., A.S.C.).
- 20th Divl. M.T. Co. (267 Co., A.S.C.).
- 24th Divl. M.T. Co. (342 Co., A.S.C.).
- 61st Divl. M.T. Co. (302 Co., A.S.C.).
- Divl. M.T. Co. (Co., A.S.C.).

No. 611 Co., A.S.C. (attached Heavy Artillery).
No. 17 Medium Ordnance Mobile Workshop.
Nos. 23 and 27 Light Ordnance Mobile Workshops.
275th Area Employment Co.

XIX. ARMY CORPS.

H.Q., XIX. Army Corps.
Corps Cavalry.
H.Q., Corps Heavy Artillery.
V/XIX. Heavy Trench Mortar Battery, R.G.A.
19th Cyclist Battalion.

Corps Signal Troops
- "T" Corps Signal Co.
- Nos. 66 and 96 (Motor) Airline Sections.
- "AR" and "AY" Cable Sections.
- No. 2 Messenger Dog Section.

"T" Corps M.T. Column
- 19th Corps Troops M.T. Co. (883 Co., A.S.C.).
- 31st Divl. M.T. Co. (259 Co., A.S.C.).
- 35th Divl. M.T. Co. (304 Co., A.S.C.).
- 41st Divl. M.T. Co. (498 Co., A.S.C.).
- M.T. Co. (Co., A.S.C.).
- M.T. Co. (Co., A.S.C.).

No. 884 Co., A.S.C. (attached Heavy Artillery).
No. 9 Medium Ordnance Mobile Workshop.
Nos. 11 and 12 Light Ordnance Mobile Workshops.
277th Area Employment Co.

CORPS TROOPS—continued.

XXII. ARMY CORPS.

H.Q., XXII. Army Corps.

Corps Cavalry—Composite Regt.
- H.Q.
- 4th Aus. L.H. Regt. ("A" & "B" Sqns.).
- 1 Sqn. Otago Mtd. Rif.

H.Q., Corps Heavy Artillery.
V/XXII. Heavy Trench Mortar Battery, R.G.A.
New Zealand Cyclist Bn.
No. 7 Group of Sharpshooters (Lovat's Scouts).

Corps Signal Troops
- "Y" Corps Sig. Co.
- Nos. 31 and 84 (Motor) Airline Sections.
- "AK" and "BD" Cable Sections.

"Y" Corps M.T. Column
- 22nd Corps Troops M.T. Co. (687 Co., A.S.C.).
- 4th Divl. M.T. Co. (65 Co., A.S.C.).
- 11th Divl. M.T. Co. (714 Co., A.S.C.).
- 51st Divl. M.T. Co. (265 Co., A.S.C.).
- 56th Divl. M.T. Co. (263 Co., A.S.C.).
- 63rd Divl. M.T. Co. (701 Co., A.S.C.).
- Divl. M.T. Co. (Co., A.S.C.).

No. 403 Co., A.S.C. (attached Heavy Artillery).
Nos. 18, 20 Medium Ordnance Mobile Workshops.
Nos. 2, 55, 62 Light Ordnance Mobile Workshops.
267th Area Employment Co.

AUSTRALIAN ARMY CORPS.

H.Q., Australian Army Corps.
Corps Cavalry—13th Regt. L.H.
H.Q., Corps Heavy Artillery.
V/Aus. Heavy Trench Mortar Battery, A.F.A.
Australian Cyclist Battalion.

Corps Signal Troops
- Australian Corps Sig. Co.
- Nos. 1 and 2 Australian (Motor) Airline Sections.
- Nos. 1 and 2 Australian Cable Sections.

Australian Corps M.T. Column
- 6th Australian (Corps Troops) M.T. Co.
- 1st Australian M.T. Co.
- 2nd Australian M.T. Co.
- 3rd Australian M.T. Co.
- 4th Australian M.T. Co.
- 5th Australian M.T. Co.

No. 272 Co., A.S.C. (attached Heavy Artillery).
Nos.   Medium Ordnance Mobile Workshops.
No. 47 Light Ordnance Mobile Workshop.

CANADIAN ARMY CORPS.

H.Q., Canadian Army Corps.
Corps Cavalry—Canadian Light Horse.
   Royal North West Mounted Police.
H.Q., Corps Heavy Artillery.
Canadian Cyclist Bn.
1st and 2nd Canadian Motor M.G. Bdes.

Corps Signal Troops
- H.Q., Canadian Corps Sig. Co.
- No. 1 Cdn. and 2 Cdn. (Motor) Airline Sections.
- "CE," "CF," "CG" and "CH" Cable Sections.

Nos. 1, 2, 3, 4 Canadian Infantry Works Companies.

Canadian Corps M.T. Column
- Canadian Corps Troops M.T. Co. (721 Co., A.S.C.).
- 1st Canadian Divl. M.T. Co. (415 Co., A.S.C.).
- 2nd Canadian Divl. M.T. Co. (722 Co., A.S.C.).
- 3rd Canadian Divl. M.T. Co. (724 Co., A.S.C.).
- 4th Canadian Divl. M.T. Co. (785 Co., A.S.C.).

Canadian M.M.G. M.T. Co. (1119 Co., C.A.S.C.).
Canadian Engineers M.T. Co. (1120 Co., C.A.S.C.).
No. 402 Co., A.S.C. (attached Heavy Artillery).
No. 8 Canadian Medium Ordnance Mobile Workshop.
Nos. 8 Cdn., 26 Cdn. Light Ordnance Mobile Workshops.
5th, 6th, 7th, 8th and 9th Canadian Area Employment Cos.

CORPS TROOPS—*continued.*

PORTUGUESE ARMY CORPS.

7391	H.Q., Portuguese Army Corps.
7392	Portuguese Cyclist Bn.—2 Companies.
7393	H.Q., Corps Artillery.
7394/7404	Corps Heavy Artillery—H.Q. and 10 Batteries.
7405	H.Q., Portuguese Engineers—
7406	1st Portuguese Army Troops Co.
7407	2nd Portuguese Army Troops Co.
7408	1st Portuguese Tunnelling Co.
7409	Searchlight Company.
7410	Engineer M.T. Column.
7411/7413	Corps Signal Troops { Portuguese Corps Signal Section. / Motor Airline Section. / Portuguese Wireless Section. }
7414/7416	Portuguese Amm. Sub-Park.
7417/7420	Corps Supply Column { Corps Troops Supply Column. / 1st Portuguese Divl. Supply Section. / 2nd Portuguese Divl. Supply Section. }
7421	H.Q., Portuguese Medical Services—
	1st and 2nd Portuguese F. Amb.
7425	Portuguese Artillery Light Workshop.
	Portuguese Corps Labour Co.
	Portuguese Punishment Bn.

DIVISIONS.

1st CAVALRY DIVISION.

1st Cavalry Brigade.	2nd Cavalry Brigade.	9th Cavalry Brigade.
Headquarters.	Headquarters.	Headquarters.
2nd D.G.	4th D.G.	8th Hrs.
5th D.G.	9th Lrs.	15th Hrs.
11th Hrs.	18th Hrs.	19th Hrs.
"I" Batt., R.H.A.	"H" Batt., R.H.A.	"Y" Batt., R.H.A.
(6—13-pr. guns)	(6—13-pr. guns)	(6—13-pr. guns)
1st Cav. M.G. Sqn.	2nd Cav. M.G. Sqn.	9th Cav. M.G. Sqn.
1st Signal Troop.	2nd Signal Troop.	9th Signal Troop.

Divisional Troops.

H.Q., 1st Cav. Div.
7th Bde. R.H.A. and Amm. Column.
1st F. Sqn., R.E.
1st Sig. Sqn.
H.Q., 1st Cav. Divl. A.S.C. (27 Co., A.S.C.).
1st Cav. Divl. M.T. Co. (57 Co., A.S.C.).
1st Cav. Divl. Aux. (Horse) Co. (574 Co., A.S.C.).
1st, 3rd and 9th Cav. F. Ambs.
1st, 10th and 39th Mobile Vet. Sections.
771st Divl. Employment Co.

2nd CAVALRY DIVISION.

3rd Cavalry Brigade.	4th Cavalry Brigade.	5th Cavalry Brigade.
Headquarters.	Headquarters.	Headquarters.
4th Hrs.	6th D.G.	2nd Dns.
5th Lrs.	3rd Hrs.	12th Lrs.
16th Lrs.	1/1st Oxfordshire Hrs.	20th Hrs.
"D" Batt., R.H.A.	"J" Batt., R.H.A.	"E" Batt., R.H.A.
(6—13-pr. guns)	(6—13-pr. guns)	(6—13-pr. guns)
3rd Cav. M.G. Sqn.	4th Cav. M.G. Sqn.	5th Cav. M.G. Sqn.
3rd Signal Troop.	4th Signal Troop.	5th Signal Troop.

Divisional Troops.

H.Q., 2nd Cav. Div.
3rd Bde. R.H.A. and Amm. Column.
2nd F. Sqn., R.E.
2nd Sig. Sqn.
H.Q., 2nd Cav. Divl. A.S.C. (424 Co., A.S.C.).
2nd Cav. Divl. M.T. Co. (46 Co., A.S.C.).
2nd Cav. Divl. Aux. (Horse) Co. (575 Co., A.S.C.).
2nd, 4th and 5th Cav. F. Ambs.
7th, 8th and 9th Mobile Vet. Sections.
772nd Divl. Employment Co.

Divisions—*continued*.

3rd CAVALRY DIVISION.

6th Cavalry Brigade.
Headquarters.
3rd D.G.
1st Dns.
10th Hrs.
" C " Batt., R.H.A.
(6—13-pr. guns)

———

6th Cav. M.G. Sqn.
6th Signal Troop.

7th Cavalry Brigade.
Headquarters.
7th D.G.
6th (Innis.) Dns.
17th Lrs.
" K " Batt., R.H.A.
(6—13-pr. guns)

———

7th Cav. M.G. Sqn.
7th Signal Troop.

Canadian Cavalry Brigade.
Headquarters.
Royal Canadian Dns.
Lord Strathcona's Horse.
Fort Garry Horse.
Royal Canadian H.A. Bde.
(2 Batts. of 4—13-pr. guns)

Canadian Cav. M.G. Sqn.
Canadian Signal Troop.

Divisional Troops.

H.Q., 3rd Cav. Div.
4th Bde. R.H.A. and Amm. Column.
3rd F. Sqn., R.E.
3rd Sig. Sqn.
H.Q. 3rd Cav. Divl. A.S.C. (81 Co., A.S.C.).
3rd Cav. Divl. M.T. Co. (73 Co., A.S.C.).
3rd Cav. Divl. Aux. (Horse) Co. (576 Co., A.S.C.).
6th, 7th and Cdn Cav. F. Ambs.
13th, 14th and " A " Cdn. Mobile Vet. Sections.
773rd Divl. Employment Co.

Divisions—*continued.*

GUARDS DIVISION.

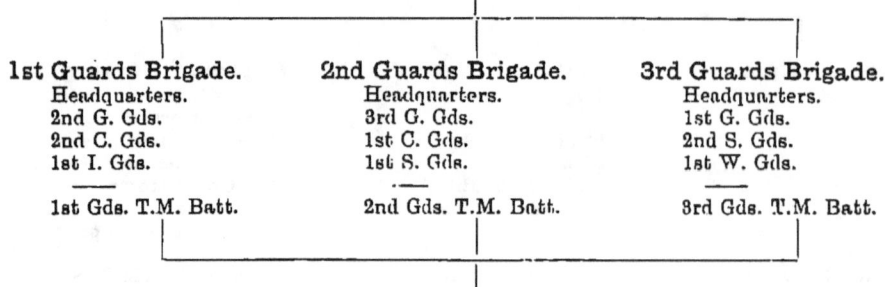

1st Guards Brigade.	2nd Guards Brigade.	3rd Guards Brigade.
Headquarters.	Headquarters.	Headquarters.
2nd G. Gds.	3rd G. Gds.	1st G. Gds.
2nd C. Gds.	1st C. Gds.	2nd S. Gds.
1st I. Gds.	1st S. Gds.	1st W. Gds.
1st Gds. T.M. Batt.	2nd Gds. T.M. Batt.	3rd Gds. T.M. Batt.

Divisional Troops.

H.Q., Guards Division.
H.Q., Divisional Artillery.
74th Bde., R.F.A. (" A," " B," " C," " D " Batts.) (18—18-prs. and 6—4·5-in. howrs.).
75th Bde., R.F.A. (" A," " B," " C," " D " Batts.) (18—18-prs. and 6—4·5-in. howrs.).
X/G. Trench Mortar Battery, R.A.
Y/G. Trench Mortar Battery, R.A.
Guards Divl. Amm. Column.
H.Q., Divisional Engineers.
55th, 75th, and 76th F. Cos., R.E.
Guards Divl. Sig. Co.
Pioneer Bn., 4th C. Gds.
No. 4 Bn. Machine Gun Guards.
Guards Divl. Train (11, 124, 168 and 436 Cos., A.S.C.).
3rd, 4th and 9th F. Ambs.
46th Mobile Vet. Section.
Guards Divl. Employment Co.

1st DIVISION.

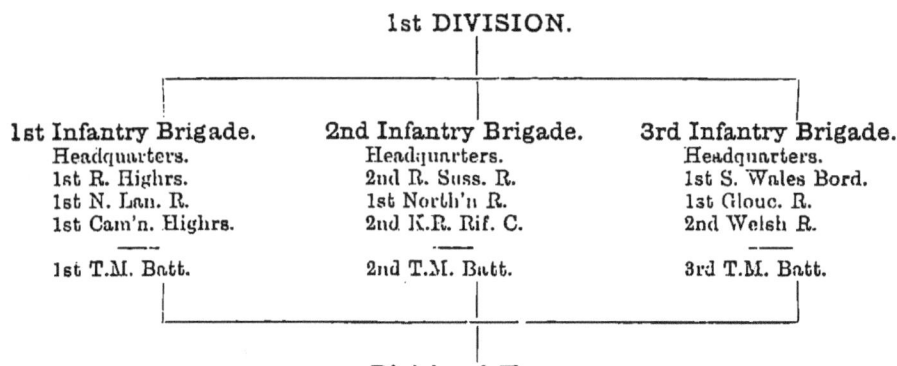

1st Infantry Brigade.	2nd Infantry Brigade.	3rd Infantry Brigade.
Headquarters.	Headquarters.	Headquarters.
1st R. Highrs.	2nd R. Suss. R.	1st S. Wales Bord.
1st N. Lan. R.	1st North'n R.	1st Glouc. R.
1st Cam'n. Highrs.	2nd K.R. Rif. C.	2nd Welsh R.
1st T.M. Batt.	2nd T.M. Batt.	3rd T.M. Batt.

Divisional Troops.

H.Q., 1st Div.
H.Q., Divisional Artillery.
25th Bde., R.F.A. (113, 114, 115 Batts. and 40 Batt.) (18—18-prs. and 6—4·5-in. howrs.).
39th Bde., R.F.A. (46, 51, 54 Batts. and 30 Batt.) (18—18-prs. and 6—4·5-in. howrs.).
X/I. Trench Mortar Battery, R.A.
Y/I. Trench Mortar Battery, R.A.
1st Divl. Amm. Column.
H.Q., Divisional Engineers.
23rd and 26th F. Cos., R.E.
409th (Lowland) F. Co., R.E. (T.).
1st Divl. Sig. Co.
Pioneer Bn., 1/6th Welsh R. (T.).
No. 1 Bn. M.G. Corps.
1st Divl. Train (7, 13, 16 and 36 Cos., A.S.C.).
1st, 2nd and 141st F. Ambs.
2nd Mobile Vet. Section.
204th Divl. Employment Co.

Divisions—*continued.*

2nd DIVISION.

5th Infantry Brigade.	6th Infantry Brigade.	99th Infantry Brigade.
Headquarters.	Headquarters.	Headquarters.
24th R. Fus.	17th R. Fus.	23rd R. Fus.
2nd Oxf. & Bucks. L.I.	1st L'pool R.	1st R. Berks. R.
2nd High. L.I.	2nd S. Staff. R.	1st K.R. Rif. C.
5th T.M. Batt.	6th T.M. Batt.	99th T.M. Batt.

Divisional Troops.

H.Q., 2nd Div.
H.Q., Divisional Artillery.
36th Bde., R.F.A. (15, 48, 71 Batts. and " D " Batt.) (18—18-prs. and 6—4˙5-in. howrs.).
41st Bde., R.F.A. (9, 16, 17 Batts. and 47 Batt.) (18—18-prs. and 6—4˙5-in. howrs.).
X/2 Trench Mortar Battery, R.A.
Y/2 Trench Mortar Battery, R.A.
2nd Divl. Amm. Column.
H.Q., Divisional Engineers.
5th and 226th F. Cos., R.E.
483rd (E. Anglian) F. Co., R.E. (T.).
2nd Divl. Sig. Co.
Pioneer Bn., 10th Bn. D. of Corn. L.I.
No. 2 Bn. M.G. Corps.
2nd Divl. Train (28, 31, 35 and 172 Cos., A.S.C.).
5th, 6th and 100th F. Ambs.
3rd Mobile Vet. Section.
205th Divl. Employment Co.

3rd DIVISION.

8th Infantry Brigade.	9th Infantry Brigade.	76th Infantry Brigade.
Headquarters.	Headquarters.	Headquarters.
2nd R. Scots.	1st North'd Fus.	8th R. Lanc. R.
1st R. Sc. Fus.	4th R. Fus.	2nd Suff. R.
7th Shrop. L.I.	13th L'pool. R.	1st Gord. Highrs.
8th T.M. Batt.	9th T.M. Batt.	76th T.M. Batt.

Divisional Troops.

H.Q., 3rd Div.
H.Q., Divisional Artillery.
40th Bde., R.F.A. (6, 23, 49 Batts. and 130 Batt.) (18—18-prs. and 6—4˙5-in. howrs.).
42nd Bde., R.F.A. (29, 41, 45 Batts. and 129 Batt.) (18—18-prs. and 6—4˙5-in. howrs.).
X/3 Trench Mortar Battery, R.A.
Y/3 Trench Mortar Battery, R.A.
3rd Divl. Amm. Column
H.Q., Divisional Engineers.
56th F., Co., R.E.
438th (Cheshire) F. Co., R.E. (T.)
529th (E. Riding) F. Co., R.E. (T.).
3rd Divl. Sig. Co.
Pioneer Bn.—20th (Pioneer) Bn., K.R. Rif. C.
No. 3 Bn. M.G. Corps.
3rd Divl. Train (15, 21, 22 and 29 Cos., A.S.C.).
7th, 8th and 142nd F. Ambs.
11th Mobile Vet. Section.
206th Divl. Employment Co.

4th DIVISION.

10th Infantry Brigade.
Headquarters.
1st R. War. R.
2nd W. Riding Regt
2nd Sea. Highrs.

10th T.M. Batt.

11th Infantry Brigade.
Headquarters.
1st Som. L.I.
1st Hamps. R.
1st Rif. Bde.

11th T.M. Batt.

12th Infantry Brigade.
Headquarters.
1st R. Lanc. Regt.
2nd Lan. Fus.
2nd Essex Regt.

12th T.M. Batt.

Divisional Troops.
H.Q., 4th Div.
H.Q., Divisional Artillery.
29th Bde., R.F.A. (125, 126, 127 Batts. and 128 Batt.) (18—18-prs. and 6—4·5-in. howrs.).
32nd Bde., R.F.A. (27, 134, 135 Batts. and 86 Batt.) (18—18-prs. and 6—4·5-in. howrs.).
X/4 Trench Mortar Battery, R.A.
Y/4 Trench Mortar Battery, R.A.
4th Divl. Amm. Column.
H.Q., Divisional Engineers.
9th F. Co., R.E.
526th (Durham) F. Co., R.E. (T.).
406th (Renfrew) F. Co., R.E. (T.).
4th Divl. Sig. Co.
Pioneer Bn.—21st Bn. W. York. R.
No. 4 Bn. M.G. Corps.
4th Divl. Train (18, 25, 32 and 38 Cos., A.S.C.).
10th, 11th and 12th F. Ambs.
4th Mobile Vet. Section.
207th Divl. Employment Co.

5th DIVISION.

13th Infantry Brigade.
Headquarters.
16th R. War. R.
2nd K.O. Sco. Bord.
1st R.W. Kent R.

13th T.M. Batt.

15th Infantry Brigade.
Headquarters.
1st Norf. R.
1st Bedf. R.
1st Ches. R.

15th T.M. Batt.

95th Infantry Brigade.
Headquarters.
1st Devon. R.
1st E. Surr. R.
1st D. Corn. L.I.

95th T.M. Batt.

Divisional Troops.
H.Q., 5th Div.
H.Q., Divisional Artillery.
15th Bde., R.F.A. (52, 80, "A" and "D" Batts.) (18—18-prs. and 6—4·5-in. howrs.).
27th Bde., R.F.A. (119, 120, 121 Batts. and 37 Batt.) (18—18-prs. and 6—4·5-in. howrs.).
X/5 Trench Mortar Battery.
Y/5 Trench Mortar Battery.
5th Divl. Amm. Column.
H.Q., Divisional Engineers.
59th, 491st and 527th F. Cos., R.E.
5th Divl. Sig. Co.
Pioneer Bn.—14th R. War. R.
No. 5 Bn. M.G. Corps.
5th Divl. Train (4, 6, 33 and 37 Cos., A.S.C.).
13th, 14th and 15th F. Ambs.
5th Mobile Vet. Section.
208th Divl. Employment Co.

Divisions—*continued.*

6th DIVISION.

16th Infantry Brigade.
Headquarters.
1st E. Kent R.
1st Shrops. L.I.
2nd York. & Lanc. R.

16th T.M. Batt.

18th Infantry Brigade.
Headquarters.
1st W. York. R.
11th Essex R.
2nd Durh. L.I.

18th T.M. Batt.

71st Infantry Brigade.
Headquarters.
9th Norf. R.
1st Leic. R.
2nd Notts. & Derby R.

71st T.M. Batt.

Divisional Troops.

H.Q., 6th Div.
H.Q., Divisional Artillery.
2nd Bde., R.F.A. (21, 42, 53 Batts. and 87 Batt.) (18—18-prs. and 6—4·5-in. howrs.).
24th Bde., R.F.A. (110, 111, 112 Batts. and 43 Batt.) (18—18 prs. and 6—4·5-in. howrs.).
X/6 Trench Mortar Battery, R.A.
Y/6 Trench Mortar Battery, R.A.
6th Divl. Amm. Column.
H.Q., Divisional Engineers.
12th F. Co., R.E.
459th (W. Riding) F. Co., R.E. (T.).
509th (London) F. Co., R.E. (T.).
6th Divl. Sig. Co.
Pioneer Bn.—11th Bn. Leic. R. (Pioneers).
No. 6 Bn. M.G. Corps
6th Divl. Train (17, 19, 23 and 24 Cos., A.S.C.)
16th, 17th and 18th F. Ambs.
6th Mobile Vet. Section.
209th Divl. Employment Co.

8th DIVISION.

23rd Infantry Brigade.
Headquarters.
2nd Devon R.
2nd W. York. R.
2nd Midd'x. R.

23rd T.M. Batt.

24th Infantry Brigade.
Headquarters.
1st Worc. R.
1st Notts. and Derby R.
2nd North'n. R.

24th T.M. Batt.

25th Infantry Brigade.
Headquarters.
2nd E. Lan. R.
2nd R. Berks. R.
2nd Rif. Brig.

25th T.M. Batt.

Divisional Troops.

H.Q., 8th Div.
H.Q., Divisional Artillery.
33rd Bde., R.F.A. (32, 33, 36 Batts. and 55 Batt.) (18—18-prs. and 6—4·5-in. howrs.).
45th Bde., R.F.A. (1, 3, 5 Batts. and 57 Batt.) (18—18-prs. and 6—4·5-in. howrs.).
X/8 Trench Mortar Battery, R.A.
Y/8 Trench Mortar Battery, R.A.
8th Divl. Amm. Column.
H.Q., Divisional Engineers.
2nd and 15th F. Cos., R.E.
490th (Home Counties) F. Co., R.E. (T.).
8th Divl. Sig. Co.
Pioneer Bn.—1/7th Bn. Durh. L.I.
No. 8 Bn. M.G. Corps.
8th Divl. Train (41, 84, 85 and 87 Cos., A.S.C.).
24th, 25th and 26th F. Ambs.
15th Mobile Vet. Section.
211th Divl. Employment Co.

Divisions—*continued.*

9th (SCOTTISH) DIVISION.

26th Infantry Brigade.	27th Infantry Brigade.	28th Infantry Brigade.
Headquarters.	Headquarters.	Headquarters.
8th R. Highrs.	11th R. Scots.	2nd R. Sco. Fus.
7th Sea. Highrs.	12th R. Scots.	9th Sco. Rif.
5th Cam'n Highrs.	6th K.O. Sco. Bord.	R. Newfoundland Bn.
26th T.M. Batt.	27th T.M. Batt.	28th T.M. Batt.

Divisional Troops.

H.Q., 9th (Scottish) Div.
H.Q., Divisional Artillery.
50th Bde., R.F.A. (" A," " B," " C," " D " Batts.) (18—18-prs. and 6—4·5-in. howrs.).
51st Bde., R.F.A. (" A," " B," " C," " D " Batts.) (18—18-prs. and 6—4·5-in. howrs.).
X/9 Trench Mortar Battery, R.A.
Y/9 Trench Mortar Battery, R.A.
9th Divl. Amm. Column.
H.Q., Divisional Engineers.
63rd, 64th and 90th F. Cos., R.E.
9th Divl. Sig. Co.
Pioneer Bn., 9th Sea. Highrs.
No. 9 Bn. M.G. Corps.
9th Divl. Train (104-107 Cos., A.S.C.).
27th, 28th and 2/1st E. Lancs. F. Ambs.
21st Mobile Vet. Section.
212th Divl. Employment Co.

11th DIVISION.

32nd Infantry Brigade.	33rd Infantry Brigade.	34th Infantry Brigade.
Headquarters.	Headquarters.	Headquarters.
9th (York Hrs.) W. York. R.	6th Lincs. R.	8th North'd Fus.
2nd York. R.	7th S. Staff. R.	5th Dorset R.
6th York. and Lanc. R.	9th Notts. & Derby. R.	11th Manch. R.
32nd T.M. Batt.	33rd T.M. Batt.	34th T.M. Batt.

Divisional Troops.

H.Q., 11th Div.
H.Q., Divisional Artillery.
58th Bde., R.F.A., (" A," " B," " C," " D " Batts.) (18—18-prs. and 6—4·5-in. howrs.).
59th Bde., R.F.A., (" A," " B," " C," " D " Batts.) (18—18-prs. and 6—4·5-in. howrs.).
X/11 Trench Mortar Battery, R.A
Y/11 Trench Mortar Battery, R.A.
11/th Divl. Amm. Column.
H.Q., Divisional Engineers.
67th, 68th and 86th F. Cos., R.E.
11th Divl. Sig. Co.
Pioneer Bn.—6th E. York. R.
No. 11 Bn. M.G. Corps.
11th Div. Train (479-482 Cos., A.S.C.).
33rd, 34th and 35th F. Ambs.
22nd Mobile Vet. Section.
213th Divl. Employment Co.

12th (EASTERN) DIVISION.

35th Infantry Brigade.	36th Infantry Brigade.	37th Infantry Brigade.
Headquarters.	Headquarters.	Headquarters.
7th Norf. R.	9th R. Fus.	6th R.W. Surr. R.
9th Essex R.	7th R. Suss. R.	6th E. Kent R.
1/1st Camb. R.	5th R. Berks. R.	6th R.W. Kent R.
35th T.M. Batt.	36th T.M. Batt.	37th T.M. Batt.

Divisional Troops.

H.Q., 12th (Eastern) Div.
H.Q., Divisional Artillery.
62nd Bde., R.F.A. (" A," " B," " C," " D " Batts.) (18—18-prs. and 6—4·5-in. howrs.).
63rd Bde., R.F.A. (" A," " B," " C," " D " Batts.) (18—18-prs. and 6—4·5-in. howrs.).
X/12 Trench Mortar Battery, R.A.
Y/12 Trench Mortar Battery, R.A.
12th Divl. Amm. Column.
H.Q., Divisional Engineers.
69th, 70th and 87th F. Cos., R.E.
12th Divl. Sig. Co.
Pioneer Bn., 5th North'n R.
No. 12 Bn. M.G. Corps.
12th Divl. Train (116-119 Cos., A.S.C.).
36th, 37th, and 38th F. Ambs.
23rd Mobile Vet. Section.
214th Divl. Employment Co.

14th DIVISION.

41st Infantry Brigade.	42nd Infantry Brigade.	43rd Infantry Brigade.
Headquarters.	Headquarters.	Headquarters.
18th York & Lanc. R.	6th (Wilts. Yeo.) Wilts. R.	12th Suff. R.
29th Durh. L.I.	16th Manch. R.	20th Midd'x R.
33rd Lond. R. (Rif. Bde.).	14th Arg. & Suth'd Highrs.	10th High. L.I.
41st T.M. Batt.	42nd T.M. Batt.	43rd T.M. Batt.

Divisional Troops.

H.Q., 14th Div.
H.Q., Divisional Artillery.
46th Bde., R.F.A. (" A," " B," " C," " D " Batts.) (18—18-prs. and 6—4·5-in. howrs.).
47th Bde., R.F.A. (" A," " B," " C," " D " Batts.) (18—18-prs. and 6—4·5-in. howrs.).
14th Divl. Amm. Column.
H.Q., Divisional Engineers.
61st, 62nd and 89th F. Cos., R.E.
14th Divl. Sig. Co.
Pioneer Bn., 15th N. Lanc. R.
No. 14 Bn., M.G. Corps.
14th Divl. Train (100-103 Cos., A.S.C.).
42nd, 43rd and 44th F. Ambs.
26th Mobile Vet. Section.
215th Divl. Employment Co.

Divisions—continued.

15th (SCOTTISH) DIVISION.

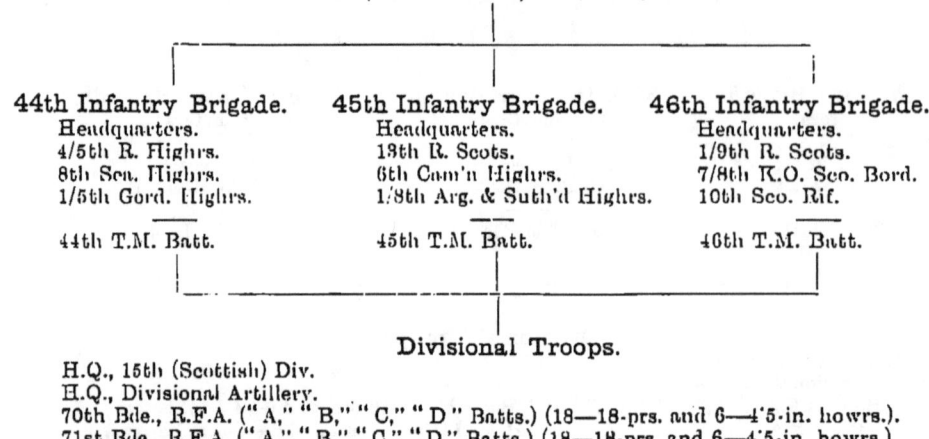

44th Infantry Brigade.
Headquarters.
4/5th R. Highrs.
8th Sea. Highrs.
1/5th Gord. Highrs.

44th T.M. Batt.

45th Infantry Brigade.
Headquarters.
13th R. Scots.
6th Cam'n Highrs.
1/8th Arg. & Suth'd Highrs.

45th T.M. Batt.

46th Infantry Brigade.
Headquarters.
1/9th R. Scots.
7/8th K.O. Sco. Bord.
10th Sco. Rif.

46th T.M. Batt.

Divisional Troops.

H.Q., 15th (Scottish) Div.
H.Q., Divisional Artillery.
70th Bde., R.F.A. ("A," "B," "C," "D" Batts.) (18—18-prs. and 6—4·5-in. howrs.).
71st Bde., R.F.A. ("A," "B," "C," "D" Batts.) (18—18-prs. and 6—4·5-in. howrs.).
X/15 Trench Mortar Battery, R.A.
Y/15 Trench Mortar Battery, R.A.
15th Divl. Amm. Column.
H.Q., Divisional Engineers.
73rd, 74th and 91st F. Cos., R.E.
15th Divl. Sig. Co.
Pioneer Bn., 9th Gord. Highrs.
No. 15 Bn. M.G. Corps.
15th Divl. Train (138-141 Cos., A.S.C.).
45th, 46th and 47th F. Ambs.
27th Mobile Vet. Section.
216th Divl. Employment Co.

16th DIVISION.

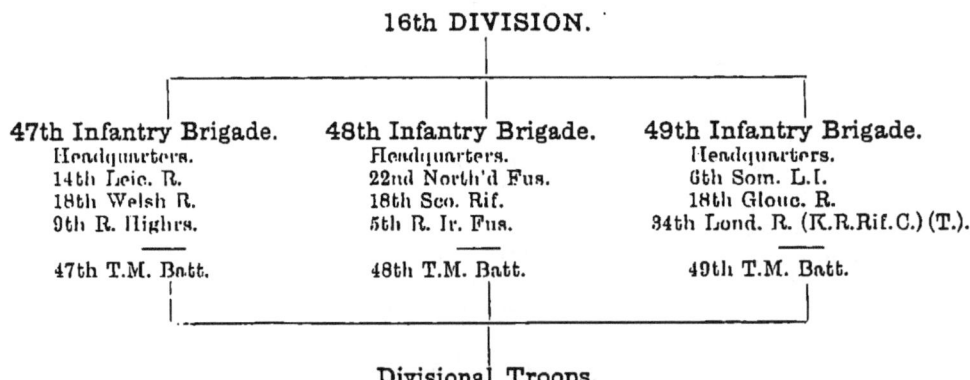

47th Infantry Brigade.
Headquarters.
14th Leic. R.
18th Welsh R.
9th R. Highrs.

47th T.M. Batt.

48th Infantry Brigade.
Headquarters.
22nd North'd Fus.
18th Sco. Rif.
5th R. Ir. Fus.

48th T.M. Batt.

49th Infantry Brigade.
Headquarters.
6th Som. L.I.
18th Glouc. R.
34th Lond. R. (K.R.Rif.C.) (T.).

49th T.M. Batt.

Divisional Troops.

H.Q., 16th Div.
H.Q., Divisional Artillery.
177th Bde., R.F.A. ("A," "B," "C," "D" Batts.) (18—18-prs. and 6—4·5-in. howrs.).
180th Bde., R.F.A. ("A," "B," "C," "D" Batts.) (18—18-prs. and 6—4·5-in. howrs.).
16th Divl. Amm. Column.
H.Q., Divisional Engineers.
155th, 156th and 157th F. Cos., R.E.
16th Divl. Sig. Co.
Pioneer Bn., 11th Hamps. R.
No. 16 Bn. M.G. Corps.
16th Divl. Train (142-145 Cos., A.S.C.).
111th, 112th and 113th F. Ambs.
47th Mobile Vet. Section.
217th Divl. Employment Co.

Divisions—*continued*.

17th (NORTHERN) DIVISION.

50th Infantry Brigade.
Headquarters.
10th W. York. R.
7th E. York. R.
6th Dorset. R.

50th T.M. Batt.

51st Infantry Brigade.
Headquarters.
7th Lincs. R.
7th (Westmoreland and Cumberland Yeo.) Bord. R.
10th Notts. & Derby R.

51st T.M. Batt.

52nd Infantry Brigade.
Headquarters.
10th Lanc. Fus.
9th W. Rid. R.
12th (Duke of Lancaster's Yeo.) Manch. R.

52nd T.M. Batt.

Divisional Troops.

H.Q., 17th (Northern) Div.
H.Q., Divisional Artillery.
78th Bde., R.F.A. ("A," "B," "C," "D" Batts.) (18—18-prs. and 6—4·5-in. howrs.).
79th Bde., R.F.A. ("A," "B," "C," "D" Batts.) (18—18-prs. and 6—4·5-in. howrs.).
X/17 Trench Mortar Battery, R.A.
Y/17 Trench Mortar Battery, R.A.
17th Divl. Amm. Column.
H.Q., Divisional Engineers.
77th, 78th and 93rd F. Cos., R.E.
17th Divl. Sig. Co.
Pioneer Bn., 7th York. & Lanc. R.
No. 17 Bn. M.G. Corps.
17th Divl. Train (146-149 Cos., A.S.C.).
51st, 52nd and 53rd F. Ambs.
29th Mobile Vet. Section.
218th Divl. Employment Co.

18th (EASTERN) DIVISION.

53rd Infantry Brigade.
Headquarters.
10th Essex R.
8th R. Berks. R.
7th R. W. Kent R.

53rd T.M. Batt.

54th Infantry Brigade.
Headquarters.
11th R. Fus.
2nd Bedf. R.
6th North'n R.

54th T.M. Batt.

55th Infantry Brigade.
Headquarters.
7th R. W. Surr. R.
7th E. Kent R.
8th E. Surr. R.

55th T.M. Batt.

Divisional Troops.

H.Q., 18th (Eastern) Div.
H.Q., Divisional Artillery.
82nd Bde., R.F.A. ("A," "B," "C," "D" Batts.) (18—18-prs. and 6—4·5-in. howrs.).
83rd Bde., R.F.A. ("A," "B," "C," "D" Batts.) (18—18-prs. and 6—4·5-in. howrs.).
X/18 Trench Mortar Battery, R.A.
Y/18 Trench Mortar Battery, R.A.
18th Divl. Amm. Column.
H.Q., Divisional Engineers.
79th, 80th and 92nd F. Cos., R.E.
18th Divl. Sig. Co.
Pioneer Bn., 8th R. Suss. R.
No. 18 Bn. M.G. Corps.
18th Divl. Train (150-153 Cos., A.S.C.).
54th, 55th and 56th F. Ambs.
30th Mobile Vet. Section.
219th Divl. Employment Co.

Divisions—*continued*.

19th (WESTERN) DIVISION.

56th Infantry Brigade.	57th Infantry Brigade.	58th Infantry Brigade.
Headquarters.	Headquarters.	Headquarters.
9th Ches. R.	10th R. War. R.	9th R. W. Fus.
1/4th Shrops. L.I.	8th Glouc. R.	9th Welsh R.
8th N. Staff. R.	3rd Worc. R.	2nd Wilts R.
56th T.M. Batt.	57th T.M. Batt.	58th T.M. Batt.

Divisional Troops.

H.Q., 19th (Western) Div.
H.Q., Divisional Artillery.
87th Bde., R.F.A. ("A," "B," "C," "D" Batts.) (18—18-prs. and 6—4·5-in. howrs.).
88th Bde., R.F.A. ("A," "B," "C," "D" Batts.) (18—18-prs. and 6—4·5-in. howrs.).
X/19 Trench Mortar Battery, R.A.
Y/19 Trench Mortar Battery, R.A.
19th Divl. Amm. Column.
H.Q., Divisional Engineers.
81st, 82nd and 94th F. Cos., R.E.
19th Divl. Sig. Co.
Pioneer Bn., 5th S. Wales Bord.
No. 19 Bn. M.G. Corps.
19th Divl. Train (154-157 Cos., A.S.C.).
57th, 58th and 59th F. Ambs.
31st Mobile Vet. Section.
220th Divl. Employment Co.

20th (LIGHT) DIVISION.

59th Infantry Brigade.	60th Infantry Brigade.	61st Infantry Brigade.
Headquarters.	Headquarters.	Headquarters.
2nd Sco. Rif.	6th Shrops. L.I.	12th L'pool. R.
11th K.R. Rif. C.	12th K.R. Rif. C.	7th Som. L.I.
11th Rif. Brig.	12th Rif. Brig.	7th D. of Corn. L.I.
59th T.M. Batt.	60th T.M. Batt.	61st T.M. Batt.

Divisional Troops.

H.Q., 20th (Light) Div.
H.Q., Divisional Artillery.
91st Bde., R.F.A. ("A," "B," "C," "D" Batts.) (18—18-prs. and 6—4·5-in. howrs.).
92nd Bde., R.F.A. ("A," "B," "C," "D" Batts.) (18—18-prs. and 6—4·5-in. howrs.).
X/20 Trench Mortar Battery, R.A.
Y/20 Trench Mortar Battery, R.A.
20th Divl. Amm. Column.
H.Q., Divisional Engineers.
83rd, 84th and 96th F. Cos. R.E.
20th Divl. Sig. Co.
Pioneer Bn., 11th Durh. L.I.
No. 20 Bn. M.G. Corps.
20th Divl. Train (158-161 Cos., A.S.C.).
60th, 61st and 62nd F. Ambs.
32nd Mobile Vet. Section.
221st Divl. Employment Co.

Divisions—*continued.*

21st DIVISION.

62nd Infantry Brigade.	64th Infantry Brigade.	110th Infantry Brigade.
Headquarters.	Headquarters.	Headquarters.
12/18th North'd. Fus.	1st E. York. R.	6th Leic. R.
1st Linc. R.	9th Yorks. L.I.	7th Leic. R.
2nd Linc. R.	15th Durh. L.I.	1st Wilts. R.
62nd T.M. Batt.	64th T.M. Batt.	110th T.M. Batt.

Divisional Troops.

H.Q., 21st Div.
H.Q., Divisional Artillery.
94th Bde., R.F.A. ("A," "B," "C," "D" Batts.) (18—18-prs. and 6—4·5-in. howrs.).
95th Bde., R.F.A. ("A," "B," "C," "D" Batts.) (18—18-prs. and 6—4·5-in. howrs.).
X/21 Trench Mortar Battery, R.A.
Y/21 Trench Mortar Battery, R.A.
21st Divl. Amm. Column.
H.Q., Divisional Engineers.
97th, 98th and 126th F. Cos., R.E.
21st Divl. Sig. Co.
Pioneer Bn., 14th North'd Fus.
No. 21 Bn. M.G. Corps.
21st Divl. Train (182-185 Cos., A.S.C.).
63rd, 64th, and 65th Field Ambs.
33rd Mobile Vet. Section.
222nd Divl. Employment Co.

24th DIVISION.

17th Infantry Brigade.	72nd Infantry Brigade.	73rd Infantry Brigade.
Headquarters.	Headquarters.	Headquarters.
8th R.W. Surr. R.	9th E. Surr. R.	9th R. Suss. R.
1st R. Fus.	8th R.W. Kent R.	7th North'n. R.
3rd Rif. Brig.	1st N. Staff. R.	13th Midd'x. R.
17th T.M. Batt.	72nd T.M. Batt.	73rd T.M. Batt.

Divisional Troops.

H.Q., 24th Div.
H.Q., Divisional Artillery.
106th Bde., R.F.A. ("A," "B," "C," "D" Batts.) (18—18-prs. and 6—4·5-in. howrs.).
107th Bde., R.F.A. ("A," "B," "C," "D" Batts.) (18—18-prs. and 6—4·5-in. howrs.).
X/24 Trench Mortar Battery, R.A.
Y/24 Trench Mortar Battery, R.A.
24th Divl. Amm. Column.
H.Q., Divisional Engineers.
103rd, 104th, 129th F. Cos., R.E.
24th Divl. Sig. Co.
Pioneer Bn., 12th Notts. & Derby. R.
No. 24 Bn. M.G. Corps.
24th Divl. Train (194-197 Cos., A.S.C.).
72nd, 73rd and 74th F. Ambs.
36th Mobile Vet. Section.
224th Divl. Employment Co.

25th DIVISION.

7th Infantry Brigade.	74th Infantry Brigade.	75th Infantry Brigade.
Headquarters.	Headquarters.	Headquarters.
9th Devon R.	9th Yorks. R.	1/8th R. War. R.
20th Manch. R.	11th Notts. & Derby. R.	1/5th Glouc. R.
21st Manch. R.	13th Durh. L.I.	1/8th Worc. R.

Divisional Troops.

H.Q., 25th Div.
H.Q., Divisional Artillery.
110th Bde., R.F.A. ("A," "B," "C," "D" Batts.) (18—18-prs. and 6—4·5-in. howrs.).
112th Bde., R.F.A. ("A," "B," "C," "D" Batts.) (18—18-prs. and 6—4·5-in. howrs.).
X/25 Trench Mortar Battery, R.A.
Y/25 Trench Mortar Battery, R.A.
25th Divl. Amm. Column.
H.Q., Divisional Engineers.
105th, 106th and 130th F. Cos., R.E.
25th Divl. Sig. Co.
Pioneer Bn., 11th S. Lan. R.
No. 25 Bn. M.G. Corps.
25th Divl. Train (198-201 Cos., A.S.C.).
75th, 76th and 77th F. Ambs.
37th Mobile Vet. Section.
225th Divl. Employment Co.

29th DIVISION.

86th Infantry Brigade.	87th Infantry Brigade.	88th Infantry Brigade.
Headquarters.	Headquarters.	Headquarters.
2nd R. Fus.	2nd S. Wales Bord.	4th Worc. R.
1st Lan. Fus.	1st K.O. Sco. Bord.	2nd Hamps. R.
1st R. Dub. Fus.	1st Bord. R.	2nd Leins. R.
86th T.M. Batt.	87th T.M. Batt.	88th T.M. Batt.

Divisional Troops.

H.Q., 29th Div.
H.Q., Divisional Artillery.
15th Bde., R.H.A. ("B," "L," and 1/1st Warwickshire Batts., R.H.A., and 460th Batt., R.F.A.)
 (18—18-prs. and 6—4·5-in. howrs.).
17th Bde., R.F.A. (13th, 26th, 92nd and "D" Batts.) (18—18-prs. and 6—4·5-in. howrs.).
X/29 Trench Mortar Battery, R.A.
Y/29 Trench Mortar Battery, R.A.
29th Divl. Amm. Column.
H.Q., Divisional Engineers.
455th (W. Riding) F. Co., R.E. (T.).
497th (Kent) F. Co., R.E. (T.).
510th (London) F. Co., R.E. (T.)
1/1st London Divl. Sig. Co. (T.).
Pioneer Bn., 1/2nd Mon. R. (T.).
No. 29 Bn. M.G. Corps.
29th Divl. Train (225-228 Cos., A.S.C.).
87th, 88th, 89th F. Ambs.
18th Mobile Vet. Section.
226th Divl. Employment Co.

Divisions—continued.

30th DIVISION.

21st Infantry Brigade.	89th Infantry Brigade.	90th Infantry Brigade.
Headquarters.	Headquarters.	Headquarters.
7th R. Ir. R.	2nd S. Lan. R.	2/14th Lond. R.
1/6th Ches. R.	7/8th R. Innis. Fus.	2/15th Lond. R.
2/23rd Lond. R.	2/17th Lond. R.	2/16th Lond. R.
21st T.M. Batt.	89th T.M. Batt.	90th T.M. Batt.

Divisional Troops.

H.Q., 30th Div.
H.Q., Divisional Artillery.
148th Bde., R.F.A. (" A," " B," " C," " D " Batts.) (18—18-prs. and 6—4·5-in. howrs.).
149th Bde., R.F.A. (" A," " B," " C," " D " Batts.) (18—18-prs. and 6—4·5-in. howrs.).
X/30 Trench Mortar Battery, R.A.
Y/30 Trench Mortar Battery, R.A.
30th Divl. Amm. Column.
H.Q., Divisional Engineers.
200th, 201st, and 202nd F. Cos., R.E.
30th Divl. Sig. Co.
Pioneer Bn., 6th S.W. Bord.
No. 30 Bn. M.G. Corps.
30th Divl. Train (186-189 Cos., A.S.C.).
96th, 97th, and 98th F. Ambs.
40th Mobile Vet. Section.
227th Divl. Employment Co.

31st DIVISION.

92nd Infantry Brigade.	93rd Infantry Brigade.	94th (Yeo.) Infantry Brigade.
Headquarters.	Headquarters.	Headquarters.
10th E. York. R.	15th W. York. R.	12th Norf. R.
11th E. York. R.	13th York. & Lan. R.	12th R. Sco. Fus.
11th E. Lan. R.	18th Durh. L.I.	24th R. Welsh Fus.
92nd T.M. Batt.	93rd T.M. Batt.	94th T.M. Batt.

Divisional Troops.

H.Q., 31st Div.
H.Q., Divisional Artillery.
165th Bde., R.F.A. (" A," " B," " C," " D " Batts.) (18—18-prs. and 6—4·5-in. howrs.).
170th Bde., R.F.A. (" A," " B," " C," " D " Batts.) (18—18-prs. and 6—4·5-in. howrs.).
X/31 Trench Mortar Battery, R.A.
Y/31 Trench Mortar Battery, R.A.
31st Divl. Amm. Column.
H.Q., Divisional Engineers.
210th, 211th and 223rd F. Cos., R.E.
31st Divl. Sig. Co.
Pioneer Bn., 12th Yorks. L.I.
No. 31 Bn. M.G. Corps.
31st Divl. Train (221-223 and 279 Cos., A.S.C.).
93rd, 94th and 95th F. Ambs.
41st Mobile Vet. Section.
228th Divl. Employment Co.

Divisions—continued.

32nd DIVISION.

14th Infantry Brigade.
Headquarters.
5/6th R. Scots (T.).
1st Dorset. R.
15th High. L.I.

14th T.M. Batt.

96th Infantry Brigade.
Headquarters.
15th Lan. Fus.
16th Lan. Fus.
2nd Manch. R.

96th T.M. Batt.

97th Infantry Brigade.
Headquarters.
1/5th Bord. R.
2nd York. L.I.
10th Arg. & Suth'd. Highs.

97th T.M. Batt.

Divisional Troops.

H.Q., 32nd Div.
H.Q., Divisional Artillery.
161st Bde., R.F.A. ("A," "B," "C," "D" Batts.) (18—18-prs. and 6—4·5-in. howrs.).
168th Bde., R.F.A. ("A," "B," "C," "D" Batts.) (18—18 prs. and 6—4·5-in. howrs.).
X/32 Trench Mortar Battery, R.A.
Y/32 Trench Mortar Battery, R.A.
32nd Divl. Amm. Column.
H.Q., Divisional Engineers.
206th, 218th and 219th F. Cos. R.E.
32nd Divl. Sig. Co.
Pioneer Bn., 16th High. L.I.
No. 32 Bn. M.G. Corps.
32nd Divl. Train (202-205 Cos., A.S.C.).
90th, 91st and 92nd F. Ambs.
42nd Mobile Vet. Section.
229th Divl. Employment Co.

33rd DIVISION.

19th Infantry Brigade.
Headquarters.
1st R. W. Surr. R.
1st Sco. Rif.
5/6th Sco. Rif. (T.).

19th T.M. Batt.

98th Infantry Brigade.
Headquarters.
4th L'pool R. (Ex. S.R.).
1st Midd'x. R.
2nd Arg. & Suth'd. Highs.

98th T.M. Batt.

100th Infantry Brigade.
Headquarters.
2nd Worc. R.
16th K.R. Rif. C.
1/9 High. L.I. (T.).

100th T.M. Batt.

Divisional Troops.

H.Q., 33rd Div.
H.Q., Divisional Artillery.
156th Bde., R.F.A. ("A," "B," "C," "D" Batts.) (18—18-prs. and 6—4·5-in. howrs.).
162nd Bde., R.F.A. ("A," "B," "C," "D" Batts.) (18—18-prs. and 6—4·5-in. howrs.).
X/33 Trench Mortar Battery, R.A.
Y/33 Trench Mortar Battery, R.A.
33rd Divl. Amm. Column.
H.Q., Divisional Engineers.
11th, 212th and 222nd F. Cos., R.E.
33rd Divl. Sig. Co.
Pioneer Bn., 18th Midd'x. R.
No. 33 Bn. M.G. Corps.
33rd Divl. Train (8, 170, 171 and 173 Cos., A.S.C.).
19th, 99th and 101st F. Ambs.
43rd Mobile Vet. Section.
230th Divl. Employment Co.

Divisions—continued.

34th DIVISION.

101st Infantry Brigade.	102nd Infantry Brigade.	103rd Infantry Brigade.
Headquarters.	Headquarters.	Headquarters.
2/4th R. W. Surr. R.	1/4th Ches. R.	1/5th K.O. Sco. Bord.
4th Suss. R.	1/7th Ches. R.	1/8th Sco. Rif.
2nd N. Lan. R.	1/1st Hereford R.	1/5th Arg. & Suth'd. Highrs.
101st T.M. Batt.	102nd T.M. Batt.	103rd T.M. Batt.

Divisional Troops.

H.Q. 34th Div.
H.Q., Divisional Artillery.
152nd Bde., R.F.A. ("A," "B," "C," "D" Batts.) (18—18-prs. and 6—4·5-in. howrs.).
160th Bde., R.F.A. ("A," "B," "C," "D" Batts.) (18—18-prs. and 6—4·5-in. howrs.).
X/34 Trench Mortar Battery, R.A.
Y/34 Trench Mortar Battery, R.A.
34th Divl. Amm. Column.
H.Q., Divisional Engineers.
207th, 208th and 209th F. Cos., R.E.
34th Divl. Sig. Co.
Pioneer Bn., 2/4th Som. L.I.
No. 34 Bn. M.G. Corps.
34th Divl. Train (229-232 Cos., A.S.C.).
102nd, 103rd and 104th F. Ambs.
44th Mobile Vet. Section.
231st Divl. Employment Co.

35th DIVISION.

104th Infantry Brigade.	105th Infantry Brigade.	106th Infantry Brigade.
Headquarters.	Headquarters.	Headquarters.
17th Lan. Fus.	15th Ches. R.	17th R. Scots.
18th Lan. Fus.	15th Notts & Derby R.	12th High. L.I.
19th Durh. L.I.	4th N. Staff. R.	18th (Glasgow Yeo.) High. L.I.
104th T.M. Batt.	105th T.M. Batt.	106th T.M. Batt.

Divisional Troops.

H.Q. 35th Div.
H.Q., Divisional Artillery.
157th Bde., R.F.A. ("A," "B," "C," "D" Batts.) (18—18-prs. and 6—4·5-in. howrs.).
159th Bde., R.F.A. ("A," "B," "C," "D" Batts.) (18—18-prs. and 6—4·5-in. howrs.).
X/35 Trench Mortar Battery, R.A.
Y/35 Trench Mortar Battery, R.A.
35th Divl. Amm. Column.
H.Q., Divisional Engineers.
203rd, 204th and 205th F. Cos., R.E.
35th Divl. Sig. Co.
Pioneer Bn., 19th North'd. Fus.
No. 35 Bn. M.G. Corps.
35th Divl. Train (233-236 Cos., A.S.C.)
105th, 106th, and 107th F. Ambs.
45th Mobile Vet. Section.
232nd Divl. Employment Co

Divisions—*continued.*

36th (ULSTER) DIVISION.

107th Infantry Brigade.	108th Infantry Brigade.	109th Infantry Brigade.
Headquarters.	Headquarters.	Headquarters.
1st R. Ir. Rif.	12th R. Ir. Rif.	1st R. Innis. Fus.
2nd R. Ir. Rif.	1st R. Ir. Fus.	2nd R. Innis. Fus.
15th R. Ir. Rif.	9th (N. Irish Horse) R. Ir. Fus.	9th R. Innis. Fus.
107th T.M. Batt.	108th T.M. Batt.	109th T.M. Batt.

Divisional Troops.

H.Q., 36th (Ulster) Div.
H.Q., Divisional Artillery.
153rd Bde., R.F.A. ("A," "B," "C," "D" Batts.) (18—18-prs. and 6—4˙5-in. howrs.).
173rd Bde., R.F.A. ("A," "B," "C," "D" Batts.) (18—18-prs. and 6—4˙5-in. howrs.).
X/36 Trench Mortar Battery, R.A.
Y/36 Trench Mortar Battery, R.A.
36th Divl. Amm. Column.
H.Q., Divisional Engineers.
121st, 122nd and 150th F. Cos., R.E.
36th Divl. Sig. Co.
Pioneer Bn., 16th R. Ir. Rif.
No. 36 Bn. M.G. Corps.
36th Divl. Train (251-254 Cos., A.S.C.)
108th, 109th and 110th F. Ambs.
48th Mobile Vet. Section.
238rd Divl. Employment Co.

37th DIVISION.

63rd Infantry Brigade.	111th Infantry Brigade.	112th Infantry Brigade.
Headquarters.	Headquarters.	Headquarters.
8th Linc. R.	10th R. Fus.	13th R. Fus.
8th Som. L.I.	13th K.R. Rif. C.	1st Essex R.
4th Midd'x. R.	13th Rif. Brig.	1/1st Herts. R.
63rd T.M. Batt.	111th T.M. Batt.	112th T.M. Batt.

Divisional Troops.

H.Q., 37th Div.
H.Q., Divisional Artillery.
123rd Bde., R.F.A. ("A," "B," "C," "D" Batts.) (18—18-prs. and 6—4˙5-in. howrs.).
124th Bde., R.F.A. ("A," "B," "C," "D" Batts.) (18—18-prs. and 6—4˙5-in. howrs.).
X/37 Trench Mortar Battery, R.A.
Y/37 Trench Mortar Battery, R.A.
37th Divl. Amm. Column.
H.Q., Divisional Engineers.
152nd, 153rd and 154th F. Cos., R.E.
37th Divl. Sig. Co.
Pioneer Bn., 9th N. Staff. R.
No. 37 Bn. M.G. Corps.
37th Divl. Train (288-291 Cos., A.S.C.).
48th, 49th and 50th F. Ambs.
28th Mobile Vet. Section.
234th Divl. Employment Co.

Divisions—*continued.*

38th (WELSH) DIVISION.

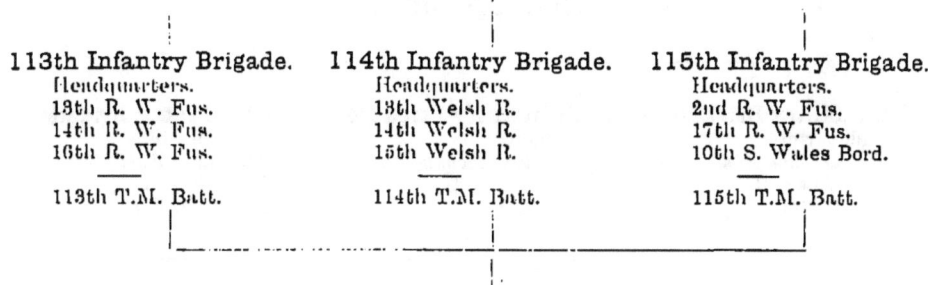

113th Infantry Brigade.	114th Infantry Brigade.	115th Infantry Brigade.
Headquarters.	Headquarters.	Headquarters.
13th R. W. Fus.	13th Welsh R.	2nd R. W. Fus.
14th R. W. Fus.	14th Welsh R.	17th R. W. Fus.
16th R. W. Fus.	15th Welsh R.	10th S. Wales Bord.
113th T.M. Batt.	114th T.M. Batt.	115th T.M. Batt.

Divisional Troops.

H.Q., 38th (Welsh) Division.
H.Q., Divisional Artillery.
121st Bde., R.F.A. ("A," "B," "C," "D" Batts.) (18—18-prs. and 6—4'5-in. howrs.).
122nd Bde., R.F.A. ("A," "B," "C," "D" Batts.) (18—18-prs. and 6—4'5-in. howrs.).
X/38 Trench Mortar Battery, R.A.
Y/38 Trench Mortar Battery, R.A.
38th Divl. Amm. Column.
H.Q., Divisional Engineers.
123rd, 124th and 151st F. Cos., R.E.
38th Divl. Sig. Co.
Pioneer Bn., 19th Welsh R.
No. 38 Bn. M.G. Corps.
38th Divl. Train (330-333 Cos., A.S.C.).
129th, 130th and 131st F. Ambs.
49th Mobile Vet. Section.
235th Divl. Employment Co.

39th DIVISION.

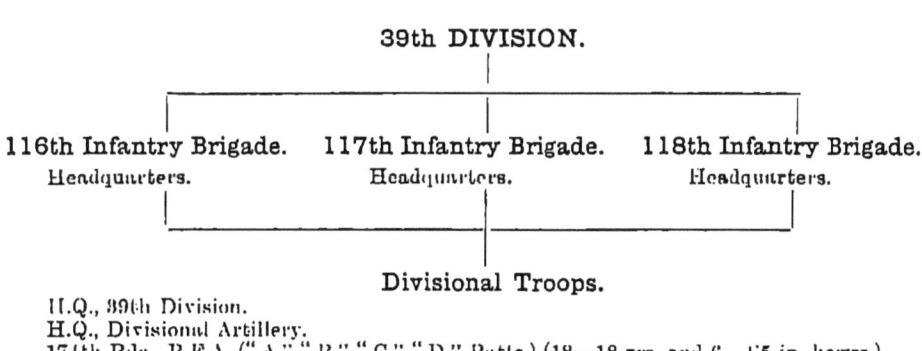

116th Infantry Brigade.	117th Infantry Brigade.	118th Infantry Brigade.
Headquarters.	Headquarters.	Headquarters.

Divisional Troops.

H.Q., 39th Division.
H.Q., Divisional Artillery.
174th Bde., R.F.A. ("A," "B," "C," "D" Batts.) (18—18-prs. and 6—4'5-in. howrs.)
186th Bde., R.F.A. ("A," "B," "C," "D" Batts.) (18—18-prs. and 6—4'5-in. howrs.)
39th Divl. Amm. Column.
H.Q., Divisional Engineers.
225th, 227th and 234th F. Cos., R.E.
39th Divl. Sig. Co.
4th E. Lan. R.
7th Notts & Derby. R.
39th Divl. Train (284-287 Cos., A.S.C.).
132nd, 133rd and 134th F. Ambs.
50th Mobile Vet. Section.
236th Divl. Employment Co.

40th DIVISION.

119th Infantry Brigade.	120th Infantry Brigade.	121st Infantry Brigade.
Headquarters.	Headquarters.	Headquarters.
13th R. Innis. Fus.	10th K.O. Sco. Bord.	23rd Lan. Fus.
13th E. Lan. R.	15th Yorks. L.I.	23rd Ches. R.
12th N. Staff. R.	11th Cam'n Highrs.	8th R. Ir. Regt.

Divisional Troops.

H.Q., 40th Division.
H.Q., Divisional Artillery.
178th Bde., R.F.A. (" A," " B," " C," " D " Batts.) (18—18-prs. and 6—4·5-in. howrs.).
181st Bde., R.F.A. (" A," " B," " C," " D " Batts.) (18—18-prs. and 6—4·5-in. howrs.).
40th Divl. Amm. Column.
H.Q., Divisional Engineers.
224th, 229th and 231st F. Cos., R.E.
40th Divl. Sig. Co.
Pioneer Bn., 17th Worc. R.
40th Divl. Train (292–295 Cos., A.S.C.).
135th, 136th and 137th F. Ambs.
51st Mobile Vet. Section.
237th Divl. Employment Co.

41st DIVISION.

122nd Infantry Brigade.	123rd Infantry Brigade.	124th Infantry Brigade.
Headquarters.	Headquarters.	Headquarters.
12th E. Surrey R.	11th R.W. Surrey R.	10th R.W. Surrey R.
15th (Hampshire Carabineers) Hamps. R.	10th R.W. Kent. R.	26th R. Fus.
18th K. R. Rif. Corps.	23rd Middx. R.	20th Durham L.I.
122nd T.M. Batt.	123rd T.M. Batt.	124th T.M. Batt.

Divisional Troops.

H.Q., 41st Div.
H.Q., Divl. Artillery.
187th Bde., R.F.A. (" A," "B," " C," " D " Batts.) (18—18-prs. and 6—4·5-in. howrs.)
190th Bde., R.F.A. (" A," " B," " C," " D " Batts.) (18—18-prs. and 6—4·5-in. howrs.)
X/41 Trench Mortar Battery, R.A.
Y/41 Trench Mortar Battery, R.A.
41st Divl. Amm. Column.
228th, 233rd and 237th Field Cos., R.E.
41st Divl. Sig. Co., R.E.
Pioneer Batt., 19th Middx. R.
No. 41 Bn. M.G. Corps.
41st Divl. Train (Nos. 296–299 Cos., A.S.C.)
138th, 139th, 140th Field Ambs.
52nd Mobile Vet. Section.
238th Divl. Employment Co.

Divisions—*continued.*

42nd (EAST LANCASHIRE) DIVISION (T.).

125th Infantry Brigade.	126th Infantry Brigade.	127th Infantry Brigade.
Headquarters.	Headquarters.	Headquarters.
1/5th Lan. Fus.	1/5th E. Lan. R.	1/5th Manch. R.
1/7th Lan. Fus.	1/8th Manch. R.	1/6th Manch. R.
1/8th Lan. Fus.	1/10th Manch. R.	1/7th Manch. R.
125th T.M. Batt.	126th T.M. Batt.	127th T.M. Batt.

Divisional Troops.

H.Q., 42nd (East Lancashire) Division.
H.Q., Divisional Artillery.
210th Bde., R.F.A. (" A," " B," " C," " D " Batts.) (18—18-prs. and 6—4·5-in. howrs.).
211th Bde., R.F.A. (" A," " B," " C," " D " Batts.) (18—18-prs. and 6—4·5-in. howrs.).
X/42 Trench Mortar Battery, R.A.
Y/42 Trench Mortar Battery, R.A.
42nd Divl. Amm. Column.
H.Q., Divisional Engineers.
427th, 428th, and 429th (E. Lanc.) F. Cos., R.E.
42nd Divl. Sig. Co.
Pioneer Batt., 1/7th North'd. Fus.
No. 42 Bn. M.G. Corps.
42nd Divl. Train (428-431 Cos., A.S.C.).
1/1st, 1/2nd and 1/3rd E. Lancashire F. Ambs.
19th Mobile Vet. Section.
239th Divl. Employment Co.

46th (NORTH. MIDLAND) DIVISION (T.).

137th Infantry Brigade.	138th Infantry Brigade.	139th Infantry Brigade.
Headquarters.	Headquarters.	Headquarters.
1/5th S. Staff. R.	1/5th Linc. R.	1/5th Notts & Derby R.
1/6th S. Staff. R.	1/4th Leic. R.	1/6th Notts & Derby R.
1/6th N. Staff. R.	1/5th Leic. R.	1/8th Notts & Derby R.
137th T.M. Batt.	138th T.M. Batt.	139th T.M. Batt.

Divisional Troops.

H.Q., 46th (N. Midland) Div.
H.Q., Divisional Artillery.
230th (N. Midland) Bde., R.F.A. (" A," " B," " C," " D " Batts.) (18—18-prs. and 6—4·5-in. howrs.).
231st (N. Midland) Bde., R.F.A. (" A," " B," " C," " D " Batts.) (18—18-prs. and 6—4·5-in. howrs.).
X/46 Trench Mortar Battery, R.A.
Y/46 Trench Mortar Battery, R.A.
46th Divl. Amm. Column.
H.Q., Divisional Engineers.
465th, 466th and 468th (N. Midland) F. Coys., R.E.
46th Divl. Sig. Coy.
Pioneer Bn., 1/1st Mon. R. (T.).
No. 46 Bn. M.G. Corps.
46th Divl. Train (451-454 Cos., A.S.C.).
1/1st, 1/2nd and 1/3rd N. Midland F. Ambs.
1/1st N. Midland Mobile Vet. Section.
240th Divl. Employment Co.

Divisions—continued.

47th (LONDON) DIVISION (T.).

140th Infantry Brigade.
Headquarters.
1/15th London R.
1/17th London R.
1/21st London R.

140th T.M. Batt.

141st Infantry Brigade.
Headquarters.
1/18th London R.
1/19th London R.
1/20th London R.

141st T.M. Batt.

142nd Infantry Brigade.
Headquarters.
1/22nd London R.
1/23rd London R.
1/24th London R.

142nd T.M. Batt.

Divisional Troops.

H.Q., 47th (London) Div.
H.Q., Divisional Artillery.
235th (London) Bde., R.F.A. ("A," "B," "C," "D" Batts.) (18—18-prs. and 6—4·5-in. howrs.).
236th (London) Bde., R.F.A. ("A," "B," "C," "D" Batts.) (18—18-prs. and 6—4·5-in. howrs.).
X/47 Trench Mortar Battery, R.A.
Y/47 Trench Mortar Battery, R.A.
47th Divl. Amm. Column.
H.Q., Divisional Engineers.
517th, 518th and 520th (London) F. Cos., R.E.
47th Divl. Sig. Co.
Pioneer Bn., 1/4th R.W. Fus. (T.).
No. 47 Bn. M.G. Corps.
47th Divl. Train (455-458 Cos., A.S.C.).
1/4th, 1/5th and 1/6th (London) F. Ambs.
1/2nd (London) Mobile Vet. Section.
241st Divl. Employment Co.

49th (WEST RIDING) DIVISION (T.).

146th Infantry Brigade.
Headquarters.
1/5th W. York. R.
1/6th W. York. R.
1/7th W. York. R.

146th T.M. Batt.

147th Infantry Brigade.
Headquarters.
1/4th W. Rid. R.
1/6th W. Rid. R.
1/7th W. Rid. R.

147th T.M. Batt.

148th Infantry Brigade.
Headquarters.
1/4th Yorks. L.I.
1/4th York. & Lanc. R.
1/5th York. & Lanc. R.

148th T.M. Batt.

Divisional Troops.

H.Q., 49th (W. Riding) Div.
H.Q., Divisional Artillery.
245th (W. Riding) Bde., R.F.A. ("A," "B," "C," "D" Batts.)(18—18-prs. and 6—4·5-in. howrs)
246th (W. Riding) Bde., R.F.A. ("A," "B," "C," "D" Batts.)(18—18-prs. and 6—4·5-in. howrs..)
X/49 Trench Mortar Battery, R.A.
Y/49 Trench Mortar Battery, R.A.
49th Divl. Amm. Column.
H.Q., Divisional Engineers.
57th Field Co., R.E.
456th and 458th (W. Riding) F. Co., R.E.
49th Divl. Sig. Co.
Pioneer Bn., 19th Lan. Fus.
No. 49 Bn. M.G. Corps.
49th Divl. Train (463-466 Cos., A.S.C.).
1/1st, 1/2nd, and 1/3rd W. Riding F. Ambs.
1/1st W. Riding Mobile Vet. Section.
243rd Divl. Employment Co.

Divisions—continued.

50th (NORTHUMBRIAN) DIVISION (T.).

149th Infantry Brigade.
Headquarters.
3rd R. Fus.
13th R. Highrs.
2nd Dub. Fus.

149th T.M. Batt.

150th Infantry Brigade.
Headquarters.
2nd North'd Fus.
7th Wilts. R.
2nd Muns. Fus.

150th T.M. Batt.

151st Infantry Brigade.
Headquarters.
6th R. Innis. Fus.
1st Yorks. L.I.
4th K.R. Rif. C.

151st T.M. Batt.

Divisional Troops.

H.Q., 50th (Northumbrian) Div.
H.Q., Divisional Artillery.
250th (Northumbrian) Bde., R.F.A. ("A," "B," "C," "D" Batts.) (18—18-prs. and 6—4·5-in. howrs.).
251st (Northumbrian) Bde., R.F.A. ("A," "B," "C," "D" Batts.) (18—18-prs. and 6—4·5-in. howrs.).
X/50 Trench Mortar Battery, R.A.
Y/50 Trench Mortar Battery, R.A.
50th Divl. Amm. Column.
H.Q., Divisional Engineers.
7th Field Co., R.E.
446th and 447th (Northumbrian) F. Cos., R.E.
50th Divl. Sig. Co.
Pioneer Bn., 5th R. Ir. Regt.
No. 50 Bn. M.G. Corps.
50th Divl. Train (467-470 Cos., A.S.C.).
1/1st, 1/3rd, and 2/2nd Northumbrian F. Ambs.
1/1st Northumbrian Mobile Vet. Section.
244th Divl. Employment Co.

51st (HIGHLAND) DIVISION (T.).

152nd Infantry Brigade.
Headquarters.
1/5th Sea. Highrs.
1/6th Sea. Highrs.
6/7th Gord. Highrs.

152nd T.M. Batt.

153rd Infantry Brigade.
Headquarters.
1/6th R. Highrs.
1/7th R. Highrs.
1/6th Arg. & Suth'd Highrs.

153rd T.M. Batt.

154th Infantry Brigade.
Headquarters.
1/4th Sea. Highrs.
1/4th Gord. Highrs.
1/7th Arg. & Suth'd Highrs.

154th T.M. Batt.

Divisional Troops.

H.Q., 51st (Highland) Div.
H.Q., Divisional Artillery.
255th (Highland) Bde., R.F.A. ("A," "B," "C," "D" Batts.) (18—18-prs. and 6—4·5-in. howrs.).
256th (Highland) Bde., R.F.A. ("A," "B," "C," "D" Batts.) (18—18-prs. and 6—4·5-in. howrs.).
X/51 Trench Mortar Battery, R.A.
Y/51 Trench Mortar Battery, R.A.
51st Divl. Amm. Column.
H.Q., Divisional Engineers.
400th, 401st and 404th (Highland) F. Cos., R.E.
51st Divl. Sig. Co.
Pioneer Bn., 1/8th R. Scots (T.).
No. 51 Bn. M.G. Corps.
51st Divl. Train (471-474 Cos., A.S.C.).
1/2nd, 1/3rd and 2/1st Highland F. Ambs.
1/1st Highland Mobile Vet. Section.
245th Divl. Employment Co.

Divisions—continued.

52nd (LOWLAND) DIVISION (T.).

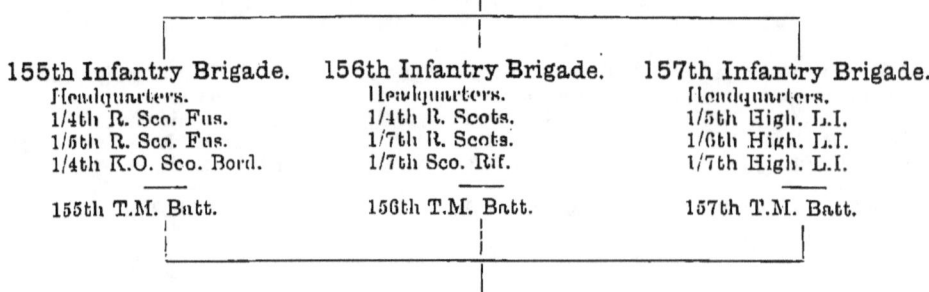

155th Infantry Brigade.
Headquarters.
1/4th R. Sco. Fus.
1/5th R. Sco. Fus.
1/4th K.O. Sco. Bord.

155th T.M. Batt.

156th Infantry Brigade.
Headquarters.
1/4th R. Scots.
1/7th R. Scots.
1/7th Sco. Rif.

156th T.M. Batt.

157th Infantry Brigade.
Headquarters.
1/5th High. L.I.
1/6th High. L.I.
1/7th High. L.I.

157th T.M. Batt.

Divisional Troops.

H.Q., 52nd (Lowland) Div.
H.Q., Divisional Artillery.
9th Bde., R.F.A. (19th, 20th, 28th and D/69th Batts.) (18—18-prs. and 6—4·5-in. howrs.).
56th Bde., R.F.A. ("A," "B," "C," and 527 Batts.) (18—18-prs. and 6—4·5-in. howrs.).
X/52 Trench Mortar Battery, R.A.
Y/52 Trench Mortar Battery, R.A.
52nd Divl. Amm. Column.
H.Q., Divisional Engineers.
410th, 412th and 413th F. Cos., R.E.
52nd Divl. Sig. Co.
Pioneer Bn., 17th North'd Fus.
No. 52 Bn. M.G. Corps.
52nd Divl. Train (217-220 Cos., A.S.C.).
1st, 2nd and 3rd Lowland F. Ambs.
1/1st Lowland Mobile Vet. Section.
984th Divl. Employment Co.

55th (WEST LANCASHIRE) DIVISION (T.).

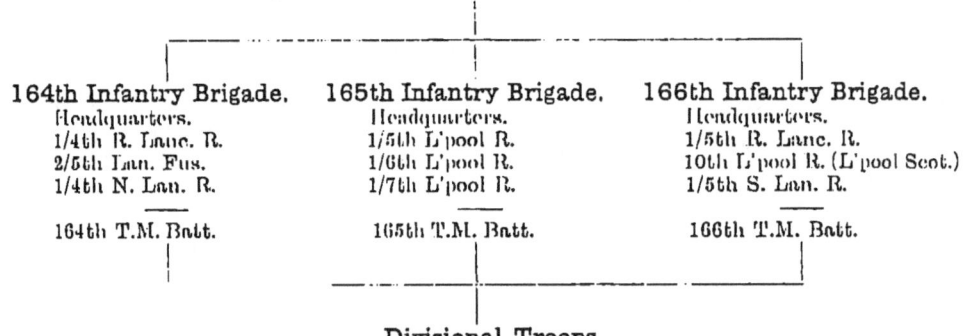

164th Infantry Brigade.
Headquarters.
1/4th R. Lanc. R.
2/5th Lan. Fus.
1/4th N. Lan. R.

164th T.M. Batt.

165th Infantry Brigade.
Headquarters.
1/5th L'pool R.
1/6th L'pool R.
1/7th L'pool R.

165th T.M. Batt.

166th Infantry Brigade.
Headquarters.
1/5th R. Lanc. R.
10th L'pool R. (L'pool Scot.)
1/5th S. Lan. R.

166th T.M. Batt.

Divisional Troops.

H.Q., 55th (W. Lanc.) Div.
H.Q., Divisional Artillery.
275th (W. Lanc.) Bde. R.F.A. ("A," "B," "C," "D" Batts.) (18—18-prs. and 6—4·5-in. howrs.).
276th (W. Lanc.) Bde. R.F.A. ("A," "B," "C," "D" Batts.) (18—18-prs. and 6—4·5-in. howrs.).
X/55 Trench Mortar Battery, R.A.
Y/55 Trench Mortar Battery, R.A.
55th Divl. Amm. Column.
H.Q., Divisional Engineers.
419th, 422nd and 423rd (W. Lancs.) F. Cos., R.E.
55th Divl. Sig. Co.
Pioneer Bn., 1/4th S. Lanc. R.
No. 55 Bn. M.G. Corps.
55th Divl. Train (95-98 Cos., A.S.C.).
1/3rd, 2/1st W. Lanc., and 2/1st Wessex F. Ambs.
1/1st W. Lanc. Mobile Vet. Section.
246th Divl. Employment Co.

Divisions—continued.

61st (SOUTH MIDLAND) DIVISION (T.).

182nd Infantry Brigade.
Headquarters.
2/6th R. War. R.
2/7th R. War. R.
2/8th Worc. R.

182nd T.M. Batt.

183rd Infantry Brigade.
Headquarters.
9th (North'd Hrs.) North'd Fus.
11th Suff. R.
1st E. Lan. R.

183rd T.M. Batt.

184th Infantry Brigade.
Headquarters.
2/5th Glouc. R.
2/4th Oxf. and Bucks L. I.
2/4 R. Berks. R.

184th T.M. Batt.

Divisional Troops.

H.Q., 61st (S. Midland) Div.
H.Q., Divisional Artillery.
306th (S. Midland) Bde., R.F.A. ("A," "B," "C," "D" Batts.)(18—18-prs. and 6—4·5-in. howrs.).
307th (S. Midland) Bde., R.F.A. ("A," "B," "C," "D" Batts.)(18—18-prs. and 6—4·5-in. howrs.).
X/61 Trench Mortar Battery, R.A.
Y/61 Trench Mortar Battery, R.A.
61st Divl. Amm. Column.
H.Q., Divisional Engineers.
476th, 478th and 479th (S. Midland) F. Cos., R.E.
61st Divl. Sig. Co.
Pioneer Bn., 1/5th Duke of Cornwall's L.I.
No. 61 Bn. M.G. Corps.
61st Divl. Train (521-524 Cos., A.S.C.).
2/1st, 2/2nd and 2/3rd S. Midland F. Ambs.
61st (S. Midland) Mobile Vet. Section.
251st Divl. Employment Co.

62nd (WEST RIDING) DIVISION (T.).

185th Infantry Brigade.
Headquarters.
1/5th Devon R.
8th W. Yorks. R.
2/20th Lond. R.

185th T.M. Batt.

186th Infantry Brigade.
Headquarters.
2/4th W. Riding R.
5th W. Riding R.
2/4th Hamps. R.

186th T.M. Batt.

187th Infantry Brigade.
Headquarters.
2/4th K.O.Y.L.I.
5th K.O.Y.L.I.
2/4th York & Lanc. R.

187th T.M. Batt.

Divisional Troops.

H.Q., 62nd (West Riding) Division.
H.Q., Divisional Artillery.
310th Bde., R.F.A. (A, B, C, D Batts.) (18—18-prs. and 6—4·5-in. howrs.).
312th Bde., R.F.A. (A, B, C, D Batts.) (18—18-prs. and 6—4·5-in. howrs.).
X/62 Trench Mortar Battery, R.A.
Y/62 Trench Mortar Battery, R.A.
62nd Divl. Amm. Column.
H.Q., Divisional Engineers.
457th, 460th and 461st (West Riding) F. Cos., R.E.
62nd Divl. Sig. Co.
Pioneer Bn., 1/9th Durh. L.I.
No. 62 Bn. M.G. Corps.
62nd Divl. Train (525-528 Cos., A.S.C.).
2/1st, 2/2nd and 2/3rd West Riding F. Ambs.
2/1st West Riding Mobile Vet. Section.
252nd Divl. Employment Co.

Divisions—continued.

63rd (ROYAL NAVAL) DIVISION.

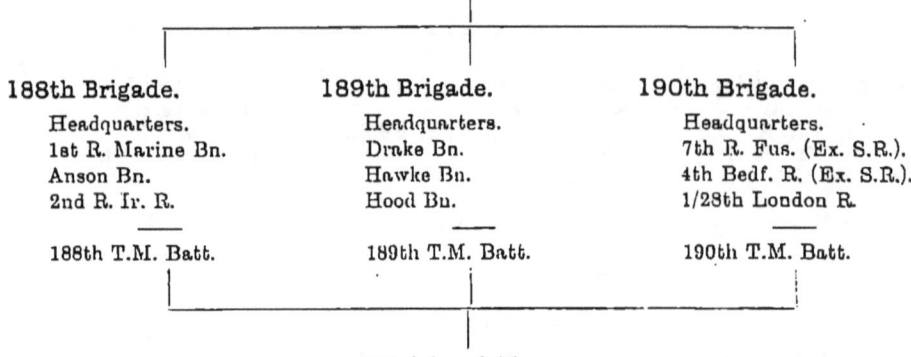

188th Brigade.
Headquarters.
1st R. Marine Bn.
Anson Bn.
2nd R. Ir. R.

188th T.M. Batt.

189th Brigade.
Headquarters.
Drake Bn.
Hawke Bn.
Hood Bn.

189th T.M. Batt.

190th Brigade.
Headquarters.
7th R. Fus. (Ex. S.R.).
4th Bedf. R. (Ex. S.R.).
1/28th London R.

190th T.M. Batt.

Divisional Troops.

H.Q., R.N. Div.
H.Q., Divisional Artillery.
223rd (Home Counties) Bde., R.F.A. ("A," "B," "C," "D" Batts.) (18—18-prs. and 6—4·5-in howrs.).
317th (Northumbrian) Bde., R.F.A. ("A," "B," "C," "D" Batts.) (18—18-prs. and 6—4·5-in. howrs.).
X/63 Trench Mortar Battery, R.A.
Y/63 Trench Mortar Battery, R.A.
63rd Divl. Amm. Column.
H.Q., Divisional Engineers.
247th, 248th and 249th F. Cos., R.E.
63rd Divl. Sig. Co.
Pioneer Bn., 14th Bn. Worc. R.
No. 63 Bn. M.G. Corps.
63rd Divl. Train (761-764 Cos., A.S.C.).
148th, 149th 150th (R. Naval) F. Ambs.
53rd Mobile Vet. Section.
63rd Divl. Employment Co.

66th (EAST LANCASHIRE) DIVISION (T.).

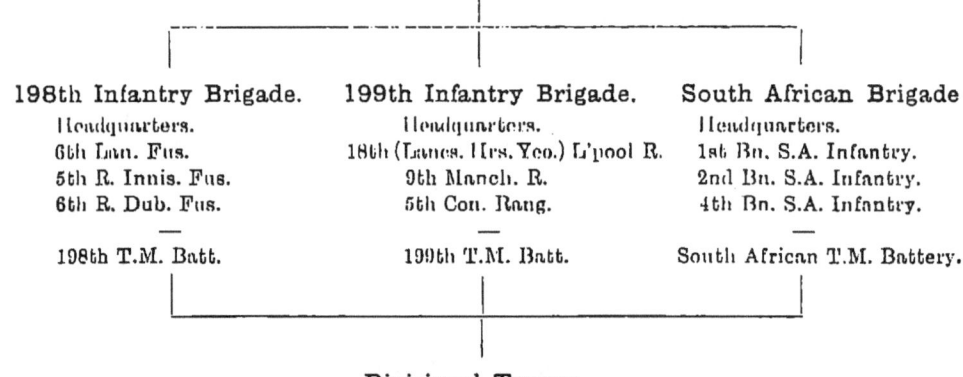

198th Infantry Brigade.
Headquarters.
6th Lan. Fus.
5th R. Innis. Fus.
6th R. Dub. Fus.

198th T.M. Batt.

199th Infantry Brigade.
Headquarters.
18th (Lancs. Hrs. Yeo.) L'pool R.
9th Manch. R.
5th Con. Rang.

199th T.M. Batt.

South African Brigade
Headquarters.
1st Bn. S.A. Infantry.
2nd Bn. S.A. Infantry.
4th Bn. S.A. Infantry.

South African T.M. Battery.

Divisional Troops.

H.Q., 66th (East Lancashire) Division.
H.Q. Divisional Artillery.
330th Bde., R.F.A. (" A," " B," " C," " D " Batts.) (18—18-prs. and 6—4·5-in. howrs.).
331st Bde., R.F.A. (" A," " B," " C," " D " Batts.) (18—18-prs. and 6—4·5-in. howrs.).
66th Divl. Amm. Column.
H.Q., Divisional Engineers.
430th, 431st, and 432nd (E. Lan.) F. Cos., R.E.
66th Divl. Sig. Co.
Pioneer Bn., 9th Glouc. R.
66th Divl. Train (541-544 Cos., A.S.C.).
2/2nd and 2/3rd E. Lancashire and S.A. F. Ambs.
1/1st E. Lan. Mobile Vet. Section.
254th Divl. Employment Co.

74th (YEOMANRY) DIVISION.

229th Infantry Bde.	230th Infantry Bde.	231st Infantry Bde.
Headquarters.	Headquarters.	Headquarters.
14th R. Highrs.	10th E. Kent R.	25th R. W. Fus.
12th Som. L.I.	15th Suff. R.	24th Welsh R.
16th Devon R.	16th R. Suss. R.	10th Shrops. L.I.
229th T.M. Batt.	230th T.M. Batt.	231st T.M. Batt.

Divisional Troops.

H.Q., 74th (Yeomanry) Division.
H.Q., Divisional Artillery.
44th Bde., R.F.A. (340, 382, 425 and "D" Batts.) (18—18-prs. and 6—4·5-in. howrs).
117th Bde., R.F.A. ("A," "B," 366 and "D" Batts.) (18—18-prs. and 6—4·5-in. howrs).
X/74 Trench Mortar Battery, R.A.
Y/74 Trench Mortar Battery, R.A.
74th Divl. Amm. Column.
H.Q., Divisional Engineers.
No. 5 Fd. Co., Royal Anglesey R.E.
No. 5 Fd. Co., Royal Monmouth R.E.
439th Fd. Co., R.E.
74th Divl. Signal Co.
Pioneer Bn., 12th N. Lanc. R.
No. 74 Bn., M.G. Corps.
74th Divl. Train (447–450 Cos., A.S.C.).
229th, 230th, 231st Field Ambs.
59th Mobile Vet. Section.
87th Sanitary Section.
985th Divisional Employment Co.

1st AUSTRALIAN DIVISION.

1st Australian Infantry Bde.	2nd Australian Infantry Bde.	3rd Australian Infantry Bde.
Headquarters.	Headquarters.	Headquarters.
1st Australian Bn.	5th Australian Bn.	9th Australian Bn.
2nd Australian Bn.	6th Australian Bn.	10th Australian Bn.
3rd Australian Bn.	7th Australian Bn.	11th Australian Bn.
4th Australian Bn.	8th Australian Bn.	12th Australian Bn.
1st Aus. T.M. Batt.	2nd Aus. T.M. Batt.	3rd Aus. T.M. Batt.

Divisional Troops.

H.Q., 1st Australian Div.
H.Q., Divisional Artillery.
1st Bde. Australian Field Artillery (1st, 2nd, 3rd Batts. and 101st Batt.) (18—18-prs. and 6—4·5-in. howrs.).
2nd Bde. Australian Field Artillery (4th, 5th, 6th Batts. and 102nd Batt.) (18—18-prs. and 6—4·5-in. howrs.).
X/1 A. Trench Mortar Battery, A.F.A.
Y/1 A. Trench Mortar Battery, A.F.A.
H.Q., Divisional Engineers.
1st Australian Divl. Amm. Column.
1st, 2nd, 3rd Australian F. Cos.
1st Australian Divl. Sig. Co.
1st Australian Pioneer Bn.
No. 1 Aus. Bn. M.G. Corps.
1st Australian Divl. Train (1-4 Cos., Aus. A.S.C.).
1st, 2nd, 3rd Australian F. Ambs.
1st Australian Mobile Vet. Section.

Divisions—continued.

2nd AUSTRALIAN DIVISION.

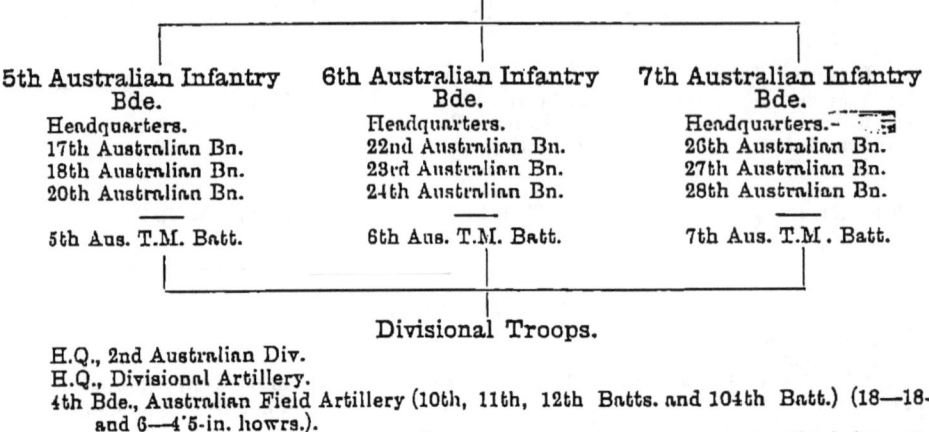

5th Australian Infantry Bde.	6th Australian Infantry Bde.	7th Australian Infantry Bde.
Headquarters.	Headquarters.	Headquarters.
17th Australian Bn.	22nd Australian Bn.	26th Australian Bn.
18th Australian Bn.	23rd Australian Bn.	27th Australian Bn.
20th Australian Bn.	24th Australian Bn.	28th Australian Bn.
5th Aus. T.M. Batt.	6th Aus. T.M. Batt.	7th Aus. T.M. Batt.

Divisional Troops.

H.Q., 2nd Australian Div.
H.Q., Divisional Artillery.
4th Bde., Australian Field Artillery (10th, 11th, 12th Batts. and 104th Batt.) (18—18-prs. and 6—4·5-in. howrs.).
5th Bde., Australian Field Artillery (13th, 14th, 15th Batts. and 105th Batt.) (18—18-prs. and 6—4·5-in. howrs.).
X/2 A. Trench Mortar Battery, A.F.A.
Y/2 A. Trench Mortar Battery, A.F.A.
2nd Australian Divl. Amm. Column.
H.Q., Divisional Engineers.
5th, 6th, 7th Australian F. Cos.
2nd Australian Divl. Sig. Co.
2nd Australian Pioneer Bn.
No. 2 Aus. Bn. M.G. Corps.
2nd Australian Divl. Train (15, 16, 17, 20 Cos., Aus. A.S.C.).
5th, 6th, 7th Australian F. Ambs.
2nd Australian Mobile Vet. Section.

3rd AUSTRALIAN DIVISION.

9th Australian Infantry Bde.	10th Australian Infantry Bde.	11th Australian Infantry Bde.
Headquarters.	Headquarters.	Headquarters.
33rd Australian Bn.	38th Australian Bn.	41st Australian Bn.
34th Australian Bn.	39th Australian Bn.	43rd Australian Bn.
35th Australian Bn.	40th Australian Bn.	44th Australian Bn.
9th Aus. T.M. Batt.	10th Aus. T.M. Batt.	11th Aus. T.M. Batt.

Divisional Troops.

H.Q., 3rd Australian Div.
H.Q., Divisional Artillery.
7th Bde., Australian Field Artillery (25th, 26th, 27th Batts. and 107th Batt.) (18—18-prs and 6—4·5-in. howrs.).
8th Bde., Australian Field Artillery (29th, 30th, 31st Batts. and 108th Batt.) (18—18-prs. and 6—4·5-in. howrs.).
X/3 A. Trench Mortar Battery, A.F.A.
Y/3 A. Trench Mortar Battery, A.F.A.
3rd Australian Divl. Amm. Column.
H.Q., Divisional Engineers.
9th, 10th, 11th Australian F. Cos.
3rd Australian Divl. Sig. Co.
3rd Australian Pioneer Bn.
No. 3 Aus. Bn. M.G. Corps.
3rd Australian Divl. Train (22-25 Cos., Aus. A.S.C.).
9th, 10th, 11th Australian F. Ambs.
3rd Australian Mobile Vet. Section.

Divisions—continued.

4th AUSTRALIAN DIVISION.

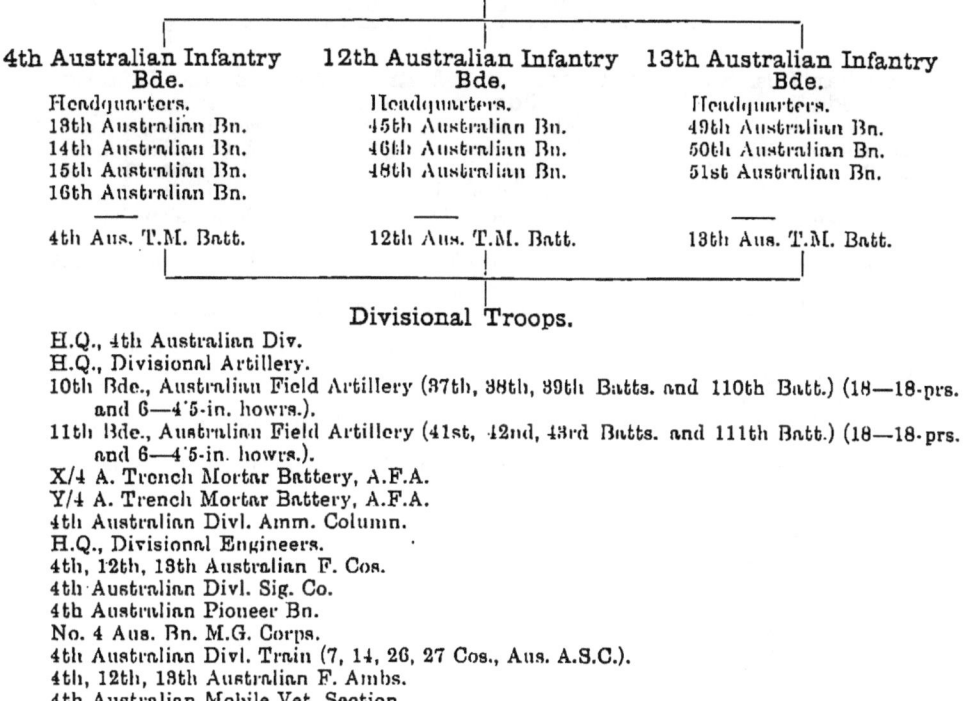

4th Australian Infantry Bde.	12th Australian Infantry Bde.	13th Australian Infantry Bde.
Headquarters.	Headquarters.	Headquarters.
13th Australian Bn.	45th Australian Bn.	49th Australian Bn.
14th Australian Bn.	46th Australian Bn.	50th Australian Bn.
15th Australian Bn.	48th Australian Bn.	51st Australian Bn.
16th Australian Bn.		
4th Aus. T.M. Batt.	12th Aus. T.M. Batt.	13th Aus. T.M. Batt.

Divisional Troops.

H.Q., 4th Australian Div.
H.Q., Divisional Artillery.
10th Bde., Australian Field Artillery (37th, 38th, 39th Batts. and 110th Batt.) (18—18-prs. and 6—4·5-in. howrs.).
11th Bde., Australian Field Artillery (41st, 42nd, 43rd Batts. and 111th Batt.) (18—18-prs. and 6—4·5-in. howrs.).
X/4 A. Trench Mortar Battery, A.F.A.
Y/4 A. Trench Mortar Battery, A.F.A.
4th Australian Divl. Amm. Column.
H.Q., Divisional Engineers.
4th, 12th, 13th Australian F. Cos.
4th Australian Divl. Sig. Co.
4th Australian Pioneer Bn.
No. 4 Aus. Bn. M.G. Corps.
4th Australian Divl. Train (7, 14, 26, 27 Cos., Aus. A.S.C.).
4th, 12th, 13th Australian F. Ambs.
4th Australian Mobile Vet. Section.

5th AUSTRALIAN DIVISION.

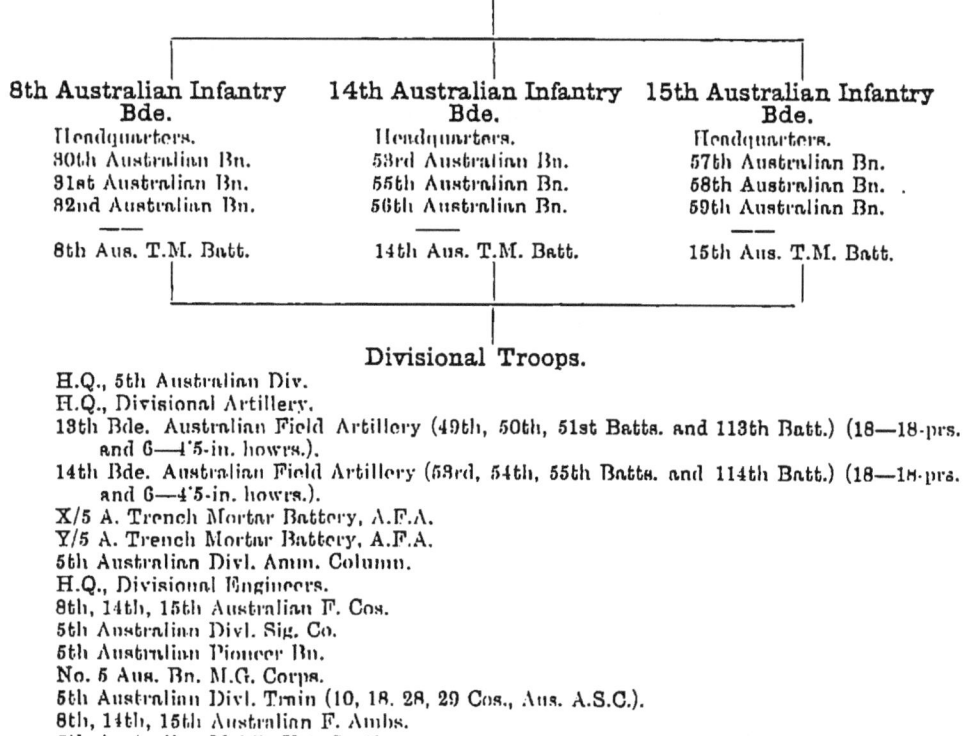

8th Australian Infantry Bde.	14th Australian Infantry Bde.	15th Australian Infantry Bde.
Headquarters.	Headquarters.	Headquarters.
30th Australian Bn.	53rd Australian Bn.	57th Australian Bn.
31st Australian Bn.	55th Australian Bn.	58th Australian Bn.
32nd Australian Bn.	56th Australian Bn.	59th Australian Bn.
8th Aus. T.M. Batt.	14th Aus. T.M. Batt.	15th Aus. T.M. Batt.

Divisional Troops.

H.Q., 5th Australian Div.
H.Q., Divisional Artillery.
13th Bde. Australian Field Artillery (49th, 50th, 51st Batts. and 113th Batt.) (18—18-prs. and 6—4·5-in. howrs.).
14th Bde. Australian Field Artillery (53rd, 54th, 55th Batts. and 114th Batt.) (18—18-prs. and 6—4·5-in. howrs.).
X/5 A. Trench Mortar Battery, A.F.A.
Y/5 A. Trench Mortar Battery, A.F.A.
5th Australian Divl. Amm. Column.
H.Q., Divisional Engineers.
8th, 14th, 15th Australian F. Cos.
5th Australian Divl. Sig. Co.
5th Australian Pioneer Bn.
No. 5 Aus. Bn. M.G. Corps.
5th Australian Divl. Train (10, 18, 28, 29 Cos., Aus. A.S.C.).
8th, 14th, 15th Australian F. Ambs.
5th Australian Mobile Vet. Section.

Divisions—*continued.*

1st CANADIAN DIVISION.

1st Canadian Infantry Bde.	2nd Canadian Infantry Bde.	3rd Canadian Infantry Bde.
Headquarters.	Headquarters.	Headquarters.
1st Canadian Bn.	5th Canadian Bn.	13th Canadian Bn.
2nd Canadian Bn.	7th Canadian Bn.	14th Canadian Bn.
3rd Canadian Bn.	8th Canadian Bn.	15th Canadian Bn.
4th Canadian Bn.	10th Canadian Bn.	16th Canadian Bn.
1st Canadian T.M. Batt.	2nd Canadian T.M. Batt.	3rd Canadian T.M. Batt.

Divisional Troops.

H.Q., 1st Canadian Div.
H.Q., Divisional Artillery.
1st Bde. Canadian Field Artillery (1, 3, 4 and 2 (D) Cdn. Batts.) (18—18-prs. and 6—4·5-in. howrs.).
2nd Bde. Canadian Field Artillery (5, 6, 7 and 48 (D) Cdn. Batts.) (18—18-prs. and 6—4·5-in. howrs.).
V 1 C. Heavy Trench Mortar Battery, R.A.
X 1 C. Trench Mortar Battery, R.A.
Y 1 C. Trench Mortar Battery, R.A.
1st Canadian Divl. Amm. Column.
H.Q., 1st Brigade Canadian Engineers.
1st, 2nd and 3rd Bns., C.E.
1st Pontoon Bridging Transport Unit, C.E.
1st Canadian Divl. Sig. Co.
No. 1 Bn. Canadian M.G. Corps.
1st Canadian Divl. Train (437-440 Cos., A.S.C.).
1st, 2nd and 3rd Canadian Fd. Ambs.
1st Canadian Mobile Vet. Section.
1st Canadian Divl. Employment Co.

2nd CANADIAN DIVISION.

4th Canadian Infantry Bde.	5th Canadian Infantry Bde.	6th Canadian Infantry Bde.
Headquarters.	Headquarters.	Headquarters.
18th (Western Ontario) Canadian Bn.	22nd Canadian Bn.	27th Canadian Bn.
19th (Central Ontario) Canadian Bn.	24th Canadian Bn., Vic. Rf. of Canada	28th Canadian Bn.
20th (Central Ontario) Canadian Bn.	25th Canadian Bn.	29th Canadian Bn.
21st (Eastern Ontario) Canadian Bn.	26th Canadian Bn.	31st Canadian Bn.
4th Canadian T.M. Batt.	5th Canadian T.M. Batt.	6th Canadian T.M. Batt.

Divisional Troops.

H.Q., 2nd Canadian Div.
H.Q., Divisional Artillery.
5th Bde., Canadian Field Artillery (17, 18, 20, and 23 (D) Cdn. Batts.) (18—18-prs. and 6—4·5-in. howrs.).
6th Bde., Canadian Field Artillery (15, 16, 25 and 22 (D) Cdn. Batts.) (18—18-prs. and 6—4·5-in. howrs.).
V 2 C. Heavy Trench Mortar Battery, R.A.
X 2 C. Trench Mortar Battery, R.A.
Y 2 C. Trench Mortar Battery, R.A.
2nd Canadian Divl. Amm. Column.
H.Q., 2nd Brigade Canadian Engineers.
4th, 5th and 6th Bns., C.E.
2nd Pontoon Bridging Transport Unit, C.E.
2nd Canadian Divl. Sig. Co.
No. 2 Bn. Canadian M.G. Corps.
2nd Canadian Divl. Train (672-675 Cos., A.S.C.).
4th, 5th, 6th Canadian F. Ambs.
2nd Canadian Mobile Vet. Section.
2nd Canadian Divl. Employment Co.

Divisions—continued.

3rd CANADIAN DIVISION.

7th Canadian Infantry Bde.	8th Canadian Infantry Bde.	9th Canadian Infantry Bde.
Headquarters.	Headquarters.	Headquarters.
P.P.C.L.I.	1st C'dn. Mtd. Rifle Bn.	43rd Canadian Bn.
Royal C'dn. Regt.	2nd C'dn. Mtd. Rifle Bn.	52nd Canadian Bn.
42nd (Montreal) Highrs.	4th C'dn. Mtd. Rifle Bn.	58th Canadian Bn.
49th (Edmonton) Regt.	5th C'dn. Mtd. Rifle Bn.	116th Canadian Bn.
7th Canadian T.M. Batt.	8th Canadian T.M. Batt.	9th Canadian T.M. Batt.

Divisional Troops.

H.Q., 3rd Canadian Div.
H.Q., Divisional Artillery.
9th Bde., Canadian Field Artillery (31, 33, 45 and 36 Cdn. Batts.) (18—18-prs. and 6—4·5-in. howrs.).
10th Bde., Canadian Field Artillery (38, 39, 40 and 35 Cdn. Batts.) (18—18-prs. and 6—4·5-in. howrs.).
V 3 C. Heavy Trench Mortar Battery, R.A.
X 3 C. Trench Mortar Battery, R.A.
Y 3 C. Trench Mortar Battery, R.A.
3rd Canadian Divl. Amm. Column.
H.Q., 3rd Brigade Canadian Engineers.
7th, 8th and 9th Bns., C.E.
3rd Pontoon Bridging Transport Unit, C.E.
3rd Canadian Divl. Sig. Co.
No. 3 Bn. Canadian M.G. Corps.
3rd Canadian Divl. Train (676-679 Cos., A.S.C.).
8th, 9th 10th Canadian F. Ambs.
3rd Canadian Mobile Vet. Section.
3rd Canadian Divl. Employment Co.

4th CANADIAN DIVISION.

10th Canadian Infantry Bde.	11th Canadian Infantry Bde.	12th Canadian Infantry Bde.
Headquarters.	Headquarters.	Headquarters.
44th Canadian Bn.	54th Canadian Bn.	38th Canadian Bn.
46th Canadian Bn.	75th Canadian Bn.	72nd Canadian Bn.
47th Canadian Bn.	87th Canadian Bn.	78th Canadian Bn.
50th Canadian Bn.	102nd Canadian Bn.	85th Canadian Bn.
10th Canadian T.M. Batt.	11th Canadian T.M. Batt.	12th Canadian T.M. Batt.

Divisional Troops.

H.Q., 4th Canadian Div.
H.Q., Divisional Artillery.
3rd Bde., Canadian Field Artillery (10, 11, 12 and 9 (D) Cdn. Batts.) (18—18-prs. and 6—4·5-in. howrs.).
4th Bde., Canadian Field Artillery (13, 19, 27 and 21 (D) Cdn. Batts.) (18—18-prs. and 6—4·5-in. howrs.).
V 4 C. Heavy Trench Mortar Battery, R.A.
X 4 C. Trench Mortar Battery, R.A.
Y 4 C. Trench Mortar Battery, R.A.
4th Canadian Divl. Amm. Column.
H.Q., 4th Brigade Canadian Engineers.
10th, 11th and 12th Bns., C.E.
4th Pontoon Bridging Transport Unit, C.E.
4th Canadian Divl. Sig. Co.
No. 4 Bn. Canadian M.G. Corps.
4th Canadian Divl. Train (794-797 Cos., A.S.C.).
11th, 12th, 13th Canadian F. Ambs.
4th Canadian Mobile Vet. Section.
4th Canadian Divl. Employment Co.

Divisions—*continued.*

NEW ZEALAND DIVISION.

1st New Zealand Inf. Bde.	2nd New Zealand Inf. Bde.	3rd New Zealand (Rifle) Bde.
Headquarters.	Headquarters.	Headquarters.
1st Auckland Regt.	1st Canterbury Regt.	1st Battalion.
2nd Auckland Regt.	2nd Canterbury Regt.	2nd Battalion.
1st Wellington Regt.	1st Otago Regt.	3rd Battalion.
2nd Wellington Regt.	2nd Otago Regt.	4th Battalion.
1st N.Z. T.M. Batt.	2nd N.Z. T.M. Batt.	3rd N.Z. T.M. Batt.

Divisional Troops.

H.Q. New Zealand Div.
H.Q., Divisional Artillery.
1st Bde. New Zealand Field Artillery (1st, 3rd, 7th Batts. and 15th Batt.) (18—18-prs. and 6—4·5-in. howrs.).
3rd Bde. New Zealand Field Artillery (11th, 12th, 13th Batts. and 4th Batt.) (18—18-prs. and 6—4·5-in. howrs.).
X/New Zealand Trench Mortar Battery, N.Z.F.A.
Y/New Zealand Trench Mortar Battery, N.Z.F.A.
New Zealand Divl. Amm. Column.
H.Q., Divisional Engineers.
1st, 2nd, 3rd, 4th New Zealand F. Cos., N.Z.E.
New Zealand Divl. Sig. Co.
New Zealand Pioneer Bn.
N.Z. Bn. M.G. Corps.
New Zealand Divl. Train (749-752 Cos., A.S.C.).
1st, 2nd, 3rd, 4th New Zealand F. Ambs.
1st New Zealand Mobile Vet. Section.

1st PORTUGUESE DIVISION.

	1st Infantry Bde.		2nd Infantry Bde.		3rd Infantry Bde.
7430	1st Infantry Bde.	7438	2nd Infantry Bde.	7446	3rd Infantry Bde.
7431	Headquarters.	7439	Headquarters.	7447	Headquarters.
7433	1st Inf. Bn.	7441	4th Inf. Bn.	7449	7th Inf. Bn.
7432	2nd Inf. Bn.	7440	5th Inf. Bn.	7450	8th Inf. Bn.
7435	3rd Inf. Bn.	7442	6th Inf. Bn.	7448	9th Inf. Bn.
7437	1st Light T.M. Batt.	7445	2nd Light T.M. Batt.	7453	3rd Light T.M. Batt.

Divisional Troops.

H.Q., 1st Portuguese Division.
H.Q., 1st Portuguese Divisional Artillery.
7454/7458 3rd Bde. Field Artillery (12—75 mm. and 4—4·5-in. howrs.).
7459/7463 4th Bde. Field Artillery (12—75 mm. and 4—4·5-in. howrs.).
7464/7468 6th Bde. Field Artillery (12—75 mm. and 4—4·5-in. howrs.).
7470 1st Medium Trench Mortar Battery.
7471 2nd Medium Trench Mortar Battery.
      1st Portuguese Divisional Ammunition Column.
      H.Q., 1st Portuguese Divisional Engineers.
7474 1st Field Co., Engineers.
7475 2nd Field Co., Engineers.
      3rd Field Co., Engineers.
7476 1st Pioneer Battalion.
7477 1st Portuguese Divl. Signal Co.
7478 1st Portuguese Divl. Train.
7479 4th, 5th and 6th Portuguese F. Ambs.
7483 1st Portuguese Divl. Mobile Vet. Section.
      1st Portuguese Machine Gun Battalion.
      1st Portuguese Sanitary Section.

Divisions—*continued.*

2nd PORTUGUESE DIVISION.

7490 4th Infantry Bde.	7498 5th Infantry Bde.
7491 Headquarters.	7499 Headquarters.
7492 3/20th Infantry Bn.	7500 10/13th Infantry Bn.
7493 8/29th Infantry Bn.	7501 1/2nd Infantry Bn.
7494 5th Infantry Bn.	7502 17th Infantry Bn.
7496 4th M.G. Co.	7504 5th M.G. Co.

Divisional Troops.

H.Q., 2nd Portuguese Division.
7514/7518   1st Bde. Field Artillery (without guns).
7519/7522   2nd Bde. Field Artillery (without guns).
7523/7526   5th Bde. Field Artillery (without guns).
7527   2nd Heavy Trench Mortar Battery.
7528   4th Medium Trench Mortar Battery.
7529   5th Medium Trench Mortar Battery.
7530   6th Medium Trench Mortar Battery.
        Machine Gun Depot.
7535   2nd Portuguese Divl. Signal Co.
7536   2nd Portuguese Divl. Train.
7537   3rd, 8th and 9th Portuguese F. Ambs.
7541   2nd Portuguese Divl. Mobile Vet. Section.

TRANSPORTATION UNITS.

Headquarters for Groups of B.G. Operating Cos. Nos. 1 to 6.
Headquarters Light Railway Workshops.
Loco. Supt. Headquarters (Broad Gauge) Nos. 1 and 2.
Carriage and Wagon Supt. H.Q. (Broad Gauge) No. 1.
Headquarters Groups of Quarries Nos. 1 to 3.
Headquarters Docks, Nos. 1 to 6, and Mediterranean L. of C.
Headquarters Port Construction, Nos. 1 to 3.

Operating Companies (Broad Gauge)—
> Nos. 1, 2, 3, 4, 5, 6, 7, 9, 11, 12, 13, 14, 15, 20, 21, 22, 23, 24, 25, 26, 27, 28, 29, 30, 31, 34, 40, 41, 42, 43, 44, 45, 46, 47, 48, 49, 50, 51, 52, 53, 58 (Canadian), 64 and 65. 92 (S.A.), 93 (S.A.). 4, 5 and 6 (Aus.).

Operating Companies (Light Railway)—
> Nos. 1, 2, 3, 4, 5 (N.Z.), 6, 9, 10, 11, 12, 13 (Canadian), 14, 29, 30, 31, 32, 33, 34 and 54. 1, 2 (Aus.).

H.Q.R.C.E.s—1, 2, 3, 4, 5 and Communications.

Railway Construction Companies (Broad Gauge)—
> Nos. 8, 10, 109, 110, 111, 112, 113, 114, 118, 119, 120, 259, 260, 261, 262, 263, 264, 268, 269, 271, 275, 277, 278, 279, 280, 281, 282, 295, 296, 297 and 298 Cos. R.E.
> No. 3 Railway Co., Royal Anglesey R.E. (S.R.)
> No. 2 Railway Co., Royal Monmouth R.E. (S.R.)
> No. 3 Railway Co., Royal Monmouth R.E. (S.R.)
> H.Q., and Nos. 1 and 2 Cos. Canadian Overseas Railway Construction Corps.

Railway Survey and Reconnaissance Sections, R.E.—Nos. 1 to 7.

Engine Crew Company—85th Canadian.

Workshop Companies (Broad Gauge)—Nos. 61, 62, 63, 78, 79 and 80.

Wagon Erecting Companies (Broad Gauge)—Nos. 16, 17, 18, 66, 67, 69 (Cdn.) and 70.

Miscellaneous Trades Companies (Broad Gauge)—Nos. 37, 38, 39, 82, 83 and 84 (S.A.).

Miscellaneous Trades Companies (Light Railway)—Nos. 23 and 24.

Workshop Companies (Light Railway)—Nos. 25, 26 and 28.

Trains Crew Companies (Light Railway)—Nos. 18, 19, 20, 21 and 22.

Railway Troops—1st, 2nd, 3rd, 4th, 5th, 6th, 7th, 8th, 9th, 10th, 11th, 12th and 13th Canadian Battalions.

Road Construction Companies—
> Nos. 301, 302, 303, 304, 305, 306, 307, 308, 309, 310, 311, 312, 313, 314, 315, 316, 317, 318, 319, 330, 331, 332, 333, 334, 335, 336, 337, 338, 339, 340, 341, 342, 343, 344, 345, 346, 347, 349.
> Steam Roller Repair Co., No. 1.

Quarry Companies—
> Nos. 198, 199, 320, 321, 322, 323, 324, 325, 326, 327, 328, 329 and 348.
> Quarry Maintenance Section.

Railway Traffic Sections—Nos. 1 to 13.

Inland Water Transport Sections—Nos. 1 to 16, 24 to 27.

Railway Telegraph Companies (Signals)—Nos. 1 to 8.

Railway Signal and Interlocking Company—No. 200.

Port Construction Companies (C.E.P.C.)—Nos. 1, 2, 3, 4, 5, 6, 7, 8, 11 and 12.

Electric Sections, R.E.—Nos. 1, 2 and 3.

Transportation Stores Depots—Nos. 1 and 2.

Transportation Stores Depot—No. 3 (I.W.T.).

Transportation Stores Companies—Nos. 1 to 13.

Transportation (Works) Companies—Nos. 220 to 224.

Light Railway Forward Companies—Nos. 231, 232, 234 to 240, 3 Aus.

Portuguese Construction Battalion—No. 1.

LINE OF COMMUNICATION UNITS.

I.—ROYAL ARTILLERY.

(12-in. guns on railway mountings.)
No. 529 (1—12-in. gun).

(2—12-in. howitzers on railway mountings.)
No. 109.

ANTI-AIRCRAFT ARTILLERY—
H.Q., L. of C., A.A. Defence Commander.
No. 175 Section (2—13-pr. guns).
No. 176 Section (2—13-pr. guns).

Northern Group, A.A. Area.
- No. 68 Section (2—13-pr. guns).
- No. 113 Section (2—13-pr. guns).
- No. 147 Section (2—13-pr. guns).
- No. 163 Section (2—13-pr. guns).
- No. 201 Section (2—3-in. guns).
- No. 203 Section (2—3-in. guns).
- No. 204 Section (2—3-in. guns).
- No. 207 Section (2—3-in. guns).
- No. 212 Section (2—3-in. guns).
- No. 224 Section (2—3-in. guns).
- No. 237 (2—3-in guns).
- No. 240 (2—3-in guns).
- No. 241 (2—3-in guns).
- No. 243 Section (2—3-in. guns).
- No. 244 Section (2—3-in. guns).

Central Group, A.A. Area.
- No. 1 Section (2—12-pr. guns).
- No. 27 Section (2—13-pr. guns).
- No. 29 Section (2—3-in. guns).
- No. 114 Section (2—13-pr. guns).
- No. 161 Section (2—13-pr. guns).
- No. 209 Section (2—3-in. guns).
- No. 210 Section (2—3-in. guns).
- No. 234 Section (2—3-in. guns).
- No. 235 Section (2—3-in. guns).

Southern Group, A.A. Area.
- No. 2 Section (2—12-pr. guns).
- No. 3 Section (2—12-pr. guns).
- No. 10 Section (2—13-pr. guns).
- No. 28 Section (2—3-in. guns).
- No. 36 Section (2—13-pr. guns).
- No. 17 Section (2—13-pr. guns).
- No. 160 Section (2—13-pr. guns).
- No. 213 Section (2—3-in. guns).
- No. 215 Section (2—3-in. guns).
- No. 229 Section (2—3-in. guns).
- No. 231 Section (2—3-in. guns).
- No. 233 Section (2—3-in. guns).
- No. 238 Section (2—3-in. guns).

Base Ports, A.A. Area.
- No. 4 Section (2—12-pr. guns).
- No. 5 Section (2—12-pr. guns).
- No. 13 Section (2—3-in. guns).
- No. 45 Section (2—13-pr. guns).
- No. 83 Section (2—13-pr. guns).
- No. 105 Section (2—13-pr. guns).
- No. 149 Section (2—13-pr. guns).
- No. 150 Section (2—13-pr. guns).
- No. 157 Section (2—13-pr. guns).
- No. 169 Section (2—13-pr. guns).
- No. 170 Section (2—13-pr. guns).
- No. 221 Section (2—3-in. guns).
- No. 223 Section (2—3-in. guns).
- No. 239 Section (2—3-in. guns).
- No. 242 Section (2—3-in. guns).
- No. 245 Section (2—3-in. guns).
- No. 246 Section (2—3-in. guns).

Independent Force A.A. Defence Commander.

"W" A.A. Bty.
- No. 108 Section (2—13-pr. guns).
- No. 112 Section (2—13-pr. guns).
- No. 167 Section (2—13-pr. guns).
- No. 206 Section (2—13-pr. guns).

"X" A.A. Bty.
- No. 51 Section (2—3-in. guns).
- No. 211 Section (2—3-in. guns).
- No. 222 Section (2—3-in. guns).
- No. 228 Section (2—3-in. guns).

No. 172 Section (2—13-pr. guns).
No. 173 Section (2—13-pr. guns).
R.M.A. (Anti-Aircraft) Workshops.

II.—ROYAL ENGINEERS.

"L" Signal Bn., R.E.
355th Electrical and Mechanical Co., R.E.
356th Electrical and Mechanical Co., R.E.
51st, 52nd, 58th, 60th, 159th, 240th, 241st, 242nd, 243rd, 244th, 1501st, 1502nd, 1503rd, 1504th, 1505th, 1506th, Artizan Works Cos., R.E.
1st Base Park Co., R.E.
32nd Base Park Co., R.E.
24th Base Park Co., R.E.

Anti-Aircraft Searchlight Sections.
Northern Group.—Nos. 12, 19, 33, 35, 38, 43, 46, 48, 62 Sections.
Central Group.—Nos. 23, 49, 51, 53, 63, 65, 66, 68, 74 Sections.
Southern Group.—Nos. 41, 47, 52, 54, 60, 67, 70, 71, 72, 77 Sections.
Base Ports Group.—Nos. 26, 37, 57, 59 Sections.
Nancy Area.—Nos. 10, 27, 56, 61, 73.
Nos. 4, 5 and 6 Barge Filtration Units (I.W.T.).
1st and 2nd Stores Depots.
No. 6 Survey Section, R.E.
Nos. 3 and 5 Telegraph Construction Cos.

III.—INFANTRY.

197th Infantry Brigade.
Headquarters.
18th North'd Fus.
23rd North'd Fus.
25th North'd Fus.
10th Linc. R.
16th Rif. Brig.
7th Suff. R.
16th Notts. & Derby R.
17th K.R. Rif. C.
13th Glouc. R.
14th High. L.I.

197th T.M. Batt.

10th Cam'n Highrs.
13th (Garr.) Bn., N. Staff. R.
1st Garrison Bn., Suff. R. (1 Co.)
43rd Garrison Bn. R. Fus.
Nos. 10 to 44 Garrison Cos.
44th Garrison Bn. R. Fus.
Nos. 8 to 12 A.A. Cos.

L. of C. Units—*continued.*

IV.—ARMY SERVICE CORPS.

SUPPLY.

Lines of Communication Supply Cos.—
Nos. 2 to 17, 29 to 31, 38.

Depot Units of Supply.—
Nos. 1 to 15 Canadian.
Nos. 1 to 25 Australian.
Nos. 1 to 5 New Zealand.

Field Bakeries.—
Nos. 2 to 9, 11 to 17.
Nos. 1 to 4 Canadian.
Nos. 1 to 5 Australian.
No. 1 New Zealand.

Field Butcheries.—
Nos. 1 to 10, 12 to 16.
Nos. 1, 2 and 3 Canadian.
Nos. 1 to 5 Australian.
No. 1 New Zealand.

Railhead Supply Detachments.—
Nos. 1 to 6, 8 to 18, 20 to 26, 30 to 34, 36 to 51, 53 to 61, 63, 65 to 67.
Nos. 1 to 3 Canadian.
No. 1 Australian.

HORSE TRANSPORT.—
Army Service Corps Base Depots.
Auxiliary (Horse) Companies.—
Nos. 224, 255, 280, 281, 361, 372, 501, 879 and 929 Cos., A.S.C.
Advanced Horse Transport Depot.

MECHANICAL TRANSPORT.—
Auxiliary (Petrol) Companies.—
Nos. 3, 4, 5, 6, 20, 35, 39, 40, 43, 55, 57, 58, 59, 78, 102, 118, 123.
Auxiliary (Steam) Companies.—
Nos. 7, 8, 71 and 76.
Auxiliary (Amb. Car) Companies.—
Nos. 41, 47 and 48.
Advanced M.T. Depots.—
Nos. 1 and 2.
Base M.T. Depots.—
Nos. 1 and 2.
Heavy Repair Shops, A.S.C.—
Nos. 1, 2, 3, 4, 5.
Workshop for A.A. Guns.—
No. 7 (1082 Co., A.S.C.).
Water Tank (M.T.) Co.—
No. 4 (987 Co., A.S.C.).
M.T. School of Instruction.

V.—ROYAL ARMY MEDICAL CORPS.

General Hospitals.—
Nos. 2, 3, 4, 5, 6, 7, 8, 10, 14, 20, 22, 24, 25, 26, 30, 35, 39, 47, 51, 53, 54, 55, 56, 57, 58, 59, 72, 73, 74, 81 and 83.
Australian General Hospitals.—
Nos. 1, 2 and 3.
Canadian General Hospitals.—
Nos. 1, 2, 3, 6, 7 and 8.
No. 1 South African General Hospital.
Stationary Hospitals.—
Nos. 1 to 8, 11, 12, 14, 25, 32, 40, 41, 42, 46 and 52 New Zealand.
Paris, Marseilles, Abancourt, St. Germain and Cherbourg Stationary Hospitals.
Canadian Stationary Hospitals.—
Nos. 2, 7 to 10.
American General Hospitals.—
No. 1 (Presbyterian, U.S.A.).
No. 9 (Lakeside, U.S.A.).
No. 12 (St. Louis, U.S.A.).
No. 13 (Harvard, U.S.A.).
No. 16 (Philadelphia, U.S.A.).
No. 18 (Chicago, U.S.A.).
British Red Cross Hospitals.—
Nos. 2, 5, 6, 8, 9 and 10.
St. John's Ambulance Brigade Hospital.
37 Detention Hospitals.
25 Native Labour Detention Hospitals.
2 P. of W. Detention Hospitals.
Native Labour Hospitals.—
Nos. 1, 2, and 3 General.
Nos. 4 and 5 Stationary.

No. 7 N.L. Contingent Hospital.
Lahore Indian General Hospital.
Convalescent Depots.—
Nos. 1 to 7, 9 to 16, No. 1 Australian, W.A.A.C., Sisters.
Indian Convalescent Depot.
Canadian Officers' Convalescent Home.
Michelham Convalescent Home.
No. 4 (Prisoners of War) Convalescent Depot.
Sanitary Sections.—
Nos. 1, 2, 3, 3A, 5A, 6A, 26, 27, 44, 109, 111 and 120.
1st London Sanitary Section (T.F.)
Sanitary Squads.—
Nos. 2, 3, 4, 11, 12, 13, 18, 19, 20, 21, 22, 25, 31, 32, 36, 40, 43, 44, 50, 51, 52, 53, 54, 55, 56, 57, 60, 61, 64, 65.
Advanced Depots Medical Stores.—
Nos. 3 and 33.
Base Depots of Medical Stores.—
Nos. 1, 2, 3, 6 and 13.
Ambulance Trains.—
Nos. 1 to 12, 14 to 17, 19 to 37, and 42.
Ambulance Barge Flotillas.—
Nos. 2, 3, 4 and 5.
Amb. Train Supply Stores, Boulogne.
Motor Ambulance Convoys.
F.A.N.Y.
Scottish Red Cross Mobile Unit.

VI.—ARMY VETERINARY CORPS.

Veterinary Hospitals.—
Nos. 2 to 10, 12, 13, 14, 15, 19 and 24.
Canadian Veterinary Hospital.
Australian Veterinary Hospital.
Marseilles Veterinary Hospital.

Convalescent Horse Depots.—
Nos. 1, 2, 3 and 4.
Advanced Depots of Veterinary Stores.
Nos. 1, 2 and 3.
Base Depots of Veterinary Stores.—
Nos. 1 and 2.

VII.—ARMY ORDNANCE DEPARTMENT.

Army Ordnance Companies.—
Nos. 1, 2, 4, 5, 6, 7, 8, 10, 13, 14, 15, 17, 19, 20, 21, 22, 23, 28, 29, 33, 34, 37, 40, 41, 42, 46, 48, 49, 50, 52, 54, 59, 60, 61, 63, 67, 69, 71, 73, 74, 76, 77, 81, 86, 88, 89, 90, 91, 101, 109, 110, 116, 117, 118, 119, 120, 121, 122, 127, 128, 129, 130, 131, 132, 133 and 134.

Three Base Ordnance Depôts.
Paris Salvage Depôt.
8 to 15, ⎫
18 to 20, ⎬ Ordnance Depôts.
24 and 25 ⎭

Empties Depôt.
Two Receipts Depôts.
Two Ammunition Transit Depôts.
Two Ordnance Ammunition Repair Factories.
Three Base Ordnance Workshops.
Advanced Base Workshops.
Nineteen (Supply) Railhead Ordnance Detachments.

VIII.—LABOUR CORPS.

Labour Group Headquarters.—
Nos. 1, 2, 3, 4, 6, 7, 9, 10, 11, 13, 14, 15, 19, 20, 27, 39, 40, 44, 50, 60, 64, 72, 73, 74, 76, 78, 79, 83.

Labour Companies.—
Nos. 87, 145, 165, 716, 720, 726, 730, 732, 734, 990, 991.

Area Employment (Artizan) Companies.—
Nos. 781, 828, 829, 830, 849, 889, 936, 938, 939, 940, 941, 942, 943, 944, 945.

Area Employment Companies.—
Nos. 745, 754, 768, 769, 775, 779, 783, 784, 787, 788, 789, 794, 795, 796, 797, 798, 799, 833, 835, 836, 837, 838, 839, 842, 844, 846, 847, 850, 851, 854, 855, 856, 857, 858, 859, 860, 861, 862, 870, 871, 877, 883, 884, 885, 886, 887, 888, 890, 891, 892, 895, 897, 898, 899, 900, 901, 902, 903, 904, 905, 930, 992, 993.

Agricultural Companies.—
No. 996.

Indian Labour Corps.—
Companies Nos. 33 (Bihar), 55 (United Provinces), 78 (Burma), 79 (United Provinces), 80 (Santal), 82 (United Provinces), 84 (Garo), 85 (Kumaon).

"B" and "C" Cape Coloured Coys.

Chinese Labour Corps.—
Companies Nos. 4, 5, 6, 9 to 19 to 22, 24, 25, 27 to 30, 33 to 38, 41, 44, 48 to 54, 56 to 57, 62 to 66, 68 to 72, 75, 77, 81, 82, 87 to 89, 91 to 98, 100, 103, 105, 106, 109, 110 to 112, 120, 124, 125, 127 to 129, 132 to 138, 141 to 145, 148, 149, 151 to 156, 158 to 160, 163, 168, 169, 170, 171, 173, 175 to 181, 183, 184, 186, 187, 191, 192, 194, 195.

IX.—NON-COMBATANT CORPS.

No. 1 Northern Co.
No. 2 Northern Co.

No. 1 Southern Co.
No. 1 Eastern Co.
No. 2 Eastern Co.

No. 1 Western Co.
No. 1 Scottish Co.

X.—DETAILS, MISCELLANEOUS UNITS.

No. 14 Cav. M.G. Squadron.
Rest Camps 1 to 10, 10 Miscellaneous.
Nos. 1 and 2 L. of C. Area Reception Camps.
Nos. 1, 3, 4, 5 and 6 Officers' Camps.
120 Prisoner of War Companies.
Army Printing and Stationery Services—
  6 Depôts.
  1 Publications Department.
  3 Printing Centres.
  Technical Store.
  Photographic Section.
  Rubber Stamp Factory.
  Typewriter Repair Shop.
Canadian Overseas Railway Construction Corps.
1 to 10 Military Prisons.
G.H.Q. Machine Gun School.
G.H.Q. Lewis Gun and Light T.M. School.

FORESTRY UNITS—
  Forestry Companies, R.E.
    Nos. 361, 363, 366 to 371.
  Canadian Forestry Corps.
    4 Group Headquarters.
    9 District Headquarters.
  Canadian Forestry Companies—
    Nos. 1, 10 to 15, 19 to 24, 26 to 28, 30 to 34, 36 to 60, 69 to 80.
  No. 2 Construction Co.

REMOUNTS—
  Advanced Remount Depôts.
    Nos. 2, 4 and 5.
  Base Remount Depôts.
    Nos. 1, 2, 3, 4 and 5.
  Indian Base Remount Depôt.
  Reinforcement Training Camps—Nos. 1 and 2.

XI.—BASE DEPOTS.

British Cavalry Base Depôt (Cavalry, M.M.P., and M.F.P.).
R.H. & R.F.A. Base Depôt.
R.G.A. Base Depôt.
R.M.A. Base Depôt.
R.A.F. (No. 1 and No. 2 Aircraft) Depôt.
Nos. 1 and 2 Aeroplane Supply Depôts.
R.E. Base Depôt.
Signals Base Depôt.
Tank Corps Base Depôt.
Machine Gun Corps Base Depôt.
Cyclist Base Depôt (All R.A.M.C. and A.C.C.).
Infantry Base Depôts—
  Guards.
  A to F, H, J to M.
  Garrison Bns.
  Australian.
  Canadian.
Q.M.A.A.C.

New Zealand.
Australian General Base Depôt.
Canadian General Base Depôt.
A.S.C. Base Depôt (Horse Transport & Supply) (No. 10 Co. A.S.C.).
1st Base, M.T.
Army Veterinary Corps (No. 2 Vet. Hospital).
Transportation Troops Base Depôt.
Indian R.A. Advanced Base Depôt.
Indian General Base Depôt.
British West Indies Regts. Base Depôt.
Labour Corps Base Depôt.
Indian Labour Corps Base Depôt.
Chinese Labour Corps Base Depôt.
1 to 4 Employment Depôts.
1 to 4 Medical Board Depôts.

PORTUGUESE EXPEDITIONARY FORCE.
DEPOTS.
(I.) PERSONNEL.

1st Infantry Depôt—6th Infantry (Porto).
2nd Infantry Depôt—19th Infantry (Chaves).
3rd Infantry Depôt—30th Infantry (Braganca).
Mixed Depôt—3rd Artillery (Santarem).
        Sappers and Miners (Lisbon).
        Field Telegraphists (Lisbon).
        Bridging Train (Tancos).
        1st Group of Medical Companies (Lisbon).
        Supply Column M.T. (Entroncamento).
Cavalry Depôt—2nd Cavalry (Lisbon).

(II.) ANIMALS.

Remount Depôt—School of Equitation (Torres Novas).

(III.) STORES.

Engineer Stores Depôt } Regiment of Sappers and Miners (Lisbon).
Advanced Engineer Stores Depôt }
War Material Depôt.
Advanced War Material Depôt.
Workshop for Ammunition—7·5 Q.F.
Sanitary Stores Depôt } 1st Group of Medical Companies (Lisbon).
Advanced Sanitary Stores Depôt }
Veterinary Depôt } 2nd Regiment of Cavalry (Lisbon).
Advanced Veterinary Depôt }
Supply Depôt } 1st Group of Administrative Companies (Lisbon).
Advanced Supply Depôt }
Clothing Depôt } " " " " "
Advanced Clothing Depôt }
Ordnance Stores   " " " " "

HOSPITALS.

Surgical Hospital—1st Group of Medical Companies (Lisbon).
Medical Hospital and Convalescent Depôt—1st Group of Medical Companies (Lisbon).
Casualty Clearing Station—1st Group of Medical Companies (Lisbon).

INDEX TO ARMIES.

Army.	Corps.	Divisions.	Army.	Corps.	Divisions.
1st	VII.	—	4th	IX.	1st, 6th, 32nd, 46th.
	VIII.	8th, 12th, 49th, 52nd.		XIII.	18th, 25th, 50th, 66th.
	XXII.	4th, 11th, 51st, 56th, 63rd.		Australian	1st Aus., 2nd Aus., 3rd Aus., 4th Aus., 5th Aus.
	Canadian	1st Cdn., 2nd Cdn., 3rd Cdn., 4th Cdn.			
2nd	II.	9th, 34th.	5th	I.	15th, 16th, 58th.
	X.	29th, 30th.		III.	55th, 74th.
	XV.	14th, 36th, 40th.		XI.	47th, 57th, 59th.
	XIX.	31st, 35th, 41st.		Portug'se	1st Port'gse, 2nd Port'gse.
3rd	IV.	5th, 37th, 42nd, N.Z.			
	V.	17th, 21st, 33rd, 38th.			
	VI.	Guards, 2nd, 3rd, 62nd.			
	XVII.	19th, 20th, 24th, 61st.			

INDEX TO ARMY CORPS.

Spare Nos.	Army Corps.	Divisions.	Army	Spare Nos.	Army Corps.	Divisions.	Army
7041/7045	Cav. Corps	1st Cav., 2nd Cav., 3rd Cav.	—	6996/7000	XIII.	18th, 25th, 50th, 66th	4th
6946/6950	I.	15th, 16th, 58th	5th	7001/7005	XV.	14th, 36th, 40th	2nd
6951/6955	II.	9th, 34th	2nd	7006/7010	XVII.	19th, 20th, 24th, 61st	3rd
6956/6960	III.	55th, 74th	5th	7016/7020	XIX.	31st, 35th, 41st	2nd
6961/6965	IV.	5th, 37th, 42nd, N.Z.	3rd	7021/7025	XXII.	4th, 11th, 51st, 56th, 63rd	1st
6966/6970	V.	17th, 21st, 33rd, 38th	3rd	7026/7030	Australian	1st Aus., 2nd Aus., 3rd Aus., 4th Aus., 5th Aus.	4th
6971/6975	VI.	Guards, 2nd, 3rd, 62nd	3rd	7031/7035	Canadian	1st Cdn., 2nd Cdn., 3rd Cdn., 4th Cdn.	1st
6976/6980	VII.	—	1st				
7011/7015	VIII.	8th, 12th, 49th, 52nd	1st				
6986/6990	IX.	1st, 6th, 32nd, 46th	4th	7036/7040	Portug'se	1st Port'gse, 2nd Port'gse	5th
6991/6995	X.	29th, 30th	2nd				
	XI.	47th, 57th, 59th	5th				

INDEX TO DIVISIONS.

Spare Nos.	Division.	Corps.	Army.	Spare Nos.	Division.	Corps.	Army.
7051/7055	1st Cav.			7211/7215	38th (Welsh)	V.	3rd
7056/7060	2nd Cav.	Cav.	—	7216/7220	39th		L. of C.
7061/7065	3rd Cav.			7221/7225	40th	XV.	2nd
7066/7070	Guards	VI.	3rd	7226/7230	41st	XIX.	2nd
7071/7075	1st	IX.	4th	7231/7235	42nd (E. Lancs.)	IV.	3rd
7076/7080	2nd	VI.	3rd	7236/7240	46th (N. Midland)	IX.	4th
7081/7085	3rd	VI.	3rd	7241/7245	47th (London)	XI.	5th
7086/7090	4th	XXII.	1st	7246/7250	49th (W. Riding)	VIII.	1st
7561/7568	5th	IV.	3rd	7251/7255	50th (Northumb'n)	XIII.	4th
7091/7095	6th	IX.	4th	7256/7260	51st (Highland)	XXII.	1st
7096/7100	8th	VIII.	1st		52nd (Lowland)	VIII.	1st
7101/7105	9th (Scottish)	II.	2nd	7261/7265	55th (W. Lancs.)	III.	5th
7106/7110	11th	XXII.	1st	7266/7270	56th (London)	XXII.	1st
7111/7115	12th (Eastern)	VIII.	1st	7271/7275	57th (W. Lancs.)	XI.	5th
7116/7120	14th	XV.	2nd	7276/7280	58th (London)	I.	5th
7121/7125	15th (Scottish)	I.	5th	7281/7285	59th (N. Midland)	XI.	5th
7126/7130	16th	I.	5th	7286/7290	61st (S. Midland)	XVII.	3rd
7131/7135	17th (Northern)	V.	3rd	7291/7295	62nd (W. Riding)	VI.	3rd
7136/7140	18th (Eastern)	XIII.	4th	7296/7300	63rd (R. Naval)	XXII.	1st
7141/7145	19th (Western)	XVII.	3rd	7301/7305	66th (E. Lancs.)	XIII.	4th
7146/7150	20th (Light)	XVII.	3rd		74th (Yeo.)	III.	5th
7151/7155	21st	V.	3rd	7306/7310	1st Aus.	Australian	4th
7156/7160	24th	XVII.	3rd	7311/7315	2nd Aus.	Australian	4th
7161/7165	25th	XIII.	4th	7316/7320	3rd Aus.	Australian	4th
7166/7170	29th	X.	2nd	7321/7325	4th Aus.	Australian	4th
7171/7175	30th	X.	2nd	7326/7330	5th Aus.	Australian	4th
7176/7180	31st	XIX.	2nd	7331/7335	1st Cdn.	Cdn.	1st
7181/7185	32nd	IX.	4th	7336/7340	2nd Cdn.	Cdn.	1st
7186/7190	33rd	V.	3rd	7341/7345	3rd Cdn.	Cdn.	1st
7191/7195	34th	II.	2nd	7346/7350	4th Cdn.	Cdn.	1st
7196/7200	35th	XIX.	2nd	7351/7355	N. Zealand	IV.	3rd
7201/7205	36th (Ulster)	XV.	2nd	7356/7360	1st Portuguese	Portuguese	5th
7206/7210	37th	IV.	3rd	7361/7365	2nd Portuguese	Portuguese	5th

INDEX TO BRIGADES.

	Brigade.	Division.		Brigade.	Division.		Brigade.	Division.
1	1st Cav.	1st Cav.	71	76th	3rd	138	176th	59th
2	2nd "		72	86th		139	177th	
3	3rd "		73	87th	29th	140	178th	
4	4th "	2nd Cav.	74	88th		141	182nd	61st
5	5th "		75	89th	30th	142	183rd	
6	6th "	3rd Cav.	76	90th		143	184th	
7	7th "		77	92nd	31st	144	185th	
8	9th "	1st Cav.	78	93rd		145	186th	62nd
9	Cdn. Cav.	3rd Cav.	7740	94th (Yeo.)	31st	146	187th	
10	1st Guards		8030	95th	5th	147	188th	63rd (R.Naval)
11	2nd Guards	Guards	79	96th	32nd	148	189th	
12	3rd Guards		80	97th		149	190th	
13	4th Guards	Cav. Corps	81	98th	33rd	150	197th	L. of C.
14	1st		82	99th	2nd	151	198th	66th
15	2nd	1st	83	100th	33rd	152	199th	
16	3rd		84	101st		7765	229th	74th
17	5th	2nd	85	102nd	34th	7771	230th	
18	6th		86	103rd		7777	231st	
19	7th	25th	87	104th		153	1st Aus.	1st Aus.
20	8th	3rd	88	105th	35th	154	2nd Aus.	
21	9th		89	106th		155	3rd Aus.	
22	10th	4th	90	107th	36th	156	4th Aus.	4th Aus.
23	11th		91	108th		157	5th Aus.	
24	12th		92	109th		158	6th Aus.	2nd Aus.
8016	13th	5th	93	110th	21st	159	7th Aus.	
25	14th	32nd	94	111th	37th	160	8th Aus.	5th Aus.
8023	15th	5th	95	112th		161	9th Aus.	
26	16th	6th	96	113th	38th	162	10th Aus.	3rd Aus.
27	17th	24th	97	114th		163	11th Aus.	
28	18th	6th	98	115th		164	12th Aus.	4th Aus.
29	19th	33rd	99	116th		165	13th Aus.	
30	21st	30th	100	117th	39th	166	14th Aus.	5th Aus.
31	23rd		101	118th		167	15th Aus.	
32	24th	8th	102	119th		168	1st Cdn.	1st Cdn.
33	25th		103	120th	40th	169	2nd "	
34	26th		104	121st		170	3rd "	
35	27th	9th	105	122nd		171	4th "	2nd Cdn.
2034	28th		106	123rd	41st	172	5th "	
36	32nd		107	124th		173	6th "	
37	33rd	11th	108	125th		174	7th "	3rd Cdn.
38	34th		109	126th	42nd	175	8th "	
39	35th		110	127th		176	9th "	
40	36th	12th	111	137th		177	10th "	4th Cdn.
41	37th		112	138th	46th	178	11th "	
42	41st		113	139th		179	12th "	
43	42nd	14th	114	140th		180	1st N.Z.	N. Zealand
44	43rd		115	141st	47th	181	2nd N.Z.	
45	44th		116	142nd		182	3rd N.Z.(Rif.)	
46	45th	15th	117	146th		183	South African	66th
47	46th		118	147th	49th	184	1st Port'gu'se	
48	47th		119	148th		185	2nd "	1st P'rtgu'se
49	48th	16th	120	149th		186	3rd "	
50	49th		121	150th	50th	187	4th "	
51	50th		122	151st		188	5th "	2nd P'rtgu'se
52	51st	17th	123	152nd		189	6th "	
53	52nd		124	153rd	51st			
54	53rd		125	154th				
55	54th	18th	8051	155th				
56	55th		8057	156th	52nd			
57	56th		8063	157th				
58	57th	19th	126	164th				
59	58th		127	165th	55th			
60	59th		128	166th				
61	60th	20th	129	167th				
62	61st		130	168th	56th			
63	62nd	21th	131	169th				
64	63rd	37th	132	170th				
65	64th	21st	133	171st	57th			
66	71st	6th	134	172nd				
67	72nd	24th	135	173rd				
68	73rd		136	174th	58th			
69	74th	25th	137	175th				
70	75th							

INDEX TO UNITS.

	Unit.	Cavalry Brigade.	Cavalry Division.
	BRITISH CAVALRY.		
244	2nd D.G.	1st	1st
245	3rd D.G.	6th	3rd
246	4th D.G.	2nd	1st
247	5th D.G.	1st	1st
248	6th D.G.	4th	2nd
249	7th D.G.	7th	3rd
250	1st Dragoons	6th	3rd
251	2nd Dragoons	5th	2nd
252	3rd Hussars	4th	2nd
253	4th Hussars	3rd	2nd
254	5th Lancers	3rd	2nd
255	6th (Innis.) Dragoons	7th	3rd
257	8th Hussars	9th	1st
258	9th Lancers	2nd	1st
259	10th Hussars	6th	3rd
260	11th Hussars	1st	1st
261	12th Lancers	5th	2nd
262	15th Hussars	9th	1st
263	16th Lancers	3rd	2nd
264	17th Lancers	7th	3rd
265	17th (1 Troop)	—	G.H.Q.
266	18th Hussars	2nd	1st
267	19th Hussars	9th	1st
268	20th Hussars	5th	2nd

	Unit.	Allotment.
	AUSTRALIAN CAVALRY.	
278	4th Regt. Light Horse ("A" Sqdn.)	} C.T., XXII. A.C.
279	("B" Sqdn.)	
280	13th Regt. Light Horse	C.T., Australian A.C.
281	Otago Mtd. Rif. (1 Sqdn.)	C.T. XXII. A.C.
	CANADIAN CAVALRY.	
285	Royal Canadian Dgns.	Cdn. Cav. Bde., 3rd Cav. Div.
286	Lord Strathcona's Horse	Cdn. Cav. Bde., 3rd Cav. Div.
287	Fort Garry Horse	Cdn. Cav. Bde., 3rd Cav. Div.
288	Canadian Light Horse	C.T., Cdn. A.C.
	Royal North West Mtd. Police.	C.T., Cdn. A.C.

	Unit.	Allotment.
	YEOMANRY — SPECIAL RESERVE AND T.F.	
299	1/1st North'mb'l'd. Yeo.	C.T., III. A.C.
300	1/1st Oxfordshire Hus.	4th Cav. Bde., 2nd Cav. Div.
7554	1/1st K. Edward's Horse	C.T., XI. A.C.
	1/1st Bedford Yeo.	Cavalry Corps
	1/1st Essex Yeo.	Cavalry Corps
	1/1st Leicester Yeo.	Cavalry Corps
	1/1st N. Somerset Yeo.	Cavalry Corps
	LOVAT'S SCOUTS — (Sharpshooters).	
305	No. 1 Group	I. A.C.
306	No. 2 Group	XVII. A.C.
307	No. 3 Group	XV. A.C.
308	No. 5 Group	VI. A.C.
309	No. 6 Group	VI. A.C.
310	No. 7 Group	XXII. A.C.
311	No. 8 Group	IV. A.C.
312	No. 9 Group	VIII. A.C.
7831	No. 10 Group	IX. A.C.
	No. 11 Group	XIII. A.C.
6807	No. 12 Group	XI. A.C.
	No. 13 Group	XV. A.C.
	CAVALRY MACHINE-GUN SQUADRONS.	
	No. 1	1st Cav. Div.
	No. 2	1st Cav. Div.
	No. 3	2nd Cav. Div.
	No. 4	2nd Cav. Div.
	No. 5	2nd Cav. Div.
	No. 6	3rd Cav. Div.
	No. 7	3rd Cav. Div.
	No. 9	1st Cav. Div.
	No. 11	L. of C.
	Cdn.	3rd Cav. Div.

Index to Units—*continued.*

ROYAL ARTILLERY.

HEADQUARTERS DIVISIONAL ARTILLERY.

316	Guards	331	19th	346	39th	360	61st
317	1st	332	20th	347	40th	361	62nd
318	2nd	333	21st	348	41st	362	63rd
319	3rd	334	24th	349	42nd	363	66th
320	4th	335	25th	350	46th	7783	74th
8013	5th	336	29th	351	47th	364	1st Aus.
321	6th	337	30th	352	49th	365	2nd Aus.
322	8th	338	31st	353	50th	366	3rd Aus.
323	9th	339	32nd	354	51st	367	4th Aus.
324	11th	340	33rd	8069	52nd	368	5th Aus.
325	12th	341	34th	355	55th	369	1st Cdn.
326	14th	342	35th	356	56th	370	2nd Cdn.
327	15th	343	36th	357	57th	371	3rd Cdn.
328	16th	344	37th	358	58th	372	4th Cdn.
329	17th	345	38th	359	59th	373	N.Z.
330	18th						

	Brigade.	Batteries.	Division.		Brigade.	Batteries.	Division.
		R.H.A. (Regulars).				R.H.A. (Regulars)—*contd.*	
383/386	3rd	"D," "E," "J"	2nd Cav.	6172/6176	*14th	"F," "T," 400, 401 (R.F.A.)...	3rd Army
387/	4th	"C," "K"	3rd Cav.				
6666/6670	*5th	"G," "N," "O," "Z"	4th Army	398/402	15th	"B," "L," 1/1st Warwickshire, 460 (R.F.A.)	29th
394/397	7th	"H," "I," "Y"	1st Cav.				
				403/406	*16th	"A," "Q," "U"	4th Army

* A.F.A. Brigade.

	Battery and Brigade.	Cavalry Brigade.	Division.		Battery and Brigade.	Cavalry Brigade.	Division.
	R.H.A. (Regulars).				R.H.A. (Regulars)—*continued.*		
415	A. 16th	—	4th Army		T. 14th	—	3rd Army
416	B. 15th	Divl. T.	29th	429	U. 16th	—	4th Army
417	C. 4th	6th	3rd Cav.	430	Y. 7th	9th	1st Cav.
418	D. 3rd	3rd	2nd Cav.	431	Z. 5th	—	4th Army
419	E. 3rd	5th	2nd Cav.	432	}		
	F. 14th	—	3rd Army	295	} Canadian	Canadian	3rd Cav.
	G. 5th	—	4th Army	296	}		
421	H. 7th	2nd	1st Cav.				
422	I. 7th	1st	1st Cav.		R.H.A.—(T.F.)		
423	J. 3rd	4th	2nd Cav.	435	1 1st Warwickshire, 15th	Divl. T.	29th
424	K. 4th	7th	3rd Cav.				
425	L. 15th	Divl. T.	29th				
	N. 5th	—	4th Army				
427	O. 5th	—	4th Army				
428	Q. 16th	—	4th Army				

Index to Units—Royal Artillery—continued.

	Brigade.	Batteries.	Division.		Brigade.	Batteries.	Division.
	R.F.A. (Regulars)				**R.F.A. (Regulars)** —continued.		
436/440	2nd	21, 42, 53 and 87	6th	664/668	88th	"A," "B," "C," "D"	19th
441/445	*5th	64, 73, 81 and "D"	4th Army	669/673	91st	,, ,,	20th
8070/8074	9th	19, 20, 28 and D/69	52nd	674/678	92nd		20th
446/450	*11th	83, 84, 85 and "D"	2nd Army	679/682	*93rd	"A," "B," "C"	3rd Army
7824/7828	*14th	"A," 68, 88 and 402	4th Army	683/687	94th	"A," "B," "C," "D"	21st
8046/8050	15th	62, 80, "A" and "D"	6th	688/692	95th	,, ,,	21st
455/459	17th	13, 25, 92 and "D"	29th	6671/6675	*96th	407, 408, 409, 410	2nd Army
460/464	*18th	"A," 59, 91 and "D"	1st Army	693/697	*104th	"A," "B," "C," "D"	4th Army
465/469	*23rd	107, 108, "C" and "D"	2nd Army	698/702	106th	,, ,,	24th
470/474	24th	110, 111, 112 and 43	6th	703/707	107th	,, ,,	24th
475/479	25th	113, 114, 115 and 40	1st	708/712	*108th	,, ,,	5th Army
480/483	*26th	"A," 116 and 117	1st Army	713/717	110th	,, ,,	25th
7561/7565	27th	119, 120, 121 and 37	5th	718/722	112th	,, ,,	25th
484/488	*28th	"A," 123, 124 and 65	2nd Army	723/727	*116th	,, ,,	2nd Army
489/493	29th	125, 126, 127 and 128	4th	7789/7793	117th	"A," "B," 366 and "D"	74th
494/498	32nd	27, 134, 135 and 86	4th	728/732	*119th	"A," "B," "C," "D"	2nd Army
499/503	33rd	32, 33, 36 and 55	8th	733/737	121st	,, ,,	38th
504/508	*34th	50, 70, "C," and 56	3rd Army	738/742	122nd	,, ,,	38th
509/513	36th	15, 48, 71 and "D"	2nd	743/747	123rd	,, ,,	37th
514/518	*38th	24, 72, "A" and "D"	2nd Army	748/752	124th	,, ,,	37th
519/523	39th	46, 51, 54 and 30	1st	753/756 & 7613	*126th	"A" and "B" (2/1st H.A.C.), 2/1st Warwickshire, 411	1st Army
524/528	40th	6, 23, 49 and 130	3rd				
529/533	41st	9, 16, 17 and 47	2nd	757/761	*147th	10, 97, "A," "D"	1st Army
534/538	42nd	29, 41, 45 and 129	3rd	762/766	148th	"A," "B," "C," "D"	30th
7784/7788	44th	340, 382, 425 and "D"	74th	767/771	149th	,, ,,	30th
539/543	45th	1, 3, 5 and 67	8th	772/776	*150th	,, ,,	5th Army
544/548	46th	"A," "B," "C," "D"	14th	777/781	152nd	,, ,,	34th
549/553	47th	,, ,,	14th	782/786	153rd	,, ,,	36th
554/558	*48th	,, ,,	4th Army	787/791	*155th	,, ,,	3rd Army
559/563	50th	,, ,,	9th	792/796	156th	,, ,,	33rd
564/568	51st	,, ,,	9th	797/801	157th	,, ,,	35th
569/573	*52nd	"A," 122, "C," "D"	1st Army	802/806	*158th	,, ,,	5th Army
8075/8079	55th	"A," "B," "C" and 527	52nd	807/811	159th	,, ,,	35th
574/578	58th	"A," "B," "C," "D"	11th	812/816	160th	,, ,,	34th
579/583	59th	,, ,,	11th	817/821	161st	,, ,,	32nd
584/588	62nd	,, ,,	12th	822/826	162nd	,, ,,	33rd
589/593	63rd	,, ,,	12th	827/831	165th	,, ,,	31st
594/598	*64th	,, ,,	2nd Army	832/836	166th	,, ,,	32nd
599/603	*65th	465, 466, 504 and 505	4th Army	837/841	*169th	376, 377, 378 and 379	3rd Army
604/608	70th	"A," "B," "C," "D"	15th	842/846	170th	"A," "B," "C," "D"	31st
609/613	71st	,, ,,	15th	847/851	173rd	,, ,,	36th
6198/6202	*72nd	,, ,,	3rd Army	852/856	174th	,, ,,	36th
614/618	74th	,, ,,	Guards	6193/6197	*175th	,, ,,	1st Army
619/623	75th	,, ,,	Guards	857/861	177th	,, ,,	16th
6188/6192	*76th	,, ,,	3rd Army	862/866	178th	,, ,,	40th
624/628	*77th	,, ,,	1st Army	867/871	*179th	383, 462, 463 and 464	5th Army
629/633	78th	,, ,,	17th	872/876	180th	"A," "B," "C," "D"	16th
634/638	79th	,, ,,	17th	877/881	181st	,, ,,	40th
639/643	82nd	,, ,,	18th	882/886	186th	,, ,,	39th
644/648	83rd	,, ,,	18th	887/891	187th	,, ,,	41st
649/653	*84th	,, ,,	4th Army	892/896	*189th	34, "B," "C," "D"	1st Army
654/658	*86th	,, ,,	4th Army	897/901	190th	"A," "B," "C," "D"	41st
659/663	87th	,, ,,	19th				

	Brigade.			Batteries.		Division.
	R.F.A. (T.F.)					
961/965	210th (E. Lancashire)	...		"A," "B," "C," "D"	...	} 42nd
966/970	211th (E. Lancashire)	...		,, ,,	...	
971/975	223rd (Home Counties)	...	...	,, ,,	...	63rd
976/980	230th (N. Midland)	...	...	,, ,,	...	} 46th
981/985	231st (N. Midland)	...	...	,, ,,	...	
986/990	*232nd (N. Midland)	...	...	,, ,,	...	4th Army
991/995	235th (London)	...	...	,, ,,	...	} 47th
996/1000	236th (London)	...	...	,, ,,	...	
1001/1005	*242nd (S. Midland)	...	...	,, ,,	...	1st Army
1006/1010	245th (W. Riding)	...	...	,, ,,	...	} 49th
1011/1015	246th (W. Riding)	...	...	,, ,,	...	

* Army Field Artillery Brigade.

Index to Units—Royal Artillery—continued.

	Brigade.	Batteries.	Division.
	R.F.A. (T.F.)—continued.		
1025/1029	250th (Northumbrian)	"A," "B," "C," "D"	50th
1030/1034	251st (Northumbrian)	" "	
1035/1039	255th (Highland)	" "	51st
1040/1044	256th (Highland)	" "	
1045/1049	275th (W. Lancashire)	" "	55th
1050/1054	276th (W. Lancashire)	" "	
1055/1059	*277th (W. Lancashire)	" "	1st Army
1060/1064	280th (London)	93rd, "A," "C," "D"	56th
1065/1069	281st (London)	109th, "A," "B," "D"	
1070/1074	*282nd (London)	"A," "B," "C," "D"	1st Army
1075/1079	285th (W. Lancashire)	" "	57th
1080/1084	286th (W. Lancashire)	" "	
1085/1089	290th (London)	" "	58th
1090/1094	291st (London)	" "	
1095/1099	*293rd (London)	1/1st Shropshire (R.H.A.), 1/1st Glamorgan (R.H.A.) "C" and "D"	1st Army
1100/1104	295th (N. Midland)	"A," "B," "C," "D"	59th
1105/1109	296th (N. Midland)	" "	
1110/1114	*298th (N. Midland)	2/1st Hants (R.H.A.), 2/1st Essex (R.H.A.) "C" and "D"	4th Army
1115/1119	306th (S. Midland)	"A," "B," "C," "D"	61st
1120/1124	307th (S. Midland)	" "	
1125/1129	310th (W. Riding)	" "	62nd
1130/1134	*311th (W. Riding)	" "	1st Army
1135/1139	312th (W. Riding)	" "	62nd
1140/1144	*315th (Northumbrian)	" "	3rd Army
1145/1149	317th (Northumbrian)	" "	63rd
1150/1154	330th (E. Lancashire)	" "	66th
1155/1159	331st (E. Lancashire)	" "	

AUSTRALIAN F.A.

	Brigade.	Batteries.	Division.
1177/1181	1st Aus.	1, 2, 3, 101 Aus.	1st Aus.
1182/1186	2nd Aus.	4, 5, 6, 102 Aus.	1st Aus.
1187/1191	*3rd Aus.	7, 8, 9, 103 Aus.	4th Army
1192/1196	4th Aus.	10, 11, 12, 104 Aus.	2nd Aus.
1197/1201	5th Aus.	13, 14, 15, 105 Aus.	2nd Aus.
1202/1206	*6th Aus.	16, 17, 18, 106 Aus.	4th Army
1207/1211	7th Aus.	25, 26, 27, 107 Aus.	3rd Aus.
1212/1216	8th Aus.	29, 30, 31, 108 Aus.	3rd Aus.
1217/1221	10th Aus.	37, 38, 39, 110 Aus.	4th Aus.
1222/1226	11th Aus.	41, 42, 43, 111 Aus.	4th Aus.
1227/1231	*12th Aus.	45, 46, 47, 112 Aus.	4th Army
1232/1236	13th Aus.	49, 50, 51, 113 Aus.	5th Aus.
1237/1241	14th Aus.	53, 54, 55, 114 Aus.	5th Aus.

CANADIAN F.A.

	Brigade.	Batteries.	Division.
1250/1254	1st Cdn.	1, 3, 4, 2 (D) Cdn.	1st Cdn.
1255/1259	2nd Cdn.	5, 6, 7, 48 (D) Cdn.	1st Cdn.
1260/1264	3rd Cdn.	10, 11, 12, 9 (D) Cdn.	4th Cdn.
1265/1269	4th Cdn.	13, 19, 27, 21 (D) Cdn.	4th Cdn.
1270/1274	5th Cdn.	17, 18, 20, 23 (D) Cdn.	2nd Cdn.
1275/1279	6th Cdn.	15, 16, 25, 22 (D) Cdn.	2nd Cdn.
1280/1284	*8th Cdn.	21, 30, 32, 43 Cdn.	1st Army
1285/1289	9th Cdn.	31, 33, 45, 36 Cdn.	3rd Cdn.
1290/1294	10th Cdn.	35, 38, 39, 40 Cdn.	3rd Cdn.
1295/1299	13th Cdn.	52, 53, 55, 54 (D) Cdn.	1st Army
1300/1304	14th Cdn.	60, 61, 66, 58 (D) Cdn.	1st Army

NEW ZEALAND F.A.

	Brigade.	Batteries.	Division.
1313/1317	1st N.Z.	1, 3, 7, 15 N.Z.	N.Z.
1318/1322	*2nd N.Z.	2, 5, 6, 9 N.Z.	3rd Army
1323/1327	3rd N.Z.	4, 11, 12, 13 N.Z.	N.Z.

ROYAL GARRISON ARTILLERY.

	Brigades, R.G.A.	Army.
1330	1st (Mobile)	1st
1331	2nd (Howitzer—9·2-in.)	2nd
1332	3rd (Mixed)	2nd
1333	4th (Mixed)	2nd
1334	5th (Howitzer—8-in.)	3rd
1335	6th (Mixed)	2nd
1336	7th (Mixed)	1st
1337	8th (Howitzer—9·2-in.)	1st
1338	9th (Mobile)	4th
1339	10th (Mobile)	2nd
1340	11th (Army)	5th
1341	12th (Howitzer—8-in.)	4th
1342	13th (Mobile)	3rd
1343	14th (Howitzer—8-in.)	4th
1344	16th (Mobile)	1st
1345	17th (Mixed)	3rd
1346	18th (Howitzer—9·2-in.)	5th
1347	19th (Howitzer—9·2-in.)	1st
1348	21st (Mobile)	4th
1349	22nd (Howitzer—9·2-in.)	3rd
1350	23rd (Howitzer—9·2-in.)	4th

* Army Field Artillery Brigade.

Index to Units—Royal Artillery—continued.

	Brigades, R.G.A.	Army.		Battery.	Brigade.	Army.
	R.G.A.—continued.			**HEAVY BATTERIES.**		
1352	25th (Army)	2nd	1428	9th (6—60-pr. guns)	77th	2nd
1353	26th (Army)	1st	1429	12th ,, ,,	29th	1st
1354	27th (Mixed)	4th	1430	14th ,, ,,	92nd	3rd
1355	28th (Mixed)	5th	1431	16th ,, ,,	1st	1st
1356	29th (Mobile)	1st	1432	17th ,, ,,	67th	1st
1357	30th (Howitzer—8-in.)	1st	1433	21st ,, ,,	1st	1st
1358	31st (Army)	1st	1434	22nd ,, ,,	13th	3rd
1359	32nd (Army)	3rd	1435	23rd ,, ,,	16th	1st
1360	33rd (Howitzer—8-in.)	2nd	1436	24th ,, ,,	84th	3rd
1361	34th (Howitzer—9·2-in.)	1st	1437	25th ,, ,,	27th	4th
1362	35th (Mobile)	3rd	1438	26th ,, ,,	77th	2nd
1363	36th (Aus.) (Mixed)	2nd	1439	31st ,, ,,	81st	1st
1364	39th (Howitzer—9·2-in.)	3rd	1440	35th ,, ,,	93rd	4th
1365	40th (Howitzer—8-in.)	1st	1441	38th ,, ,,	63rd	3rd
1366	41st (Mobile)	4th	1442	48th ,, ,,	3rd	2nd
1367	42nd (Mobile)	5th	1443	71st ,, ,,	21st	4th
1368	43rd (Howitzer—9·2-in.)	2nd	1444	108th ,, ,,	46th	5th
1369	44th (S.A.) (Howitzer—8-in.)	5th	1445	109th ,, ,,	6th	2nd
1370	45th (Howitzer—9·2-in.)	1st	1446	110th ,, ,,	67th	1st
1371	46th (Mobile)	5th	1447	111th ,, ,,	85th	3rd
1372	47th (Howitzer—8-in.)	4th	1448	112th ,, ,,	3rd	2nd
1373	48th (Mobile)	1st	1449	113th ,, ,,	76th	4th
1374	49th (Howitzer—8-in.)	5th	1450	114th ,, ,,	6th	2nd
1375	50th (S.A.) (Howitzer—8-in.)	1st	1451	115th ,, ,,	7th	1st
1376	51st (Mixed)	4th	1452	116th ,, ,,	89th	4th
1377	52nd (Howitzer—9·2-in.)	5th	1453	117th ,, ,,	28th	5th
1378	53rd (Mixed)	1st	1454	119th ,, ,,	63rd	3rd
1379	54th (Howitzer—8-in.)	3rd	1455	120th ,, ,,	85th	4th
1380	55th (Army)	5th	1456	121st ,, ,,	29th	1st
1381	56th (Howitzer—9·2-in.)	3rd	1457	122nd ,, ,,	62nd	3rd
1382	57th (Army)	3rd	1458	124th ,, ,,	42nd	5th
1383	58th (Army)	3rd	1459	125th ,, ,,	7th	1st
1384	59th (Howitzer—8-in.)	2nd	1460	126th ,, ,,	62nd	3rd
1385	60th (Howitzer—9·2-in.)	3rd	1461	127th ,, ,,	92nd	3rd
1386	62nd (Mixed)	3rd	1462	128th ,, ,,	9th	4th
1387	63rd (Mobile)	3rd	1463	129th ,, ,,	92nd	3rd
1388	64th (Howitzer—8-in.)	2nd	1464	130th ,, ,,	9th	4th
1389	65th (Howitzer—9·2-in.)	2nd	1465	131st ,, ,,	4th	2nd
1390	66th (Howitzer—8-in.)	3rd	1466	132nd ,, ,,	76th	4th
1391	67th (Mixed)	1st	1467	133rd ,, ,,	48th	1st
1392	68th (Howitzer—8-in.)	4th	1468	135th ,, ,,	17th	3rd
1393	69th (Howitzer—9·2-in.)	4th	1469	136th ,, ,,	53rd	1st
1394	70th (Howitzer—9·2-in.)	2nd	1470	137th ,, ,,	51st	4th
1395	71st (Howitzer—8-in.)	4th	1471	138th ,, ,,	51st	4th
1396	72nd (Army)	2nd	1472	139th ,, ,,	85th	4th
1397	73rd (Army)	4th	1473	140th ,, ,,	36th Aus.	2nd
1398	76th (Mixed)	4th	1474	141st ,, ,,	86th	2nd
1399	77th (Mixed)	2nd	1475	142nd ,, ,,	79th	4th
1400	78th (Howitzer—8-in.)	1st	1476	144th ,, ,,	27th	4th
1411	79th (Mixed)	4th	1477	145th ,, ,,	35th	3rd
1412	81st (Mixed)	1st	1478	146th ,, ,,	16th	1st
1413	83rd (Mixed)	4th	1479	147th ,, ,,	48th	1st
1414	84th (Mixed)	3rd	1480	150th ,, ,,	10th	2nd
1415	85th (Mobile)	4th	1481	151st ,, ,,	36th Aus.	2nd
1416	86th (Mobile)	2nd	1482	152nd ,, ,,	84th	3rd
1417	87th (Mobile)	2nd	1483	154th ,, ,,	87th	2nd
1418	88th (Howitzer—8-in.)	3rd	1484	156th ,, ,,	87th	2nd
1419	89th (Howitzer—8-in.)	5th	1485	159th ,, ,,	10th	2nd
1420	90th (Howitzer—9·2-in.)	3rd	1486	1st Canadian (6—60-pr. guns)	2nd Cdn.	1st
1421	91st (Howitzer—9·2-in.)	1st	1487	2nd Canadian (6—60-pr. guns)	2nd Cdn.	1st
1422	92nd (Mobile)	3rd		**HEAVY BATTERIES (T.F.)**		
1423	93rd (Mixed)	4th	1661	1/1st Essex (6—60-pr. guns)	79th	4th
1424	98th (Howitzer—9·2-in.)	4th	1662	1/1st Highland (6—60-pr. guns)	83rd	4th
1425	99th (Howitzer—8-in.)	2nd	1663	1/1st Kent (6—60-pr. guns)	92nd	3rd
1426	1st Canadian (Howitzer—9·2-in.)	1st	1664	1/1st Lancashire (6—60-pr. guns)	46th	5th
1427	2nd Canadian (Mixed)	1st	1665	1/2nd Lancashire (6—60-pr. guns)	21st	4th
	3rd Canadian (Howitzer—8-in.)	1st	1666	2/1st Lancashire (6—60-pr. guns)	17th	3rd
			1667	1/1st London (6—60-pr. guns)	42nd	5th

Index to Units—Royal Artillery—continued.

	Battery.	Brigade.	Army.		Battery.	Brigade.	Army.
	Heavy Batteries (T.F.)—contd.				**Siege Batteries**—continued.		
1668	1/2nd London (6—60-pr. guns)	13th	3rd		(1—9·2-in. gun on railway mounting.)	—	2nd
1669	1/1st Lowland (6—60-pr. guns)	81st	1st	1730	53rd		
1670	2/1st Lowland (6—60-pr. guns)	93rd	4th		(1—9·2-in. gun on railway mounting.)	—	5th
1671	1/1st N. Mid. (Stafford) (6—60-pr. guns)	41st	4th	1733	56th (6—8-in. howrs.) ...	17th	3rd
1672	2/1st N. Mid. (6—60-pr. guns)	4th	2nd	1734	57th ,, ,, ...	89th	5th
1673	1/1st Northumbrian (6—60-pr. guns)	41st	4th	1735	58th (4—6-in. guns) ...	—	3rd
1674	1/1st W. Riding (6—60-pr. guns)	28th	5th	1736	59th (6—6-in. howrs.) ...	48th	1st
1675	1/1st Welsh (6—60-pr. guns)	53rd	1st	1737	60th (4—6-in. guns) ...	—	1st
1676	1/1st Wessex ,, ,,	86th	2nd	1738	61st (6—8-in. howrs.) ...	64th	2nd
	SIEGE BATTERIES.			1739	62nd (4—9·2-in. howrs.) ...	45th	1st
1679	1st (6—6-in. howrs.) ...	41st	4th	1740	63rd (2—12-in. howrs. on railway mountings).	—	2nd
1680	2nd ,, ,, ...	85th	4th	1741	64th (2—12-in. howrs. on railway mountings).	—	5th
1681	3rd ,, ,, ...	85th	4th	1742	*65th (1—12-in. howr.) ...	—	1st
1682	4th ,, ,, ...	46th	5th	1743	66th (6—9·2-in. howrs.) ...	2nd	2nd
1683	5th ,, ,, ...	46th	5th	1744	67th (6—8-in. howrs.) ...	62nd	3rd
1684	6th ,, ,, ...	41st	4th	1745	68th (6—6-in. howrs.) ...	89th	5th
1685	7th (4—6-in. guns) ...	—	2nd	1746	69th (6—9·2-in. howrs.) ...	83rd	4th
1686	8th ,, ,, ...	—	3rd	1747	70th (6—8-in. howrs.) ...	12th	4th
1687	9th (4—6-in. howrs.)	71st	4th	1748	71st (S.A.) (6—6-in. howrs.)...	44th S.A.	5th
1688	10th (6—9·2-in. howrs.)	52nd	5th	1749	72nd (S.A.) (6—6-in. howrs.)...	50th	1st
1689	11th (6—6-in. howrs.)	14th	4th	1750	73rd (S.A.) (6—6-in. howrs.)...	44th S.A.	5th
1690	12th (6—9·2-in. howrs.)	70th	2nd	1751	74th (S.A.) (6—6-in. howrs.)...	50th	1st
1691	13th ,, ,,	17th	3rd	1752	75th (S.A.) (6—6-in. howrs.)...	50th	1st
1692	14th (6—6-in. howrs.)	79th	4th	1753	76th (6—9·2-in. howrs.) ...	62nd	3rd
1693	15th (6—6-in. howrs.)	70th	2nd	1754	77th (6—8-in. howrs.) ...	84th	3rd
1694	16th (6—6-in. howrs.)	8th	1st	1755	78th ,, ,, ...	88th	3rd
1695	17th (6—6-in. howrs.)	71st	4th	1756	79th (4—9·2-in. howrs.) ...	67th	1st
1696	18th (2—12-in. howrs. on railway mountings).	—	5th	1757	80th (2—12-in. howrs.) ...	—	4th
1697	19th (6—8-in. howrs.)	76th	4th	1758	81st (6—6-in. howrs.) ...	48th	1st
1698	20th ,, ,, ...	44th S.A.	5th	1759	82nd (2—12-in. howrs. on railway mountings).	—	2nd
1699	21st (6—9·2-in. howrs.)	3rd	2nd	1760	83rd (2—12-in. howrs. on railway mountings).	—	3rd
1700	22nd (2—12-in. howrs. on railway mountings).	—	2nd	1761	85th (2—12-in. howrs.) ...	—	2nd
1701	23rd (4—6-in. howrs.)	30th	1st	1762	86th (2—12-in. howrs. on railway mountings).	—	1st
1702	24th (6—6-in. howrs.)	21st	4th				
1703	25th (6—8-in. howrs.)	68th	4th	1763	87th (4—6-in. howrs.) ...	78th	1st
1704	26th (4—6-in. guns)	—	3rd	1764	88th (6—6-in. howrs.) ...	3rd	2nd
1705	27th (6—6-in. howrs.)	7th	1st	1765	89th (2—12-in. howrs. on railway mountings).	—	3rd
1706	28th (6—6-in. howrs.)	7th	1st	1766	90th (6—9·2-in howrs.) ...	8th	1st
1707	29th (4—6-in. guns)	—	2nd	1767	91st ,, ,, ...	76th	4th
1708	30th (6—8-in. howrs.)	59th	2nd		(1—12-in. gun on railway mounting).	—	1st
1709	31st (4—6-in. howrs.)	33rd	2nd	1768	92nd		
1710	32nd (6—6-in. howrs.)	45th	1st		(1—12-in. gun on railway mounting).	—	3rd
1711	33rd (6—8-in. howrs.)	27th	4th				
1712	34th (6—9·2-in. howrs.)	84th	3rd	1769	93rd (6—9·2-in. howrs.) ...	69th	4th
1713	35th (4—6-in. guns on naval mountings).	—	3rd	1770	94th (6—9·2-in. howrs.) ...	23rd	4th
1714	36th (6—8-in. howrs.)	78th	1st	1771	95th (6—9·2-in. howrs.) ...	90th	3rd
1715	37th (6—6-in. howrs.)	59th	2nd	1772	96th (4—9·2-in. howrs.) ...	91st	1st
1716	38th ,, ,, ...	45th	1st	1773	99th (6—6-in. howrs.) ...	49th	5th
1717	39th (6—8-in. howrs.)	30th	1st	1774	100th (4—6-in. howrs.) ...	64th	2nd
1718	40th (4—6-in. howrs.)	40th	1st	1775	101st ,, ,, ...	64th	2nd
1719	41st (6—6-in. howrs.)	23rd	4th	1776	102nd ,, ,, ...	64th	2nd
1720	42nd (4—9·2-in. howrs.)	6th	2nd	1777	103rd (2—12-in. howrs. on railway mountings).	—	L. of C.
1721	44th (2—12-in. howrs. on railway mountings).	—	5th	1778	104th (2—12-in. howrs. on railway mountings).	—	2nd
1722	45th (2—9·2-in. guns on railway mountings).	—	2nd	1779	106th (4—6-in. howrs.) ...	56th	3rd
1723	46th (4—9·2-in. howrs.)	19th	1st	1780	108th ,, ,, ...	78th	1st
1724	47th (6—8-in. howrs.)	5th	3rd	1781	109th (4—6-in. howrs.) ...	47th	4th
1725	48th (6—9·2-in. howrs.)	84th	1st	1782	110th (6—6-in. howrs.) ...	27th	4th
1726	49th (6—6-in. howrs.)	1st	1st	1783	111th (6—6-in. howrs.) ...	6th	2nd
1727	50th (4—6-in. guns on naval mountings).	—	4th	1784	112th (6—6-in. howrs.) ...	34th	1st
				1785	113th (6—6-in. howrs.) ...	10th	2nd
1728	51st (6—6-in. howrs.)	17th	3rd	1786	114th (6—6-in. howrs.) ...	68th	4th
1729	52nd (2—12-in. howrs. on railway mountings).	—	1st	1787	115th (4—6-in. howrs.) ...	65th	2nd

* 1 Section Personnel only in addition.

Index to Units—Royal Artillery—continued.

	Battery.	Brigade.	Army.		Battery.	Brigade.	Army.
	Siege Batteries—continued.				**Siege Batteries**—continued.		
1788	116th (6—6-in. howrs.)	77th	2nd	1859	203rd (6—6-in. howrs.)	86th	2nd
1789	117th (4—9·2-in. howrs.)	18th	5th	1860	204th (6—6-in. howrs.)	16th	1st
1790	118th (6—9·2-in. howrs.)	65th	2nd	1861	205th (6—6-in. howrs.)	89th	3rd
1791	119th (6—6-in. howrs.)	77th	2nd	1862	207th " "	54th	3rd
1792	120th (6—8-in. howrs.)	66th	3rd	1863	208th (4—6-in. howrs.)	45th	1st
1793	121st (6—9·2-in. howrs.)	98th	4th	1864	210th " "	98th	4th
1794	122nd (6—6-in. howrs.)	66th	3rd	1865	211th " "	68th	4th
1795	123rd (6—6-in. howrs.)	88th	3rd	1866	212th " "	65th	2nd
1796	124th (6—9·2-in. howrs.)	93rd	4th	1867	213th (6—8-in. howrs.)	28th	5th
1797	125th (S.A.) (6—6-in. howrs.)	44th(S.A.)	5th	1868	214th (6—8-in. howrs.)	14th	4th
1798	126th (6—8-in. howrs.)	71st	4th	1869	215th (6—8-in. howrs.)	93rd	4th
1799	128th (2—12-in. hrs. on rly. mtgs.)	—	5th	1870	216th (6—6-in. howrs.)	27th	4th
1800	129th (6—9·2-in. howrs.)	4th	2nd	1871	217th (6—6-in. howrs.)	70th	2nd
1801	133rd (6—9·2-in. howrs.)	89th	3rd	1872	218th (6—6-in. howrs.)	18th	5th
1802	135th (6—8-in. howrs.)	83rd	4th	1873	219th (6—6-in. howrs.)	87th	2nd
1803	136th (6—9·2-in. howrs.)	60th	3rd	1874	220th (4—6-in. howrs.)	56th	3rd
1804	139th (4—6-in. howrs.)	78th	1st	1875	221st (6—8-in. howrs.)	33rd	2nd
1805	140th (6—6-in. howrs.)	91st	1st	1876	222nd (4—6-in. guns)	—	4th
1806	141st (6—6-in. howrs.)	28th	5th	1877	223rd (6—6-in. howrs.)	4th	2nd
1807	142nd (4—6-in. howrs.)	34th	1st	1878	224th (6—6-in. howrs.)	62nd	3rd
1808	143rd (4—9·2-in. howrs.)	27th	4th	1879	225th (4—6-in. howrs.)	89th	5th
1809	144th (4—6-in. howrs.)	56th	3rd	1880	226th (6—6-in. howrs.)	10th	2nd
1810	145th (6—8-in. howrs.)	79th	4th	1881	227th (6—8-in. howrs.)	6th	2nd
1811	146th (4—6-in. howrs.)	47th	4th	1882	228th (6—6-in. howrs.)	76th	4th
1812	147th (6—6-in. howrs.)	43rd	2nd	1883	230th (6—6-in. howrs.)	83rd	4th
1813	148th (4—9·2-in. howrs.)	28th	5th	1884	231st (6—6-in. howrs.)	93rd	4th
1814	149th (6—6-in. howrs.)	67th	1st	1885	232nd (6—6-in. howrs.)	93rd	4th
1815	150th (4—6-in. howrs.)	14th	4th	1886	233rd (6—6-in. howrs.)	76th	4th
1816	151st (6—8-in. howrs.)	99th	2nd	1887	234th (6—6-in. howrs.)	67th	1st
1817	152nd " "	3rd	2nd	1888	235th (4—6-in. howrs.)	8th	1st
1818	153rd (6—6-in. howrs.)	9th	4th	1889	236th (4—6-in. howrs.)	18th	5th
1819	154th (6—9·2-in. howrs.)	43rd	2nd	1890	237th (6—6-in. howrs.)	42nd	5th
1820	155th (6—6-in. howrs.)	36th(Aus.)	2nd	1891	238th (4—6-in. howrs.)	69th	4th
1821	156th (6—8-in. howrs.)	47th	4th	1892	239th (6—8-in. howrs.)	81st	1st
1822	157th (6—6-in. howrs.)	70th	2nd	1893	241th (6—6-in. howrs.)	30th	1st
1823	158th (6—9·2-in. howrs.)	7th	1st	1894	242nd (4—6-in. howrs.)	12th	4th
1824	160th (6—6-in. howrs.)	5th	3rd	1895	243rd (2—12-in. howrs.)	—	4th
1825	161st (6—9·2-in. howrs.)	51st	4th	1896	244th (6—6-in. howrs.)	90th	3rd
1826	162nd (6—6-in. howrs.)	67th	1st	1897	245th (6—6-in. howrs.)	6th	2nd
1827	163rd (6—6-in. howrs.)	81st	1st	1898	248th (6—6-in. howrs.)	17th	3rd
1828	164th (6—6-in. howrs.)	52nd	5th	1899	249th (6—8-in. howrs.)	53rd	1st
1829	166th (4—6-in. howrs.)	49th	5th	1900	250th (6—6-in. howrs.)	2nd	2nd
1830	168th (6—6-in. howrs.)	68th	4th	1901	251st (6—6-in. howrs.)	53rd	1st
1831	169th (6—8-in. howrs.)	51st	4th	1902	252nd (6—6-in. howrs.)	53rd	1st
1832	170th (6—6-in. howrs.)	35th	3rd	1903	253rd (6—6-in. howrs.)	22nd	3rd
1833	173rd (4—6-in. howrs.)	54th	3rd	1904	254th (6—6-in. howrs.)	1st	1st
1834	174th (6—6-in. howrs.)	79th	4th	1905	255th (6—6-in. howrs.)	51st	4th
1835	175th (6—9·2-in. howrs.)	56th	3rd	1906	256th (6—8-in. howrs.)	40th	1st
1836	177th (6—6-in. howrs.)	2nd	2nd	1907	258th (4—6-in. howrs.)	88th	3rd
1837	178th (4—6-in. howrs.)	89th	5th	1908	259th (6—6-in. howrs.)	52nd	5th
1838	179th (6—6-in. howrs.)	81st	1st	1909	260th (6—6-in. howrs.)	9th	4th
1839	180th (6—6-in. howrs.)	18th	5th	1910	261st (6—8-in. howrs.)	4th	2nd
1840	182nd (6—6-in. howrs.)	22nd	3rd	1911	262nd (6—8-in. howrs.)	54th	3rd
1841	183rd (4—6-in. howrs.)	60th	3rd	1912	263rd (4—6-in. howrs.)	12th	4th
1842	184th (6—9·2-in. howrs.)	81st	1st	1913	264th (4—6-in. howrs.)	52nd	5th
1843	185th (6—9·2-in. howrs.)	79th	4th	1914	265th (6—9·2-in. howrs.)	22nd	3rd
1844	186th (4—6-in. howrs.)	40th	1st	1915	266th (6—6-in. howrs.)	89th	3rd
1845	187th (4—6-in. guns)	—	2nd	1916	267th (6—6-in. howrs.)	35th	3rd
1846	188th (6—9·2-in. howrs.)	53rd	1st	1917	268th (6—6-in. howrs.)	3rd	2nd
1847	189th (4—6-in. guns)	—	4th	1918	270th (6—6-in. howrs.)	98th	4th
1848	190th (4—6-in. howrs.)	43rd	2nd	1919	271th (6—6-in. howrs.)	62nd	3rd
1849	191st (6—9·2-in. howrs.)	77th	2nd	1920	275th (6—8-in. howrs.)	50th(S.A.)	1st
1850	192nd (4—6-in. guns)	—	1st	1921	276th (6—6-in. howrs.)	84th	3rd
1851	193rd (6—8-in. howrs.)	7th	1st	1922	277th (4—6-in. howrs.)	90th	3rd
1852	194th (6—6-in. howrs.)	87th	2nd	1923	278th (6—6-in. howrs.)	31th	1st
1853	195th (6—6-in. howrs.)	29th	1st	1924	279th (6—6-in. howrs.)	33rd	2nd
1854	196th (4—6-in. howrs.)	10th	1st	1925	280th (6—6-in. howrs.)	16th	1st
1855	198th (4—6-in. guns)	—	2nd	1926	281st (6—6-in. howrs.)	39th	3rd
1856	199th (6—6-in. howrs.)	51th	3rd	1927	282nd (4—6-in. howrs.)	99th	2nd
1857	200th " "	5th	3rd	1928	283rd (6—6-in. howrs.)	51st	4th
7738	201st (4—6-in. howrs.)	13th	3rd	1929	284th (6—6-in. howrs.)	83rd	4th
1858	202nd (4—6-in. howrs.)	65th	2nd	1930	285th (6—6-in. howrs.)	99th	2nd

Index to Units—Royal Artillery—continued.

	Battery.	Brigade.	Army.		Battery.	Brigade.	Army.
	Siege Batteries—continued.				**Siege Batteries**—continued.		
1931	286th (6—8-in. howrs.)	77th	2nd	7595	471st {(1—14-in.gn.on rly. mtg.) / (1—14-in.gn. on rly. mtg.)}	—	4th / 1st
1932	287th (6—6-in. howrs.)	22nd	3rd	1992	479th (4—6-in. guns)	—	2nd
1933	288th (4—6-in. howrs.)	19th	1st	1993	481st (4—6-in. guns)	—	5th
1934	290th (4—6-in. howrs.)	8th	1st	1994	484th (4—6-in. guns)	—	3rd
1935	291st (6—6-in. howrs.)	69th	4th	1995	488th (4—6-in. guns)	—	1st
1936	294th (6—6-in. howrs.)	98th	4th	1996	493rd (2—12-in. howrs.)	—	1st
1937	295th (6—6-in. howrs.)	5th	3rd	6336	494th (2—12-in. howrs.)	—	4th
1938	296th (4—6-in. howrs.)	14th	4th	6186	*495th (1—12-in. howr.)	—	3rd
1939	297th (6—6-in. howrs.)	19th	1st	6796	498th (4—6-in. guns)	—	4th
1940	298th (4—6-in. howrs.)	33rd	3rd	1997	499th (4—6-in. guns)	—	4th
1941	299th (6—6-in. howrs.)	90th	3rd	1998	500th (4—6-in. guns)	—	3rd
1942	301st (6—6-in. howrs.)	4th	2nd	6180	503rd (4—6-in. guns)	—	3rd
1943	303rd (6—6-in. howrs.)	29th	1st	1999	504th (4—6-in. guns)	—	4th
1944	305th (4—6-in. howrs.)	60th	3rd	7608	514th {(1—12-in. hr. on rly. mtgs.) / (1—12-in. hr. on rly. mtgs.)}	—	1st / 5th
1945	*306th (4—6-in. howrs.)	66th	3rd		515th (1—14-in.gun on rly.mtgs.)	—	1st
1946	308th (6—6-in. howrs.)	30th	1st	7684	520th (4—6-in. guns)	—	1st
1947	309th (6—6-in. howrs.)	47th	4th	6797	521st (4—6-in. guns)	—	5th
1948	312th (4—6-in. guns)	—	4th	2000	523rd (2—9.2-in.gns.on rly. mtgs.)	—	1st
1949	319th (4—6-in. howrs.)	12th	4th	2001	524th {(1—12-in.hr. on rly. mtg.) / (1—12-in.hr. on rly. mtg.)}	—	5th / 5th
1950	321st (4—6-in. howrs.)	19th	1st	6206	525th (4—6-in. guns)	—	3rd
1951	323rd (6—6-in. howrs.)	42nd	5th		526th (4—6-in. guns)	—	2nd
1952	324th (6—6-in. howrs.)	86th	2nd	7596	527th (4—6-in. guns)	—	1st
1953	325th (6—6-in. howrs.)	66th	3rd	6037	528th (4—6-in. guns)	—	2nd
1954	326th (6—6-in. howrs.)	91st	1st		529th (1—12-in. gn. on rly. mgt.)	—	L. of C.
1955	327th (4—6-in. howrs.)	23rd	4th	7761	543rd {(1—12-in.gn.on rly. mtg.) / (1—12-in.gn. on rly. mtg.)}	—	4th / 1st
1956	328th (6—6-in. howrs.)	88th	3rd	6795	544th (4—6-in. guns)	—	5th
1957	329th (6—6-in. howrs.)	28th	5th	7890	545th (4—6-in. howrs.)	—	4th
1958	330th (4—6-in. guns)	—	5th		546th (4—6-in guns)	—	2nd
1959	331st (4—6-in. howrs.)	69th	4th	1731	1st (Aus.) (6—8-in. howrs.)	36th Aus.	2nd
1960	332nd (6—6-in. howrs.)	71st	4th	1732	2nd (Aus.) (6—9.2-in. howrs.)	36th Aus.	2nd
1961	333rd (2—12-in. hrs. on rly. mtgs.)	—	3rd	2002	1st Cdn. (6—9.2-in. howrs.)	1st Cdn.	1st
1962	335th (4—6-in. howrs.)	59th	2nd	2003	2nd Cdn. (6—6-in. howrs.)	2nd Cdn.	1st
1963	336th (6—6-in. howrs.)	84th	3rd	2004	3rd Cdn. (6—6-in. howrs.)	1st Cdn.	1st
1964	337th (4—6-in. howrs.)	91st	1st	2005	4th Cdn. (6—8-in. howrs.)	2nd Cdn.	1st
1965	342nd (4—6-in. howrs.)	60th	3rd	2006	5th Cdn. (6—9.2-in. howrs.)	2nd Cdn.	1st
1966	*343rd (1—12-in. hr. on rly. mtgs.)		3rd	2007	6th Cdn. (6—6-in. howrs.)	2nd Cdn.	1st
1967	346th (4—6-in. howrs.)	49th	5th	2008	7th Cdn. (6—6-in. howrs.)	1st Cdn.	1st
1968	349th (2—12-in. howrs.)	—	5th	2009	8th Cdn. (6—8-in. howrs.)	3rd Cdn.	1st
1969	350th (4—6-in. howrs.)	59th	2nd	2010	9th Cdn. (6—6-in. howrs.)	1st Cdn.	1st
1970	351st (6—6-in. howrs.)	43rd	2nd	7611	10th Cdn. (6—6-in. howrs.)	3rd Cdn.	1st
1971	352nd (6—6-in. howrs.)	2nd	2nd	7612	11th Cdn. (6—6-in. howrs.)	3rd Cdn.	1st
1972	353rd (6—6-in. howrs.)	36 (Aus.)	2nd	7602	12th Cdn. (6—6-in. howrs.)	3rd Cdn.	1st
1973	354th (6—6-in. howrs.)	21st	4th		1st(R.M.A.)(2—12-in. howrs.)	—	4th
1974	355th (4—6-in. howrs.)	23rd	4th		2nd(R.M.A.)(2—12-in.howrs.)	—	2nd
1975	359th (2—12-in. hrs. on rly. mtgs.)		2nd				
1976	363rd (2—9.2-in.gns.on rly. mtgs.)	—	3rd		Battery.		Army.
1977	366th (2—9.2-in.gns.on rly. mtgs.)	—	1st				
1978	374th (2—12-in. hrs. on rly. mtgs.)		4th		**HEAVY HOWITZER BRIGADE, R.M.A.**		
1979	375th (2—12-in. howrs.)		2nd				
7739	379th (4—6-in. howrs.)	13th	3rd				
1980	381st (2—12-in. hrs. on rly. mtgs.)	—	2nd	2044	No. 1—15-in. Howitzer		4th
1981	393rd (4—6-in. guns)	—	1st	2045	No. 2—15-in. Howitzer		5th
1982	405th (4—6-in. howrs.)	99th	2nd	2046	No. 3—15-in. Howitzer		3rd
1983	409th (4—6-in. guns)	—	3rd	2047	No. 4—15-in. Howitzer		2nd
6204	420th (4—6-in. howrs.)	63rd	3rd	2050	No. 8—15-in. Howitzer		1st
1984	431st (2—12-in howrs.)	—	3rd	2051	No. 10—15-in. Howitzer		3rd
1985	434th (4—6-in. guns)	—	3rd				
1986	442nd (2—9.2-in.gns.on rly. mtgs.)		3rd		**BERMUDA R.G.A.**		
6205	443rd (4—6-in. howrs.)	63rd	3rd				
1987	444th (2—12-in. hrs.on rly. mtgs.)		1st	2055	Contingent		2nd
1988	449th (4—6-in. guns)		4th				
1989	450th (4—6-in. guns)		1st				
1990	456th (1—9.2-in.gn. on rly. mgts.)		5th				
	(1—9.2-in.gn. on rly. mgts)		4th				
1991	461st (2—9.2-in.gns. on rly. mtgs.)		1st				

* 1 Section personnel only in addition.

ANTI-AIRCRAFT ARTILLERY.

2057	H.Q. 1st Army A.A. Defence Commander.	2060	H.Q. 4th Army A.A. Defence Commander.
2059	H.Q. 2nd Army A.A. Defence Commander.		H.Q. 5th Army A.A. Defence Commander.
2058	H.Q. 3rd Army A.A. Defence Commander.		

Index to Units—Royal Artillery—*continued.*

ANTI-AIRCRAFT BATTERIES.

	Battery	Army.		Battery	Army.		Battery	Army.		Battery	Army.		Battery	Army.
2064	"A"	5th	2069	"F"	4th	2074	"L"	3rd	2079	"Q"	4th		"W"	Ind. Force R.A.F.
2065	"B"	5th	2070	"G"	4th	2075	"M"	3rd	2080	"R"	2nd		"X"	Ind. Force R.A.F.
2066	"C"	1st	2071	"H"	2nd	2076	"N"	3rd	2081	"T"	2nd		"Y"	1st
2067	"D"	5th	2072	"J"	2nd	2077	"O"	3rd	2082	"U"	2nd		"Z"	4th
2068	"E"	1st	2073	"K"	1st	2078	"P"	4th						

ANTI-AIRCRAFT SECTIONS.

	Section.	Battery.	Allotment.		Section.	Battery.	Allotment.
2087	No. 1 (2—12-pr. guns)	Central Group	L. of C.	2147	No. 70 (2—13-pr. guns)	"B"	5th Army.
2088	No. 2 " "	Southern Group	L. of C.	2148	No. 71 " "	"Q"	4th Army.
2089	No. 3 " "	Southern Group	L. of C.	2149	No. 75 (2—3-in. guns)	...	G.H.Q.,
2090	No. 4 " "	Base Ports	L. of C.	2150	No. 76 " "	"T"	2nd Army.
2091	No. 5 " "	Base Ports	L. of C.	2151	No. 77 (2—13-pr. guns)	"A"	5th Army.
2092	No. 6 (2—13-pr. guns)	"F"	4th Army.	6144	No. 78 " "	"T"	2nd Army.
2093	No. 7 " "	"Y"	1st Army.	2152	No. 79 " "	"Y"	1st Army.
2094	No. 8 " "	"H"	2nd Army.	2153	No. 81 " "	"U"	2nd Army.
2095	No. 9 " "	"K"	1st Army.	2154	No. 82 " "	"G"	4th Army.
2096	No. 10 " "	Southern Group	L. of C.	2155	No. 83 " "	Base Ports	L. of C.
2097	No. 11 " "	"N"	3rd Army.	2156	No. 84 " "	"M"	3rd Army.
2098	No. 12 " "	"P"	4th Army.	2157	No. 86 " "	"O"	3rd Army.
2099	No. 13 (2—3-in. guns)	Base Ports	L. o C.	2158	No. 87 " "	"M"	3rd Army.
2100	No. 14 (2—13-pr. guns)	...	G.H.Q.,	2159	No. 88 " "	"J"	2nd Army.
2101	No. 15 " "	"Q"	4th Army.	2160	No. 89 " "	"D"	5th Army.
2102	No. 16 " "	"L"	3rd Army.	2161	No. 100 " "	"A"	5th Army.
2103	No. 17 " "	"H"	2nd Army.	2162	No. 101 " "	"B"	5th Army.
2104	No. 18 " "	"D"	5th Army.	2163	No. 104 " "	"O"	3rd Army.
2105	No. 19 " "	"J"	2nd Army.	2164	No. 105 " "	Base Ports	L. of C.
2106	No. 20 " "	"C"	1st Army.	2165	No. 107 " "	"O"	3rd Army.
2107	No. 21 " "	"U"	2nd Army.	2166	No. 108 " "	"W" Ind. Force	L. of C.
2108	No. 22 " "	"A"	5th Army.	2167	No. 109 " "	"Q"	4th Army.
2109	No. 25 " "	"K"	1st Army.	2168	No. 110 " "	"F"	4th Army.
2110	No. 26 " "	"A"	5th Army.	2169	No. 111 " "	"J"	2nd Army.
2111	No. 27 " "	Central Group	L. of C.	2170	No. 112 " "	"W" Ind. Force	L. of C.
2112	No. 28 (2—3-in. guns)	Southern Group	L. of C.	2171	No. 113 " "	Northern Group	L. of C.
2113	No. 29 " "	Central Group	L. of C.	2172	No. 114 " "	Central Group	L. of C.
2114	No. 31 (2—13-pr. guns)	"G"	4th Army.	2173	No. 115 " "	"R"	2nd Army.
2115	No. 33 " "	"B"	5th Army.	2214	No. 116 " "	"H"	2nd Army.
2116	No. 34 " "	"U"	2nd Army.	2174	No. 127 " "	"Z"	4th Army.
2117	No. 35 " "	"T"	2nd Army.	2175	No. 128 " "	"P"	4th Army.
2118	No. 36 " "	Southern Group	L. of C.	2176	No. 129 " "	"M"	3rd Army.
2119	No. 37 " "	"Z"	4th Army.	2177	No. 132 " "	"D"	5th Army.
2120	No. 39 " "	"L"	3rd Army.	2178	No. 133 " "	"Y"	1st Army.
2121	No. 40 " "	"M"	3rd Army.	2179	No. 134 " "	"K"	1st Army.
2122	No. 41 " "	"L"	3rd Army.	2180	No. 137 " "	"G"	4th Army.
2123	No. 42 " "	"R"	2nd Army.		No. 142 " "	"B"	5th Army.
2124	No. 43 " "	"T"	2nd Army.	7560	No. 143 " "	"C"	1st Army.
2125	No. 44 " "	"F"	4th Army.	7743	No. 144 " "	"H"	2nd Army.
2126	No. 45 " "	Base Ports	L. of C.	7744	No. 145 " "	"R"	2nd Army.
2127	No. 46 " "	"G"	4th Army.		No. 146 " "	"P"	4th Army.
2128	No. 47 " "	Southern Group	L. of C.		No. 147 " "	Northern Group	L. of C.
2129	No. 48 " "	"N"	3rd Army.		No. 148 " "	"Z"	4th Army.
2130	No. 49 " "	"Y"	1st Army.		No. 149 " "	Base Ports	L. of C.
2131	No. 50 " "	"N"	3rd Army.		No. 150 " "	Base Ports	L. of C.
2132	No. 51 (2—3-in. guns)	"X" Ind. Force	L. of C.	6261	No. 155 " "	"M"	3rd Army.
2133	No. 52 (2—13-pr. guns)	"P"	4th Army.	6144	No. 156 " "	"Y"	1st Army.
6148	No. 53 (2—3-in. guns)	"J"	2nd Army.		No. 157 " "	Base Ports	L. of C.
2135	No. 54 (2—13-pr. guns)	"R"	2nd Army.		No. 158 " "	"C"	1st Army.
2136	No. 56 " "	"T"	2nd Army.		No. 159 " "	"H"	2nd Army.
2137	No. 57 " "	"F"	4th Army.		No. 160 " "	Southern Group	L. of C.
2138	No. 58 " "	"O"	3rd Army.		No. 161 " "	Central Group	L. of C.
2139	No. 61 " "	"D"	5th Army.		No. 162 " "	"Y"	1st Army.
2140	No. 62 " "	"N"	3rd Army.		No. 163 " "	Northern Group	L. of C.
2141	No. 64 " "	"N"	3rd Army.		No. 164 " "	"B"	5th Army.
2142	No. 65 " "	"M"	3rd Army.		No. 165 " "	"A"	5th Army.
2143	No. 66 " "	"L"	3rd Army.		No. 166 " "	"D"	5th Army.
2144	No. 67 " "	"Q"	4th Army.		No. 167 " "	"W" Ind. Force	L. of C.
2145	No. 68 " "	Northern Group	L. of C.		No. 168 " "	"K"	1st Army.
2146	No. 69 " "	"C"	1st Army.		No. 169 " "	Base Ports	L. of C.

Index to Units—Royal Artillery—continued.

ANTI-AIRCRAFT SECTIONS—continued.

	Section.	Battery.	Allotment.		Section.	Battery.	Allotment.
	No. 170 (2—13-pr. guns)	Base Ports	L. of C.	2205	No. 226 (2—3-in. guns)	"K"	1st Army.
	No. 171 " "		2nd Army.		No. 227 " "	"Z"	4th Army.
	No. 172 " "	Ind. Force	L. of C.		No. 228 " "	"X" Ind. Force.	L. of C.
	No. 173 " "	Ind. Force	L. of C.		No. 229 " "	Southern Group	L. of C.
	No. 174 " "	"B"	5th Army.		No. 230 " "	"K"	1st Army.
	No. 175 " "				No. 231 " "	Southern Group	L. of C.
	No. 176 " "		L. of C.	6145	No. 232 " "	"R"	2nd Army.
	No. 177 " "		2nd Army.		No. 233 " "	Southern Group	L. of C.
2181	No. 201 (2—3-in. guns)	Northern Group	L. of C.		No. 234 " "	Central Group	L. of C.
2182	No. 202 " "	"G"	1st Army.		No. 235 " "	Central Group	L. of C.
2183	No. 203 " "	Northern Group	L. of C.		No. 236 " "	"Q"	4th Army.
2184	No. 204 " "	Northern Group	L. of C.		No. 237 " "	Northern Group	L. of C.
2185	No. 205 " "	"Z"	4th Army.		No. 238 " "	Southern Group	L. of C.
2186	No. 206 (2—13-pr. guns)	"W" Ind. Force	L. of C.		No. 239 " "	Base Ports	L. of C.
2187	No. 207 (2—3-in. guns)	Northern Group	L. of C.	6224	No. 240 " "	Northern Group	L. of C.
2188	No. 209 " "	Central Group	L. of C.		No. 241 " "	Northern Group	L. of C.
2189	No. 210 " "	Central Group	L. of C.		No. 242 " "	Base Ports	L. of C.
2190	No. 211 " "	"X" Ind. Force.	L. of C.		No. 243 " "	Northern Group	L. of C.
2191	No. 212 " "	Northern Group	L. of C.		No. 244 " "	Northern Group	L. of C.
2192	No. 213 " "	Southern Group	L. of C.		No. 245 " "	Base Ports	L. of C.
6142	No. 214 " "	"J"	2nd Army.		No. 246 " "	Base Ports	L. of C.
2194	No. 215 " "	Southern Group	L. of C.	2206	No. 1 R.M.A. (2—3-in. guns)	"B" R.M.A.	At. Belg. Ar.
2195	No. 216 " "	"T"	2nd Army.	2207	No. 2 R.M.A. " "	"B" R.M.A.	At. Belg. Ar.
2196	No. 217 " "	"U"	2nd Army.	2208	No. 3 R.M.A. (2—2-pr. Vickers Pom-Poms)	"B" R.M.A.	At. Belg. Ar.
2197	No. 218 " "	"D"	5th Army.				
2198	No. 219 " "	"A"	1st Army.	2209	No. 4 R.M.A. (2—2-pr. Vickers Pom-Poms)	"B" R.M.A.	At. Belg. Ar.
2199	No. 220 " "	"B"	5th Army.				
2200	No. 221 " "	Base Ports	L. of C.	2210	No. 1 Cdn. (2—13-pr. guns)	"E"	1st Army.
2201	No. 222 " "	"X" Ind. Force.	L. of C.	2211	No. 2 Cdn. " "	"E"	1st Army.
2202	No. 223 " "	Base Ports	L. of C.	2212	No. 3 Cdn. " "	"E"	1st Army.
2203	No. 224 " "	Northern Group	L. of C.	2213	No. 4 Cdn. " "	"E"	1st Army.
2204	No. 225 " "	"O"	3rd Army.		No. 5 Cdn. " "	"E"	1st Army.

HEAVY TRENCH MORTAR BATTERIES—R.G.A.

	Battery.	Corps.		Battery.	Corps.		Battery.	Division.
2229	V/I.	I.	2238	V/X.	X.	2216	V. 1C.	1st Cdn.
2230	V/II.	II.		V/XI.	XI.	2247	V. 2C.	2nd Cdn.
2231	V/III.	III.	2239	V/XIII.	XIII.	2248	V. 3C.	3rd Cdn.
2232	V/IV.	IV.	2240	V/XV.	XV.	2249	V. 4C.	4th Cdn.
2233	V/V.	V.	2241	V/XVII.	XVII.			(5th Cdn Div.
2234	V/VI.	VI.	2243	V/XIX.	XIX.	2250	V. 5C.	Arty., 1st
2235	V/VII.	VII.	2244	V/XXII.	XXII.			Army
2236	V/VIII.	VIII.	2245	V/Aus.	Aus.			
2237	V/IX.	IX.						

Index to Units—Royal Artillery—continued.

MEDIUM TRENCH MORTAR BATTERIES—R.A.

	Battery.	Division.		Battery.	Division.		Battery.	Division.
2255	X.G.	Guards.	2297	X.30.	30th.	2339	X.58.	58th.
2256	Y.G.	Guards.	2298	Y.30.	30th.	2340	Y.58.	58th.
2257	X.1.	1st.	2299	X.31.	31st.	2341	X.59.	59th.
2258	Y.1.	1st.	2300	Y.31.	31st.	2342	Y.59.	59th.
2259	X.2.	2nd.	2301	X.32.	32nd.	2343	X.61.	61st.
2260	Y.2.	2nd.	2302	Y.32.	32nd.	2344	Y.61.	61st.
2261	X.3.	3rd.	2303	X.33.	33rd.	2345	X.62.	62nd.
2262	Y.3.	3rd.	2304	Y.33.	33rd.	2346	Y.62.	62nd.
2263	X.4.	4th.	2305	X.34.	34th.	2347	X.63.	63rd.
2264	Y.4.	4th.	2306	Y.34.	34th.	2348	Y.63.	63rd.
7566	X.5.	5th.	2307	X.35.	35th.	7795	X.74.	74th.
7567	Y.5.	5th.	2308	Y.35.	35th.	7796	Y.74.	74th.
2265	X.6.	6th.	2309	X.36.	36th.	2351	X.1.A.	1st Aus.
2266	Y.6.	6th.	2310	Y.36.	36th.	2352	Y.1.A.	1st Aus.
2267	X.8.	8th.	2311	X.37.	37th.	2353	X.2.A.	2nd Aus.
2268	Y.8.	8th.	2312	Y.37.	37th.	2354	Y.2.A.	2nd Aus.
2269	X.9.	9th.	2313	X.38.	38th.	2355	X.3.A.	3rd Aus.
2270	Y.9.	9th.	2314	Y.38.	38th.	2356	Y.3.A.	3rd Aus.
2271	X.11.	11th.	2319	X.41.	41st.	2357	X.4.A.	4th Aus.
2272	Y.11.	11th.	2320	Y.41.	41st.	2358	Y.4.A.	4th Aus.
2273	X.12.	12th.	2321	X.42.	42nd.	2359	X.5.A.	5th Aus.
2274	Y.12.	12th.	2322	Y.42.	42nd.	2360	Y.5.A.	5th Aus.
2277	X.15.	15th.	2323	X.46.	46th.	2361	X.N.Z.	N.Z.
2278	Y.15.	15th.	2324	Y.46.	46th.	2362	Y.N.Z.	N.Z.
2281	X.17.	17th.	2325	X.47.	47th.	2363	X.1.C.	1st Cdn.
2282	Y.17.	17th.	2326	Y.47.	47th.	2364	Y.1.C.	1st Cdn.
2283	X.18.	18th.	2327	X.49.	49th.	2366	X.2.C.	2nd Cdn.
2284	Y.18.	18th.	2328	Y.49.	49th.	2367	Y.2.C.	2nd Cdn.
2285	X.19.	19th.	2329	X.50.	50th.	2369	X.3.C.	3rd Cdn.
2286	Y.19.	19th.	2330	Y.50.	50th.	2370	Y.3.C.	3rd Cdn.
2287	X.20.	20th.	2331	X.51.	51st.	2372	X.4.C.	4th Cdn.
2288	Y.20.	20th.	2332	Y.51.	51st.	2373	Y.4.C.	4th Cdn.
2289	X.21.	21st.		X.52.	52nd.	8010	X.5.C.	5th Cdn.
2290	Y.21.	21st.		Y.52.	52nd.		Y.5.C.	Divl. Arty. 1st Army.
2291	X.24.	24th.	2333	X.55.	55th.			
2292	Y.24.	24th.	2334	Y.55.	55th.			
2293	X.25.	25th.	2335	X.56.	56th.			
2294	Y.25.	25th.	2336	Y.56.	56th.			
2295	X.29.	29th.	2337	X.57.	57th.			
2296	Y.29.	29th.	2338	Y.57.	57th.			

LIGHT TRENCH MORTAR BATTERIES.

	Battery.	Division.		Battery.	Division.		Battery.	Division.
2391	1st Gds.	Guards	2102	9th	3rd	2110	19th	33rd
2392	2nd ,,	,,	2103	10th	4th	2111	21st	30th
2393	3rd ,,	,,	2104	11th	4th	2112	23rd	8th
	4th ,,	Cav. Corps	2105	12th	4th	2113	24th	8th
2395	1st	1st	8022	13th	5th	2114	25th	8th
2396	2nd	1st	2106	14th	32nd	2120	26th	9th
2397	3rd	1st	8029	15th	5th	2121	27th	9th
2398	5th	2nd	2107	16th	6th	2035	28th	9th
2399	6th	2nd	2108	17th	24th	2122	32nd	11th
2101	8th	3rd	2109	18th	6th			

Index to Units—Royal Artillery—continued.

LIGHT TRENCH MORTAR BATTERIES—continued.

	Battery.	Division.		Battery.	Division.		Battery.	Division.
2423	33rd	11th	2477	108th	36th	2528	183rd	61st
2424	34th	11th	2478	109th	36th	2529	184th	61st
2425	35th	12th	2479	110th	21st	2530	185th	62nd
2426	36th	12th	2480	111th	37th	2531	186th	62nd
2427	37th	12th	2481	112th	37th	2532	187th	62nd
2431	44th	15th	2482	113th	38th	2533	188th	63rd
2432	45th	15th	2483	114th	38th	2534	189th	63rd
2433	46th	15th	2484	115th	38th	2535	190th	63rd
2437	50th	17th	2491	122nd	41st		197th	L. of C.
2438	51st	17th	2492	123rd	41st		198th	66th
2439	52nd	17th	2493	124th	41st		199th	66th
2440	53rd	18th	2494	125th	42nd	7770	229th	74th
2441	54th	18th	2495	126th	42nd	7776	230th	74th
2442	55th	18th	2496	127th	42nd	7782	231st	74th
2443	56th	19th	2497	137th	46th	2539	1st Aus.	1st Aus.
2444	57th	19th	2498	138th	46th	2540	2nd Aus.	1st Aus.
2445	58th	19th	2499	139th	46th	2541	3rd Aus.	1st Aus.
2446	59th	20th	2500	140th	47th	2542	4th Aus.	4th Aus.
2447	60th	20th	2501	141st	47th	2543	5th Aus.	2nd Aus.
2448	61st	20th	2502	142nd	47th	2544	6th Aus.	2nd Aus.
2449	62nd	21st	2503	146th	49th	2545	7th Aus.	2nd Aus.
2450	63rd	37th	2504	147th	49th	2546	8th Aus.	5th Aus.
2451	64th	21st	2505	148th	49th	2547	9th Aus.	3rd Aus.
2452	71st	6th	2506	149th	50th	2548	10th Aus.	3rd Aus.
2453	72nd	24th	2507	150th	50th	2549	11th Aus.	3rd Aus.
2454	73rd	24th	2508	151st	50th	2550	12th Aus.	4th Aus.
2457	76th	3rd	2509	152nd	51st	2551	13th Aus.	4th Aus.
2458	86th	29th	2510	153rd	51st	2552	14th Aus.	5th Aus.
2459	87th	29th	2511	154th	51st	2553	15th Aus.	5th Aus.
2460	88th	29th	8056	155th	52nd	2554	1st Cdn.	1st Cdn.
2461	89th	30th	8062	156th	52nd	2555	2nd Cdn.	1st Cdn.
2462	90th	30th	8068	157th	52nd	2556	3rd Cdn.	1st Cdn.
2463	92nd	31st	2512	164th	55th	2557	4th Cdn.	2nd Cdn.
2464	93rd	31st	2513	165th	55th	2558	5th Cdn.	2nd Cdn.
7741	94th	31st	2514	166th	55th	2559	6th Cdn.	2nd Cdn.
8036	95th	5th	2515	167th	56th	2560	7th Cdn.	3rd Cdn.
2465	96th	32nd	2516	168th	56th	2561	8th Cdn.	3rd Cdn.
2466	97th	32nd	2517	169th	56th	2562	9th Cdn.	3rd Cdn.
2467	98th	33rd	2518	170th	57th	2563	10th Cdn.	4th Cdn.
2468	99th	2nd	2519	171st	57th	2564	11th Cdn.	4th Cdn.
2469	100th	33rd	2520	172nd	57th	2565	12th Cdn.	4th Cdn.
2470	101st	34th	2521	173rd	58th	2566	1st N.Z.	N.Z.
2471	102nd	34th	2522	174th	58th	2567	2nd N.Z.	N.Z.
2472	103rd	34th	2523	175th	58th	2568	3rd N.Z.	N.Z.
2473	104th	35th	2524	176th	59th	2569	S.A.	66th
2474	105th	35th	2525	177th	59th			
2475	106th	35th	2526	178th	59th			
2476	107th	36th	2527	182nd	61st			

DIVISIONAL AMMUNITION COLUMNS.

2588	Guards	2603	19th	2619	40th	2634	63rd
2589	1st	2604	20th	2620	41st	2635	66th
2590	2nd	2605	21st	2621	42nd	7794	74th
2591	3rd	2606	24th	2622	46th	2636	1st Aus.
2592	4th	2607	25th	2623	47th	2637	2nd Aus.
7568	5th	2608	29th	2624	49th	2638	3rd Aus.
2593	6th	2609	30th	2625	50th	2639	4th Aus.
2594	8th	2610	31st	2626	51st	2640	5th Aus.
2595	9th	2611	32nd	8082	52nd	2641	1st Cdn.
2596	11th	2612	33rd	2627	55th	2642	2nd Cdn.
2597	12th	2613	34th	2628	56th	2643	3rd Cdn.
2598	14th	2614	35th	2629	57th	2644	4th Cdn.
2599	15th	2615	36th	2630	58th	2645	N.Z.
2600	16th	2616	37th	2631	59th		
2601	17th	2617	38th	2632	61st		
2602	18th	2618	39th	2633	62nd		

Index to Units—ROYAL ENGINEERS.*

	Unit.	Div.		Unit.	Div.
	FIELD SQUADRONS.			Field Companies (Regular)—*continued.*	
2654	1st	1st Cav.	2726	204th	35th
2655	2nd	2nd Cav.	2727	205th	35th
2656	3rd	3rd Cav.	2728	206th	32nd
	FIELD COMPANIES (Regular).		2729	207th	34th
2661	2nd	8th	2730	208th	34th
2662	5th	2nd	2731	209th	34th
2663	7th	50th	2732	210th	31st
2664	9th	4th	2733	211th	31st
2665	11th	33rd	2734	212th	33rd
2666	12th	6th	2735	218th	32nd
2667	15th	8th	2736	219th	32nd
2668	23rd	1st	2737	222nd	33rd
2669	26th	1st	2738	223rd	31st
2670	55th	Guards	2739	224th	40th
2671	56th	3rd	2740	225th	39th
2672	57th	49th	2741	226th	2nd
8098	59th	5th	2742	227th	39th
2673	61st	14th	2743	228th	41st
2674	62nd	14th	2744	229th	40th
2675	63rd	9th	2745	231st	40th
2676	64th	9th	2746	233rd	41st
2677	67th	11th	2747	234th	39th
2678	68th	11th	2748	237th	41st
2679	69th	12th	2749	247th	63rd
2680	70th	12th	2750	248th	63rd
2681	73rd	15th	2751	249th	69th
2682	74th	15th		**FIELD COMPANIES (S.R.).**	
2683	75th	Guards		No. 5 Royal Anglesey	74th
2752	76th	Guards		No. 5 Royal Monmouth	74th
2684	77th	17th		**FIELD COMPANIES (Australian).**	
2685	78th	17th			
2686	79th	18th	2774	1st	1st Aus.
2687	80th	18th	2775	2nd	1st Aus.
2688	81st	19th	2776	3rd	1st Aus.
2689	82nd	19th	2777	4th	4th Aus.
2690	83rd	20th	2778	5th	2nd Aus.
2691	84th	20th	2779	6th	2nd Aus.
2692	86th	11th	2780	7th	2nd Aus.
2693	87th	12th	2781	8th	5th Aus.
2694	89th	14th	2782	9th	3rd Aus.
2695	90th	9th	2783	10th	3rd Aus.
2696	91st	15th	2784	11th	3rd Aus.
2697	92nd	18th	2785	12th	4th Aus.
2698	93rd	17th	2786	13th	4th Aus.
2699	94th	19th	2787	14th	5th Aus.
2700	96th	20th	2788	15th	5th Aus.
2701	97th	21st		**FIELD COMPANIES (New Zealand).**	
2702	98th	21st			
2703	103rd	24th	2807	1st	N.Z.
2704	104th	24th	2808	2nd	N.Z.
2705	105th	25th	2809	3rd	N.Z.
2706	106th	25th	2810	4th	N.Z.
2707	121st	36th		**FIELD COMPANIES (T.F.)**	
2708	122nd	36th	2811	400th (Highland)	51st
2709	123rd	38th	2812	401st („)	51st
2710	124th	38th	2813	404th („)	51st
2711	126th	21st	2814	406th (Renfrew)	4th
2712	129th	24th	2815	409th (Lowland)	1st
2713	130th	25th	8081	410th	52nd
2714	150th	36th	6170	411th	1st Army
2715	151st	38th	8085	412th	52nd
2716	152nd	37th	8086	413th	52nd
2717	153rd	37th	2816	416th (Edinburgh)	56th
2718	154th	37th	2817	419th (W. Lancs.)	55th
2719	155th	16th	2818	421st (W. Lancs.)	57th
2720	156th	16th	2819	422nd (W. Lancs.)	55th
2721	157th	16th	2820	423rd (W. Lancs.)	55th
2722	200th	30th	2821	427th (E. Lancs.)	42nd
2723	201st	30th	2822	428th (E. Lancs.)	42nd
2724	202nd	30th	2823	429th (E. Lancs.)	42nd
2725	203rd	35th	2824	430th (E. Lancs.)	66th

* For Forestry Companies see under Forestry.

Index to Units—Royal Engineers—*continued.*

	Unit.	Division.
	Field Companies (T.F.)—*continued.*	
2825	431st (E. Lancs.)	66th
2826	432nd (E. Lancs.)	66th
2827	438th (Cheshire)	3rd
7802	439th	74th
2828	446th (Northumbrian)	50th
2829	447th (,,)	50th
2830	455th (W. Riding)	29th
2831	456th (,,)	49th
2832	457th (,,)	62nd
2833	458th (,,)	49th
2834	459th (,,)	6th
2835	460th (,,)	62nd
2836	461st (,,)	62nd
2837	465th (N. Midland)	46th
2838	466th (,,)	46th
2839	467th (,,)	59th
2840	468th (,,)	46th
2841	469th (,,)	59th
2842	470th (,,)	59th
2843	476th (S. Midland)	61st
2844	478th (,,)	61st
2845	479th (,,)	61st
2846	483rd (E. Anglian)	2nd
2847	490th (Home Counties)	8th
8039	491st	5th
2848	497th (Kent)	29th
2849	502nd (Wessex)	57th
2850	503rd (,,)	58th
2851	504th (,,)	58th
2852	505th (,,)	57th
2853	509th (London)	6th
2854	510th (,,)	29th
2855	511th (,,)	58th
2856	512th (,,)	56th
2857	513th (,,)	56th
2858	517th (,,)	47th
2859	518th (,,)	47th
2860	520th (,,)	47th
2861	526th (Durham)	4th
8040	527th	5th
2862	529th (East Riding)	3rd
	546th (Kent)	4th Army
	547th (Kent)	3rd Army
	549th (Lancs.)	3rd Army
6171	550th (Glamorgan)	1st Army
7817	648th (Home Counties)	4th Army

CANADIAN ENGINEERS.

Brigade.	Battalion.	Division.
1st	1st, 2nd, 3rd	1st Cdn.
2nd	4th, 5th, 6th	2nd Cdn.
3rd	7th, 8th, 9th	3rd Cdn.
4th	10th, 11th, 12th	4th Cdn.

	Unit.	Army.
	SPECIAL BRIGADE.	
2880	H.Q. and Depot	
	SPECIAL (CYLINDER) Cos.	
2881	"A"	
2882	"B"	
2883	"C"	
2884	"D"	
2885	"E"	G.H.Q.
2886	"F"	
2887	"G"	
2888	"H"	
2889	"J"	
2890	"K"	
2891	"L"	

	Unit.	Army.
	Special Brigade—*continued.*	
	SPECIAL (CYLINDER) COS.—*con.*	
2892	"M"	
2893	"N"	
2894	"O"	G.H.Q.
2895	"P"	
2896	"Q"	
	SPECIAL (PROJECTOR) Co.	
2897	"Z"	G.H.Q.
	SPECIAL (MORTAR) Cos.	
2898	No. 1	
2899	No. 2	G.H.Q.
2900	No. 3	
2901	No. 4	
	G.H.Q. TROOPS COMPANIES.	
	29th	G.H.Q.
	ARMY TROOPS COMPANIES.	
2906	20th	2nd
2907	25th	1st
2908	42nd	5th
2909	132nd	3rd
2910	133rd	5th
2911	134th	2nd
2912	135th	5th
2913	136th	2nd
2914	138th	2nd
2915	141st	2nd
2916	142nd	3rd
2917	144th	4th
2918	145th	2nd
2919	146th	4th
2920	147th	3rd
2921	148th	5th
2922	149th	3rd
2923	167th	2nd
2924	213th	4th
2925	214th	2nd
2926	215th	5th
2927	216th	1st
2928	217th	1st
2929	221st	4th
2930	230th	5th
2931	232nd	3rd
2932	235th	2nd
2933	236th	2nd
2934	238th	4th
2935	239th	5th
	245th	2nd
2936	280th	3rd
2937	281st	5th
2938	282nd	1st
2939	283rd	4th
2940	284th	5th
2941	288th	4th
2942	289th	2nd
7691	290th	5th
2943	1st Canadian	1st
2944	2nd Canadian	1st
2945	3rd Canadian	1st
2946	4th Canadian	1st
2947	5th Canadian	1st
2948	1st Australian	4th
	ARMY TROOPS COMPANIES (T.F.).	
2956	552nd (Aberdeen)	5th
2957	554th (Dundee)	2nd
2958	556th (Glamorgan)	2nd
2959	557th (,,)	2nd
2960	559th (Hants)	3rd
2961	560th (,,)	5th
2962	565th (Wilts)	1st
2963	567th (Devon)	4th
2964	568th (,,)	1st
2965	573rd (Cornwall)	2nd

Index to Units—Royal Engineers—continued.

	Unit.	Army.		Unit.	Army.
	Army Troops Companies (T.F.)—continued.			**Searchlight Companies and Sections**—continued.	
2966	574th (Cornwall)	4th	3040	No. 22 A.A. Sec.	1st
2967	577th (Sussex)	3rd	3041	No. 23 A.A. Sec.	L. of C.
	ARMY TROOPS COMPANIES (S.R.)		3042	No. 24 A.A. Sec.	2nd
			3043	No. 25 A.A. Sec.	1st
2970	7th Royal Monmouth	3rd	3044	No. 26 A.A. Sec.	L. of C.
	SIEGE COMPANIES (Special Reserve).		3045	No. 27 A.A. Sec.	L. of C.
			3046	No. 28 A.A. Sec.	2nd
2972	1st Siege Co., Royal Anglesey	4th	3047	No. 29 A.A. Sec.	4th
2973	2nd Siege Co., Royal Anglesey	3rd	3048	No. 30 A.A. Sec.	3rd
2974	4th Siege Co., Royal Anglesey	4th	3049	No. 31 A.A. Sec.	2nd
2975	1st Siege Co., Royal Monmouth	1st	3050	No. 32 A.A. Sec.	1st
2976	4th Siege Co., Royal Monmouth	3rd	3051	No. 33 A.A. Sec.	L. of C.
2977	6th Siege Co., Royal Monmouth	2nd	3052	No. 35 A.A. Sec.	L. of C.
	TUNNELLING COMPANIES.		3053	No. 36 A.A. Sec.	4th
2979	170th	5th	3054	No. 37 A.A. Sec.	L. of C.
2980	171st	2nd	3055	No. 38 A.A. Sec.	L. of C.
2981	172nd	1st	3056	No. 39 A.A. Sec.	1st
2982	173rd	2nd	3057	No. 40 A.A. Sec.	2nd
2983	174th	3rd	3058	No. 41 A.A. Sec.	L. of C.
2984	175th	1st	3059	No. 42 A.A. Sec.	1st
2985	176th	1st	3060	No. 43 A.A. Sec.	L. of C.
2986	177th	3rd	3061	No. 44 A.A. Sec.	5th
2987	178th	3rd	3062	No. 45 A.A. Sec.	3rd
2988	179th	1st	3063	No. 46 A.A. Sec.	L. of C.
2989	180th	4th	3064	No. 47 A.A. Sec.	L. of C.
2990	181st	3rd	3065	No. 48 A.A. Sec.	L. of C.
2991	182nd	4th		No. 49 A.A. Sec.	L. of C.
2992	183rd	3rd	3066	No. 50 Field Searchlight Co.	4th
2993	184th	2nd	7745	No. 51 A.A. Sec.	L. of C.
2994	185th	1st		No. 52 A.A. Sec.	L. of C.
2995	250th	5th		No. 53 A.A. Sec.	L. of C.
2996	251st	5th		No. 54 A.A. Sec.	L. of C.
2997	252nd	3rd		No. 55 A.A. Sec.	3rd
2998	253rd	4th		No. 56 A.A. Sec.	L. of C.
2999	254th	4th		No. 57 A.A. Sec.	L. of C.
3000	255th	2nd		No. 58 A.A. Sec.	3rd
3001	256th	4th		No. 59 A.A. Sec.	L. of C.
3002	257th	5th		No. 60 A.A. Sec.	L. of C.
3003	258th	3rd		No. 61 A.A. Sec.	L. of C.
3004	1st Australian	4th		No. 62 A.A. Sec.	L. of C.
3005	2nd Australian	4th		No. 63 A.A. Sec.	L. of C.
3006	3rd Australian	5th	7746	No. 64 A.A. Sec.	2nd
3009	3rd Canadian	2nd		No. 65 A.A. Sec.	L. of C.
3010	New Zealand	3rd		No. 66 A.A. Sec.	L. of C.
	LAND DRAINAGE COMPANIES.			No. 67 A.A. Sec.	L. of C.
				No. 68 A.A. Sec.	L. of C.
3016	196th (½ Co.)	2nd		No. 69 A.A. Sec.	4th
	(½ Co.)	5th		No. 70 A.A. Sec.	L. of C.
	SEARCHLIGHT COMPANIES AND SECTIONS.			No. 71 A.A. Sec.	L. of C.
				No. 72 A.A. Sec.	L. of C.
3019	No. 1 A.A. Sec.	2nd		No. 73 A.A. Sec.	L. of C.
3020	No. 2 A.A. Sec.	3rd		No. 74 A.A. Sec.	L. of C.
3021	No. 3 A.A. Sec.	1st		No. 75 A.A. Sec.	3rd
3022	No. 4 A.A. Sec.	5th		No. 76 A.A. Sec.	3rd
3023	No. 5 A.A. Sec.	1st		No. 77 A.A. Sec.	L. of C.
3024	No. 6 A.A. Sec.	4th		A.A. Searchlight Co., Canadian Engineers.	1st
3025	No. 7 A.A. Sec.	4th		**ELECTRICAL & MECHANICAL COMPANIES.**	
3026	No. 8 A.A. Sec.	3rd			
3027	No. 9 A.A. Sec.	1st	3076	350th	1st
3028	No. 10 A.A. Sec.	L. of C.	3077	351st	5th
3029	No. 11 A.A. Sec.	2nd	3078	352nd	3rd
3030	No. 12 A.A. Sec.	L. of C.	3079	353rd	4th
3031	No. 13 A.A. Sec.	1st	3080	354th	2nd
3032	No. 14 A.A. Sec.	5th	3081	355th	L. of C.
3033	No. 15 A.A. Sec.	1st	3082	356th	L. of C.
3034	No. 16 A.A. Sec.	4th		**ARMY WORKSHOP COMPANIES, R.E.**	
3035	No. 17 A.A. Sec.	4th			
3036	No. 18 A.A. Sec.	1st	3085	No. 1	1st
3037	No. 19 A.A. Sec.	L. of C.	3086	No. 2	2nd
3038	No. 20 A.A. Sec.	5th	3087	No. 3	3rd
3039	No. 21 A.A. Sec.	3rd	3088	No. 4	4th
			3089	No. 5	5th

Index to Units—Royal Engineers—continued.

	Unit.	Army.		Unit.	Army.
	FIELD SURVEY BATTALIONS.			**ADVANCED R.E. PARKS.**	
3096	1st	1st	3188	No. 1	1st
	2nd	5th	3189	No. 2	2nd
3097	3rd	3rd	3190	No. 3	2nd
3098	4th	2nd	3191	No. 4	1st
3099	5th	4th	3192	No. 5	3rd
			3193	No. 6	4th
	SOUND RANGING SECTIONS.		3194	No. 7	3rd
3100	A	4th	3195	No. 8	3rd
3101	B	4th	3196	No. 9	5th
3102	BB	2nd	3197	No. 10	2nd
3103	C	3rd	3198	No. 11	5th
3104	CC	3rd	3199	No. 12	4th
3105	D	3rd		**ARTISAN WORKS COMPANIES**	
3106	DD	5th	3202	51st	L. of C.
3108	F	3rd	3203	52nd	L. of C.
3110	G	4th	3204	58th	L. of C.
3111	GG	2nd	3205	60th	L. of C.
3112	H	1st	6416	159th	L. of C.
3114	I	2nd	6417	240th	L. of C.
3115	J	5th	6418	241st	L. of C.
3116	K	4th	6419	242nd	L. of C.
3117	L	1st	6420	243rd	L. of C.
3118	M	2nd	6429	244th	L. of C.
3119	O	4th	3206	1501st	L. of C.
3120	P	1st	3207	1502nd	L. of C.
3121	R	4th	3208	1503rd	L. of C.
3122	S	2nd	3209	1504th	L. of C.
3123	T	1st	3210	1505th	L. of C.
3124	U	5th	3211	1506th	L. of C.
3125	W	2nd		**WORKS COMPANIES.**	
3126	Y	1st		No. 6	Ind. Force, R.A.F.
3127	Z	1st		No. 22	Ind. Force, R.A.F.
3128	Experimental	G.H.Q.		No. 39	Ind. Force, R.A.F.
	OBSERVATION GROUPS.			No. 572	Ind. Force, R.A.F.
3135	No. 1	2nd		No. 575	Ind. Force, R.A.F.
3136	No. 2	4th		No. 578	Ind. Force, R.A.F.
3137	No. 3	2nd			
3138	No. 4	1st		**TRANSPORTATION (WORKS) COMPANIES.**	
	No. 5	5th		No. 220	2nd
3140	No. 6	2nd		No. 221	5th
3141	No. 7	2nd		No. 222	3rd
3142	No. 8	5th		No. 223	1st
3143	No. 9	5th		No. 224	4th
3144	No. 10	1st		**BORING SECTIONS.**	
3145	No. 11	1st	3216	1st	3rd
3146	No. 12	2nd		2nd	5th
3147	No. 13	4th	3217	3rd	4th
3148	No. 14	4th	3218	4th	1st
3149	No. 15	3rd	3219	5th	2nd
3150	No. 16	3rd		**BARGE FILTRATION UNITS (I.W.T.).**	
3151	No. 17	3rd			
3152	No. 18	1st	3226	No. 3	4th
	No. 19	3rd	3227	No. 4	L. of C.
3154	No. 20	3rd		No. 5	L. of C.
3155	No. 21	1st	3228	No. 6	L. of C.
3157	No. 23	2nd			
3158	No. 24	4th	3233	**CAMOUFLAGE PARK**	G.H.Q.
6810	No. 27	5th		**METEOROLOGICAL SECTION.**	
	PONTOON PARKS (H.T.) *		3234	Meteorological Section	G.H.Q.
3176	1st	1st			
3177	2nd	5th			
3178	3rd	3rd			
3179	7th	2nd			
	BASE PARK COMPANIES.				
3184	1st	L. of C.			
3185	24th	L. of C.			
3186	32nd	L. of C.			

* For Pontoon Parks (M.T.) see under A.S.C.

Index to Units—ROYAL AIR FORCE.

	Unit.	Army.		Unit.	Army.
3235	1st Wing	1st	3293	No. 65 Squadron	2nd
3236	2nd Wing	2nd	3294	No. 70 Squadron	2nd
3239	9th Wing	H.Q.	3295	No. 73 Squadron	4th
3240	10th Wing	1st	7730	No. 74 Squadron	2nd
3241	11th Wing	2nd	3296	No. 79 Squadron	2nd
3242	12th Wing	3rd	3297	No. 80 Squadron	4th
3243	13th Wing	3rd	3298	No. 82 Squadron	2nd
3244	15th Wing	4th	3299	No. 83 Squadron	H.Q.
3245	22nd Wing	4th	3300	No. 84 Squadron	4th
3246	41st Wing	Ind. Force.	7762	No. 85 Squadron	4th
	51st Wing	H.Q.		No. 87 Squadron	3rd
3247	54th Wing	H.Q.	6801	No. 88 Squadron	5th
	65th Wing	2nd	6802	No. 92 Squadron	4th
6788	80th Wing	5th		No. 94 Squadron	H.Q.
6790	81st Wing	5th		No. 97 Squadron	Ind. Force.
	82nd Wing	H.Q.	7731	No. 98 Squadron	1st
	83rd Wing	Ind. Force.		No. 99 Squadron	Ind. Force.
	88th Wing	Ind. Force.	3301	No. 100 Squadron	Ind. Force.
	89th Wing	4th	3302	No. 101 Squadron	4th
	90th Wing	3rd	3303	No. 102 Squadron	3rd
3248	No. 1 Squadron	H.Q.	6789	No. 103 Squadron	5th
3249	No. 2 Squadron	5th		No. 104 Squadron	Ind. Force.
3250	No. 3 Squadron	3rd		No. 107 Squadron	H.Q.
3251	No. 4 Squadron	2nd		No. 108 Squadron	2nd
3253	No. 5 Squadron	1st		No. 110 Squadron	Ind. Force.
3254	No. 6 Squadron	4th		No. 115 Squadron	Ind. Force.
3255	No. 7 Squadron	2nd	3304	No. 148 Squadron	1st
3256	No. 8 Squadron	4th	7758	No. 149 Squadron	2nd
3257	No. 9 Squadron	4th		No. 151 Squadron	H.Q.
3258	No. 10 Squadron	2nd		No. 152 Squadron	H.Q.
3259	No. 11 Squadron	3rd	3305	No. 201 Squadron	3rd
3260	No. 12 Squadron	3rd	3306	No. 203 Squadron	1st
3261	No. 13 Squadron	3rd		No. 204 Squadron	2nd
3262	No. 15 Squadron	3rd	3307	No. 205 Squadron	H.Q.
3263	No. 16 Squadron	1st	3308	No. 206 Squadron	2nd
3264	No. 18 Squadron	H.Q.		No. 207 Squadron	H.Q.
3265	No. 19 Squadron	1st	3309	No. 208 Squadron	4th
3266	No. 20 Squadron	4th	3310	No. 209 Squadron	1st
7569	No. 21 Squadron	5th		No. 210 Squadron	3rd
3268	No. 22 Squadron	1st	3312	No. 211 Squadron	4th
3269	No. 23 Squadron	4th		No. 214 Squadron	H.Q.
3270	No. 24 Squadron	4th		No. 215 Squadron	Ind. Force.
3271	No. 25 Squadron	H.Q.		No. 216 Squadron	Ind. Force.
3272	No. 27 Squadron	H.Q.		No. 218 Squadron	4th
3273	No. 29 Squadron	2nd	3313	No. 2 (A.F.C.) Squadron	5th
3274	No. 32 Squadron	H.Q.	3314	No. 3 (A.F.C.) Squadron	4th
3275	No. 35 Squadron	4th	3315	No. 4 (A.F.C.) Squadron	5th
	No. 38 Squadron	2nd	3316	No. 1 Balloon Co.	1st
3276	No. 40 Squadron	1st	3317	No. 2 Balloon Co.	1st
3277	No. 41 Squadron	2nd	3318	No. 3 Balloon Co.	5th
8003	No. 42 Squadron	5th	3319	No. 4 Balloon Co.	1st
3278	No. 43 Squadron	H.Q.	3320	No. 5 Balloon Co.	2nd
	No. 45 Squadron	Ind. Force.	3321	No. 6 Balloon Co.	2nd
7570	No. 46 Squadron	4th	3322	No. 7 Balloon Co.	2nd
3280	No. 48 Squadron	2nd	3323	No. 8 Balloon Co.	2nd
3281	No. 49 Squadron	H.Q.	3324	No. 10 Balloon Co.	1st
3282	No. 52 Squadron	1st	3325	No. 11 Balloon Co.	5th
3283	No. 53 Squadron	2nd	3326	No. 12 Balloon Co.	3rd
3284	No. 54 Squadron	5th	3327	No. 13 Balloon Co.	4th
3285	No. 55 Squadron	Ind. Force.	3328	No. 14 Balloon Co.	4th
3286	No. 56 Squadron	3rd	3329	No. 15 Balloon Co.	4th
3287	No. 57 Squadron	3rd	3330	No. 16 Balloon Co.	3rd
3288	No. 58 Squadron	H.Q.	3331	No. 17 Balloon Co.	2nd
3289	No. 59 Squadron	3rd	3332	No. 18 Balloon Co.	3rd
3290	No. 60 Squadron	3rd	3333	No. 19 Balloon Co.	3rd
3291	No. 62 Squadron	H.Q.		No. 20 Balloon Co.	5th
7559	No. 64 Squadron	1st			

SIGNAL SERVICE.

Unit.	Allotment.	Unit.	Allotment.
"L" Signal Battalion	G.H.Q.	3rd Army Signal Company	3rd Army.
1st Army Signal Company	1st Army.	4th Army Signal Company	4th Army.
2nd Army Signal Company	2nd Army.	5th Army Signal Company	5th Army.

Index to Units—Signal Service—continued.

	Unit.	Division.		Unit.	Division.
3355	1st Sig. Sqdn.	1st Cav.	3357	3rd Sig. Sqdn.	3rd Cav.
3356	2nd Sig. Sqdn.	2nd Cav.	3445	Cav. Corps Sig. Sqdn. ...	Cav. Corps.

	Unit.	Allotment.		Unit.	Allotment.
	1st Sig. Troop	1st Cav. Bde.		6th Sig. Troop	6th Cav. Bde.
	2nd Sig. Troop	2nd Cav. Bde.		7th Sig. Troop	7th Cav. Bde.
	3rd Sig. Troop	3rd Cav. Bde.		9th Sig. Troop	9th Cav. Bde.
	4th Sig. Troop	4th Cav. Bde.		Cdn. Sig. Troop	Cdn. Cav. Bde.
	5th Sig. Troop	5th Cav. Bde.			

DIVISIONAL SIGNAL COMPANIES.

3360	Guards	3370	14th	3381	30th	3392	41st	3402	58th	3412	5th Aus.
3361	1st	3371	15th	3382	31st	3393	42nd	3403	59th	3413	1st Cdn.
3362	2nd	3372	16th	3383	32nd	3394	46th	3404	61st	3414	2nd Cdn.
3363	3rd	3373	17th	3384	33rd	3395	47th	3405	62nd	3415	3rd Cdn.
3364	4th	3374	18th	3385	34th	3396	49th	3406	63rd	3416	4th Cdn.
7574	5th	3375	19th	3386	35th	3397	50th	3407	66th	3417	N.Z.
3365	6th	3376	20th	3387	36th	3398	51st	7803	74th		
3366	8th	3377	21st	3388	37th	8087	52nd	3408	1st Aus.		
3367	9th	3378	24th	3389	38th	3399	55th	3409	2nd Aus.		
3368	11th	3379	25th	3390	39th	3400	56th	3410	3rd Aus.		
3369	12th	3380	29th	3391	40th	3401	57th	3411	4th Aus.		

	Unit.	Allotment.		Unit.	Allotment.
	CORPS SIGNAL COMPANIES.			**Motor Airline Sections**—*contd.*	
3427	"A"	I. A.C.	3472	No. 48	4th Army.
3428	"B"	II. A.C.	3473	No. 50	5th Army.
3429	"C"	III. A.C.	3474	No. 51	XV. A.C.
3430	"D"	IV. A.C.	3475	No. 52	1st Army.
3431	"E"	IX. A.C.	3476	No. 53	4th Army.
3432	"F"	VI. A.C.	3477	No. 56	G.H.Q.
3433	"G"	VII. A.C.	3479	No. 64	VIII. A.C.
	"L"	XI. A.C.	3480	No. 66	XIX. A.C.
3436	"N"	XIII. A.C.	3481	No. 70	1st Army.
3437	"O"	V. A.C.	3482	No. 76	III. A.C.
3438	"P"	XV. A.C.	3483	No. 77	IV. A.C.
3439	"R"	XVII. A.C.		No. 78	Ind. Force.
3440	"S"	VIII. A.C.	3485	No. 79	G.H.Q.
3441	"T"	XIX. A.C.	3486	No. 80	VII. A.C.
3442	"X"	X. A.C.	3487	No. 81	IX. A.C.
3443	"Y"	XXII. A.C.	3488	No. 82	G.H.Q.
3444	Cdn.	Cdn. A.C.	3489	No. 83	II. A.C.
6670	Aus.	Aus. A.C.	3490	No. 84	XXII. A.C.
			3491	No. 85	I. A.C.
	MOTOR AIRLINE SECTIONS.		3492	No. 86	V. A.C.
3449	No. 5	I. A.C.	3493	No. 87	X. A.C.
3450	No. 6	III. A.C.	3494	No. 88	5th Army
3451	No. 7	IV. A.C.	3495	No. 89	G.H.Q.
3452	No. 8	G.H.Q.	3496	No. 90	XVII. A.C.
7732	No. 9	2nd Army.	3497	No. 91	XV. A.C.
3453	No. 10	G.H.Q.	3498	No. 92	G.H.Q.
3454	No. 11	IX. A.C.	3499	No. 93	VI. A.C.
3455	No. 13	VI. Corps.	3500	No. 94	VIII. A.C.
3456	No. 16	3rd Army.	3501	No. 95	XIII. A.C.
3457	No. 18	2nd Army.	3502	No. 96	XIX. A.C.
3458	No. 19	3rd Army.	3503	No. 100	3rd Army
3459	No. 20	VII. A.C.		No. 101	XI. A.C.
	No. 27	XI. A.C.	6678	No. 1 Aus.	Aus. A.C.
3460	No. 28	5th Army.	6679	No. 2 Aus.	Aus. A.C.
3461	No. 29	1st Army		No. 1 Cdn.	Cdn. A.C.
3462	No. 30	1st Army		No. 2 Cdn.	Cdn. A.C.
3463	No. 31	XXII. A.C.			
7733	No. 32	2nd Army.		**CABLE SECTIONS.**	
3464	No. 33	II. A.C.	3511	AA	VII. A.C.
3465	No. 35	XIII. A.C.	3512	AD	Cav. Corps.
3466	No. 36	V. A.C.	3513	AK	XXII. A.C.
3467	No. 40	XVII. A.C.	3514	AN	I. A.C.
3468	No. 43	4th Army.	3515	AP	II. A.C.
3469	No. 44	G.H.Q.	3516	AR	XIX. A.C.
3470	No. 45	4th Army.		AS	XI. A.C.
3471	No. 47	X. A.C.	3517	AU	5th Army.

Index to Units—Signal Service—continued.

CABLE SECTIONS—Continued.

	Unit.	Allotment.		Unit.	Allotment.
3518	AW	VII. A.C.	3542	L	VIII. A.C.
3519	AY	XIX. A.C.	3543	LC	X. A.C.
3520	BD	XXII. A.C.	3544	LZ	1st Army.
3521	BE	XV. A.C.	3545	MM	IV. A.C.
3522	BF	XV. A.C.	7736	N	2nd Army.
3524	BL	4th Army.	3546	O	VI. A.C.
3525	BM	5th Army.	3547	OO	V. A.C.
3526	BP	1st Army.	3548	P	IV. A.C.
3527	BT	IX. A.C.	3549	QQ	3rd Army.
3528	BV	XVII. A.C.		R	XI. A.C.
3531	CC	VI. A.C.	3550	RR	5th Army.
3533	CE	Cdn. A.C.	3551	SD	VIII. A.C.
3534	CF	Cdn. A.C.	3552	SS	III. A.C.
	CG	Cdn. A.C.	3553	SV	IX. A.C.
	CH	Cdn. A.C.	3554	TT	XVII. A.C.
3535	EE	X. A.C.	3555	VV	XIII. A.C.
	F	2nd Army	3556	WE	III. A.C.
3537	GG	Cav. Corps.	7763	WT	2nd Army.
3538	GQ	V. A.C.		WW	2nd Army.
3539	H	XIII. A.C.	3558	ZZ	3rd Army.
3540	J	II. A.C.	6680	No. 1 Aus.	Aus. A.C.
3541	K	I. A.C.	6681	No. 2 Aus.	Aus. A.C.

ARMY FIELD ARTILLERY BRIGADE SIGNAL SUB-SECTIONS.

Sub-section.	Army.	Sub-section.	Army.
No. 5 (R.H.A.)	4th	No. 113	2nd
No. 14 (R.H.A.)	3rd	No. 119	2nd
No. 16 (R.H.A.)	4th	No. 126	1st
No. 5	4th	No. 147	1st
No. 11	2nd	No. 150	5th
No. 14	4th	No. 155	1st
No. 18	1st	No. 158	5th
No. 23	2nd	No. 169	1st
No. 26	1st	No. 175	1st
No. 28	2nd	No. 179	5th
No. 34	3rd	No. 189	1st
No. 38	2nd	No. 232	4th
No. 48	4th	No. 242	1st
No. 52	1st	No. 277	1st
No. 61	2nd	No. 282	1st
No. 65	4th	No. 293	1st
No. 72	3rd	No. 298	4th
No. 76	3rd	No. 311	1st
No. 77	1st	No. 315	3rd
No. 84	4th	No. 3 (Aus.)	4th
No. 86	4th	No. 6 (Aus.)	4th
No. 93	3rd	No. 12 (Aus.)	4th
No. 96	2nd	No. 8 (Cdn.)	4th
No. 104	4th	No. 2 (N.Z.)	3rd
No. 108	4th		

AREA SIGNAL DETACHMENTS.

	Army.		Army.
No. 1	1st	No. 21	3rd
No. 2	1st	No. 22	3rd
No. 3	1st	No. 23	3rd
No. 4	1st	No. 24	3rd
No. 5	5th	No. 25	3rd
No. 6	5th	No. 26	2nd
No. 7	5th	No. 27	2nd
No. 8	2nd	No. 28	2nd
No. 8A	2nd	No. 29	3rd
No. 9	2nd	No. 30	4th
No. 10	2nd	No. 31	1st
No. 11	5th	No. 32	4th
No. 12	4th	No. 33	1st
No. 13	2nd	No. 34	5th
No. 14	5th	No. 35	2nd
No. 15	4th	No. 36	2nd
No. 16	4th	No. 37	5th
No. 17	3rd	No. 38	4th
No. 18	1st	No. 39	5th
No. 19	3rd	No. 40	4th
No. 20	3rd		

Index to Units—Signal Service—continued.

BRIGADE R.G.A., SIGNAL SUB-SECTIONS.

Sub-section.	Army.	Sub-section.	Army.
No. 1	1st	No. 50	1st
No. 2	2nd	No. 51	4th
No. 3	2nd	No. 52	5th
No. 4	2nd	No. 53	1st
No. 5	4th	No. 54	3rd
No. 6	2nd	No. 55	5th
No. 7	1st	No. 56	3rd
No. 8	1st	No. 57	3rd
No. 9	4th	No. 58	3rd
No. 10	2nd	No. 59	2nd
No. 11	5th	No. 60	3rd
No. 12	4th	No. 62	3rd
No. 13	3rd	No. 63	3rd
No. 14	4th	No. 64	1st
No. 16	1st	No. 65	2nd
No. 17	3rd	No. 66	3rd
No. 18	5th	No. 67	1st
No. 19	1st	No. 68	4th
No. 21	4th	No. 69	4th
No. 22	3rd	No. 70	2nd
No. 23	4th	No. 71	4th
No. 25	2nd	No. 72	2nd
No. 26	1st	No. 73	4th
No. 27	4th	No. 76	4th
No. 28	5th	No. 77	2nd
No. 29	1st	No. 78	1st
No. 30	1st	No. 79	4th
No. 31	1st	No. 81	1st
No. 32	3rd	No. 83	4th
No. 33	2nd	No. 84	3rd
No. 34	1st	No. 85	4th
No. 35	3rd	No. 86	2nd
No. 36	2nd	No. 87	2nd
No. 39	3rd	No. 88	3rd
No. 40	1st	No. 89	4th
No. 41	4th	No. 90	3rd
No. 42	1st	No. 91	1st
No. 43	2nd	No. 92	3rd
No. 44	5th	No. 93	4th
No. 45	1st	No. 98	4th
No. 46	5th	No. 99	2nd
No. 47	4th	No. 1 Cdn.	1st
No. 48	1st	No. 2 Cdn.	1st
No. 49	5th	No. 3 Cdn.	1st

	Unit.	Allotment.		Unit.	Allotment.
	LIGHT MOTOR SET WIRELESS SECTIONS.			**LIGHT RAILWAY SIGNAL COMPANIES.**	
3568	No. 7	G.H.Q.			
3569	No. 8	G.H.Q.			
	SIGNAL CONSTRUCTION COMPANIES.		3579	No. 1	1st Army.
3572	No. 1	1st Army.	7737	No. 2	2nd Army.
7735	No. 2	2nd Army.	3581	No. 3	3rd Army.
3573	No. 3	3rd Army.	3582	No. 4	4th Army.
3574	No. 4	4th Army.	3583	No. 5	5th Army.
3575	No. 5	5th Army.			
	No. 6	Ind. Force			

PIGEON SERVICE.

	Unit.	Army.		Unit.	Army.
	MOTOR MOBILE LOFTS.			**Horse Drawn Mobile Lofts—** continued—	
	No. 1	4th			
3589	No. 3	2nd	3600	No. 7	1st
3590	No. 4	4th	3601	No. 8	5th
3591	No. 5	1st	3602	No. 9	1st
	HORSE DRAWN MOBILE LOFTS.		3603	No. 10	2nd
			3604	No. 11	5th
3594	No. 1	1st	3610	No. 17	1st
3596	No. 3	3rd	3611	No. 18	2nd
3598	No. 5	3rd	3613	No. 20	5th

Index to Units—Pigeon Service—continued.

	Unit.	Army.		Unit.	Army.
	Horse Drawn Mobile Lofts—continued—			**Horse Drawn Mobile Lofts—**continued—	
3614	No. 21	3rd		No. 120	3rd
3615	No. 22	3rd	6798	No. 121	5th
3616	No. 23	2nd		No. 123	1st
3617	No. 24	4th		No. 124	3rd
3619	No. 26	2nd		No. 125	G.H.Q.
	No. 27	2nd		No. 126	2nd
3621	No. 28	1st		No. 127	G.H.Q.
3622	No. 29	2nd		No. 128	1st
3623	No. 30	2nd		No. 129	2nd
3624	No. 31	2nd		No. 130	2nd
3625	No. 32	1st		No. 131	1st
3626	No. 33	5th		No. 132	3rd
3627	No. 34	1st		No. 133	2nd
3628	No. 35	5th		No. 134	2nd
3631	No. 38	2nd		No. 135	2nd
3633	No. 40	2nd		No. 136	3rd
3634	No. 41	2nd		No. 138	4th
3635	No. 42	2nd		No. 139	5th
3638	No. 45	5th		No. 140	5th
3639	No. 46	1st		No. 141	3rd
3641	No. 48	5th		No. 142	3rd
3642	No. 49	1st		No. 143	4th
3644	No. 51	5th		No. 144	1st
3645	No. 52	5th		No. 145	3rd
3646	No. 53	5th		No. 146	5th
3649	No. 56	2nd		No. 147	5th
3650	No. 57	2nd		No. 148	5th
3651	No. 58	2nd		No. 149	G.H.Q.
3652	No. 59	5th		No. 150	G.H.Q.
3653	No. 60	2nd		No. 152	G.H.Q.
3654	No. 61	2nd		No. 154	2nd
3655	No. 62	2nd		No. 156	5th
3656	No. 63	2nd		No. 157	G.H.Q.
3657	No. 64	2nd		No. 158	G.H.Q.
	No. 67	5th		No. 159	1st
	No. 68	3rd		No. 160	G.H.Q.
7658	No. 69	5th		No. 161	G.H.Q.
	No. 80	3rd		No. 162	G.H.Q.
	No. 82	3rd		No. 163	G.H.Q.
	No. 84	G.H.Q.		No. 164	G.H.Q.
	No. 85	2nd		No. 165	G.H.Q.
	No. 87	2nd		No. 166	G.H.Q.
	No. 88	4th		No. 167	G.H.Q.
	No. 93	2nd		No. 168	G.H.Q.
	No. 94	2nd		No. 169	G.H.Q.
	No. 95	2nd		No. 170	G.H.Q.
	No. 96	2nd			
	No. 97	2nd			
	No. 98	2nd			
	No. 99	3rd			
	No. 100	4th		**FIXED LOFTS.**	
	No. 101	4th			
	No. 102	3rd		Coudette	
	No. 103	4th		Bryas	1st
	No. 104	2nd		Fosse 7, Lens	
	No. 105	3rd		Courtrai	2nd
	No. 106	3rd		Mouscron	
	No. 107	4th		Arry	3rd
	No. 108	4th		Le-Quesnoy	4th
	No. 109	2nd		Peronne	
	No. 110	4th			
	No. 111	4th			
	No. 112	3rd			
	No. 113	5th		**MESSENGER DOG SECTIONS.**	
	No. 114	4th			
	No. 115	3rd		No. 1	2nd Army
	No. 116	3rd		No. 2	XIX. A.C.
	No. 117	4th		No. 3	5th Army
	No. 118	2nd		Central Kennel Section	L. of C.
	No. 119	G.H.Q.			

Index to Units—INFANTRY.

	Unit.	Brigade.	Division.		Unit.	Brigade.	Division.
	C. Gds.				**D. of Corn. L.I.**		
3705	1st	2nd Gds.	Gds.	8034	1st	95th	5th
3706	2nd	1st Gds.	Gds.	3750	1/5th	Pioneer Bn.	61st
3707	3rd	4th Gds.	Cav. Corps	3751	7th	61st	20th
3708	4th	Pioneer Bn.	Gds.	3752	10th	Pioneer Bn.	2nd
	G. Gds.				**Devon R.**		
3709	1st	3rd Gds.	Gds.	8031	1st	95th	5th
3710	2nd	1st Gds.	Gds.	3753	2nd	23rd	8th
3711	3rd	2nd Gds.	Gds.	6207	1/5th	185th	62nd
3712	4th	4th Gds.	Cav. Corps	7841	9th	7th	25th
				7769	16th	229th	74th
	I. Gds.				**Dorset R.**		
3713	1st	1st Gds.	Gds.	3754	1st	14th	32nd
3714	2nd	4th Gds.	Cav. Corps	3755	5th	34th	11th
	S. Gds.			3756	6th	50th	17th
3715	1st	2nd Gds.	Gds.		**R. Dub. Fus.**		
3716	2nd	3rd Gds.	Gds.	3757	1st	86th	29th
	W. Gds.			3758	2nd	149th	50th
3717	1st	3rd Gds.	Gds.		6th	198th	66th
	A. & S. Highrs.				**Durh. L.I.**		
3718	2nd	98th	33rd	3759	2nd	18th	6th
8067	1/5th	103rd	34th	7667	2/6th	177th	59th
8015	1/6th	153rd	51st	3762	1/7th	Pioneer Bn.	8th
3719	1/7th	154th	51st	3764	1/9th	Pioneer Bn.	62nd
3720	1/8th	45th	15th	3765	11th	Pioneer Bn.	20th
3721	10th	97th	32nd	7899	13th	74th	25th
3723	14th	42nd	14th	3766	15th	64th	21st
	Bedf. R.			3767	18th	93rd	31st
8026	1st	15th	5th	3768	19th	104th	35th
3724	2nd	54th	18th	3769	20th	124th	41st
3725	4th	190th	63rd	6077	29th	41st	14th
	R. Berks. R.			3771	**Essex R.** 1st	112th	37th
3728	1st	99th	2nd	3772	2nd	12th	4th
3729	2nd	25th	8th	3773	9th	35th	12th
3730	2/4th	184th	61st	3774	10th	53rd	18th
3731	5th	36th	12th	3775	11th	18th	6th
3732	8th	53rd	18th	7668	15th	177th	59th
	Bord. R.				**Glouc. R.**		
3733	1st	87th	29th	3776	1st	3rd	1st
3734	1/5th	97th	32nd	7897	1/5th	75th	25th
3735	7th (Westmorland and Cumb'd Yeo.)	51st	17th	3777	2/5th	184th	61st
				3778	8th	57th	19th
	Camb. R.				9th	Pioneer Bn.	66th
3738	1/1st	35th	12th	3779	13th	107th	L. of C.
	Camn. Highrs.			7698	18th	49th	16th
3739	1st	1st	1st		**Gord. Highrs.**		
3740	5th	26th	9th	3780	1st	76th	3rd
3741	6th	45th	15th	3781	1/4th	154th	51st
3742	10th (Lovat Scouts)	—	L. of C.	3782	1/5th	44th	15th
7754	11th	120th	40th	3783	6/7th	152nd	51st
	Ches. R.			3786	9th	Pioneer Bn.	15th
8027	1st	15th	5th		**R. Guernsey L.I.**		
6056	1/4th	102nd	34th	3787	1st	—	G.H.Q.
3743	1/5th	Pioneer Bn.	56th		**Hamps. R.**		
3744	1/6th	21st	30th	3788	1st	11th	4th
6057	1/7th	102nd	34th	3789	2nd	88th	29th
3745	9th	56th	19th	6208	2/4th	186th	62nd
3748	15th	105th	35th	3790	11th	Pioneer Bn.	16th
7666	23rd	121st	40th	3791	15th	122nd	41st
	Conn. Rang.				**Hereford R.**		
3749	5th	199th	66th	6058	1/1st	102nd	34th

Index to Units—Infantry—continued.

	Unit.	Brigade.	Division.		Unit.	Brigade.	Division.
	Herts. R.				**Lan. Fus.**		
3792	1/1st	112th	37th	3834	1st	86th	29th
				3835	2nd	12th	4th
	High. L.I.			3836	1/5th	125th	42nd
3793	2nd	5th	2nd	3837	2/5th	164th	55th
8064	1/5th	157th	52nd	3838	6th	198th	66th
8065	1/6th	157th	52nd	3839	1/7th	125th	42nd
8066	1/7th	157th	52nd	3841	1/8th	125th	42nd
3794	1/9th	100th	33rd	3843	10th	52nd	17th
3795	10th	43rd	14th	3845	15th	96th	32nd
3796	12th	106th	35th	3846	16th	96th	32nd
3797	14th	197th	L. of C.	3847	17th	104th	35th
3798	15th	14th	32nd	3848	18th	104th	35th
3799	16th	Pioneer Bn.	32nd	3849	19th	Pioneer Bn.	49th
3800	18th (Glasgow Yeo.)	106th	35th	7751	23rd	121st	40th
	H.A.C.				**E. Lan. R.**		
3801	1/1st	—	G.H.Q.	3850	1st	188rd	61st
				3851	2nd	25th	8th
	R. Innis. Fus.			3852	4th	—	39th
3802	1st	109th	36th	3853	1/5th	126th	42nd
3803	2nd	109th	36th	3855	11th	92nd	31st
	5th	198th	66th	7756	13th	119th	40th
6293	6th	161st	50th				
3804	7/8th	49th	30th		**N. Lan. R.**		
3805	9th	109th	36th	3856	1st	1st	1st
7757	13th	119th	40th	6055	2nd	101st	34th
				3857	1/4th	164th	55th
	R. Ir. Fus.			3858	2/4th	170th	57th
3806	1st	108th	36th	3859	1/5th	170th	57th
7692	5th	48th	16th	3860	2/5th	Pioneer Bn.	57th
3807	9th (N. Irish Horse)	108th	36th		12th	Pioneer Bn.	74th
				6079	15th	Pioneer Bn.	14th
	R. Ir. Regt.						
3808	2nd	188th	63rd		**S. Lan. R.**		
8088	5th	Pioneer Bn.	50th	3862	2nd	89th	30th
3809	7th (S. Irish Horse)	21st	30th	3863	1/4th	Pioneer Bn.	55th
7669	8th	121st	40th	3864	2/4th	172nd	57th
				3865	1/5th	166th	55th
	R. Ir. Rif.				11th	Pioneer Bn.	25th
3810	1st	107th	36th				
3811	2nd	107th	36th		**R. Lanc. R.**		
3812	12th	108th	36th	3867	1st	12th	4th
3813	15th	107th	36th	3868	1/4th	164th	55th
3814	16th	Pioneer Bn.	36th	3869	1/5th	166th	55th
				3870	2/5th	170th	57th
	E. Kent R.			3871	8th	76th	3rd
3815	1st	16th	6th				
3816	6th	37th	12th		**Leic. R.**		
3817	7th	55th	18th	3872	1st	71st	6th
7772	10th	230th	74th	3873	1/4th	138th	46th
				3875	1/5th	138th	46th
	R. W. Kent R.			3876	6th	110th	21st
8020	1st	13th	5th	3877	7th	110th	21st
3818	6th	37th	12th	3879	11th	Pioneer Bn.	6th
3819	7th	53rd	18th	7610	14th	47th	16th
3820	8th	72nd	24th				
3821	10th	123rd	41st		**Leins. R.**		
				3880	2nd	88th	29th
	K. R. Rif. C.				**Linc. R.**		
3822	1st	99th	2nd	3881	1st	62nd	21st
3823	2nd	2nd	1st	3882	2nd	62nd	21st
3825	4th	151st	50th	3884	1/5th	138th	46th
3827	11th	59th	20th	3886	6th	33rd	11th
3828	12th	60th	20th	3887	7th	51st	17th
3829	13th	111th	37th	3888	8th	63rd	37th
3830	16th	100th	33rd	3889	10th	197th	L. of C.
3831	17th	197th	L. of C.				
3832	18th	122nd	41st		**L'pool R.**		
3833	20th	Pioneer Bn.	3rd	3890	1st	6th	2nd
	25th	Pioneer Bn.	59th	3891	4th	98th	33rd
				3892	1/5th	165th	55th

Index to Units—Infantry—continued.

	Unit.	Brigade.	Division.		Unit.	Brigade.	Division.
	L'pool R.—contd.				**Midd'x R.**—contd.		
3893	1/6th	165th	55th	3954	19th	Pioneer Bn.	41st
3894	2/6th	171st	57th	3955	20th	43rd	14th
3895	1/7th	165th	55th	3957	23rd	123rd	41st
3896	2/7th	171st	57th	3958	No. 1 Lab. Co.	A.T.	2nd Army
3897	8th	171st	57th	3959	No. 2 Lab. Co.	A.T.	2nd Army
3898	9th	172nd	57th	3960	No. 3 Lab. Co.	A.T.	2nd Army
3899	10th (L'pool Scot.)	166th	55th	3961	No. 4 Lab. Co.	A.T.	2nd Army
3902	12th	61st	20th		No. 5 Lab. Co.	A.T.	3rd Army
3903	13th	9th	3rd		No. 6 Lab. Co.	A.T.	4th Army
3905	18th (Lanc. Hrs. Yeo.)	199th	66th		No. 7 Lab. Co.	A.T.	2nd Army
7670	25th	176th	59th		**Mon. R.**		
	London R.			3962	1/1st	Pioneer Bn.	46th
3907	1/1st	167th	56th	3963	1/2nd	Pioneer Bn.	29th
3908	1/2nd	169th	56th		**R. Muns. Fus.**		
3909	2/2nd	173rd	58th	3964	1st	172nd	57th
3910	3rd	173rd	58th	3965	2nd	150th	50th
3911	1/4th	168th	56th		**Norf. R.**		
3913	1/5th	169th	56th	8025	1st	15th	5th
3914	6th	174th	58th	3966	7th	35th	12th
3915	7th	174th	58th	3967	9th	71st	6th
3916	8th	174th	58th	7773	12th	94th	31st
3917	9th	175th	58th		**North'n R.**		
3918	2/10th	175th	58th	3968	1st	2nd	1st
3919	12th	175th	58th	3969	2nd	24th	8th
3920	1/13th	168th	56th	3970	5th	Pioneer Bn.	12th
3921	1/14th (Lon. Scot.)	168th	56th	3971	6th	54th	18th
	2/14th	90th	30th	3972	7th	73d	24th
3922	1/15th	140th	47th		**North'd Fus.**		
	2/15th	90th	30th	3973	1st	9th	3rd
3923	1/16th (Q. Westm.)	169th	56th	6272	2nd	150th	50th
	2/16th	90th	30th	3977	1/7th	Pioneer Bn.	42nd
3924	1/17th	140th	47th	3978	8th	34th	11th
	2/17th	89th	30th	3979	9th (North'd Hrs.)	183rd	61st
3925	1/18th	141st	47th	3980	12/13th	62nd	21st
3926	1/19th	141st	47th	3981	14th	Pioneer Bn.	21st
3927	1/20th	141st	47th	3982	17th	Pioneer Bn.	52nd
6209	2/20th	185th	62nd	3983	18th	197th	L. of C.
3928	1/21st	140th	47th	3984	19th	Pioneer Bn.	35th
3929	1/22nd	142nd	47th	3985	22nd	48th	16th
3930	1/23rd	142nd	47th	3986	23rd	197th	L. of C.
	2/23rd	21st	30th	3987	25th	197th	L. of C.
3931	1/24th	142nd	47th	7671	36th	178th	59th
7829	2/24th	173rd	58th		**Notts. & Derby. R.**		
3932	1/28th (Artists Rifles)	190th	63rd	3988	1st	24th	8th
6078	33rd (Rif. Bde.)	41st	14th	3989	2nd	71st	6th
7699	34th (K.R.Rif.C.) (T.)	49th	16th	3990	1/5th	139th	46th
	Manch. R.			3992	1/6th	139th	46th
3933	2nd	96th	32nd	3994	7th	—	39th
3934	1/5th	127th	42nd	3995	1/8th	139th	46th
3936	1/6th	127th	42nd	3996	9th	33rd	11th
3938	1/7th	127th	42nd	3997	10th	51st	17th
3940	1/8th	126th	42nd	7836	11th	74th	25th
3941	9th	199th	66th	3998	12th	Pioneer Bn.	24th
3942	1/10th	126th	42nd	3999	15th	105th	35th
3943	11th	34th	11th	4000	16th	197th	L. of C.
3944	12th (Duke of Lan. Yeo.)	52nd	17th		**Oxf. & Bucks. L.I.**		
3945	16th	42nd	14th	4001	2nd	5th	2nd
7835	20th	7th	25th	4002	2/4th	184th	61st
7838	21st	7th	25th	4004	11th (Garr.) Bn.		
	Midd'x R.				(1 Co.)	A.T.	2nd Army
3947	1st	98th	33rd		(1 Co.)	A.T.	4th Army
3948	2nd	23rd	8th		(2 Cos.)	A.T.	5th Army
3949	4th	63rd	37th				
3950	1/7th	167th	56th				
3951	1/8th	167th	56th				
3952	13th	73rd	24th				
3953	18th	Pioneer Bn.	33rd				

Index to Units—Infantry—*continued.*

	Unit.	Brigade.	Division.		Unit.	Brigade.	Division.
	Rif. Brig.				**K.O. Sco. Bord.**		
4005	1st	11th	4th	4046	1st	87th	29th
4006	2nd	25th	8th	8019	2nd	13th	5th
4007	3rd	17th	24th	8054	1/4th	155th	52nd
4011	11th	59th	20th	8055	1/5th	103rd	34th
4012	12th	60th	20th	4047	6th	27th	9th
4013	13th	111th	37th	4048	7/8th	46th	15th
4014	16th	197th	L. of C.	7753	10th	120th	40th
	R. Fus.				**Sco. Rif.**		
4015	1st	17th	24th	4049	1st	19th	33rd
4016	2nd	86th	29th	4050	2nd	59th	20th
6215	3rd	149th	50th	4051	5/6th	19th	33rd
4017	4th	9th	3rd	8060	1/7th	156th	52nd
4018	7th	190th	63rd	8061	1/8th	103rd	34th
4019	9th	36th	12th	4052	9th	28th	9th
4020	10th	111th	37th	4053	10th	46th	15th
4021	11th	54th	18th	7660	18th	48th	16th
4022	13th	112th	37th		**Sea. Highrs.**		
4023	17th	6th	2nd	4054	2nd	10th	4th
4024	23rd	99th	2nd	4055	1/4th	154th	51st
4025	24th	5th	2nd	4056	1/5th	152nd	51st
4026	26th	124th	41st	4057	1/6th	152nd	51st
				4058	7th	26th	9th
	43rd Garrison Bn.			4059	8th	44th	15th
	GARRISON COS.			4060	9th	Pioneer Bn.	9th
	Nos. 1 and 2		1st Army				
	Nos. 3, 4 and 16		2nd Army		**Shrops. L.I.**		
	Nos. 5, 6 and 15		3rd Army	4061	1st	16th	6th
	No. 7 and Composite			4062	1/4th	56th	19th
	Guards Co.		4th Army	4063	6th	60th	20th
	Nos. 8 and 9		5th Army	4064	7th	8th	3rd
	Nos. 10 to 14		L. of C.	7781	10th	231st	74th
	44th Garrison Bn.				**Som. L.I.**		
	ANTI-AIRCRAFT COS.			4065	1st	11th	4th
	No. 1		1st Army	6052	2/4th	Pioneer Bn.	34th
	Nos. 2 and 3		2nd Army	4066	6th	49th	16th
	Nos. 4 and 5		3rd Army	4067	7th	61st	20th
	No. 6		4th Army	4068	8th	63rd	37th
	No. 7		5th Army	7673	11th	177th	59th
	Nos. 8, 9, 10, 11, 12		L. of C.	7768	12th	229th	74th
	R. Highrs.				**N. Staff. R.**		
4027	1st	1st	1st	4069	1st	72nd	24th
4028	4/5th	44th	15th	4070	4th	105th	35th
4029	1/6th	153rd	51st	4072	1/6th	137th	46th
4030	1/7th	153rd	51st	4074	8th	56th	19th
4031	8th	26th	9th	4075	9th	Pioneer Bn.	37th
4032	9th	47th	16th	7755	12th	119th	40th
6254	13th	149th	50th	4076	13th (Garr). Bn.	—	L. of C.
7767	14th	229th	74th		**S. Staff. R.**		
	R. Scots.			4077	2nd	6th	2nd
4033	2nd	8th	3rd	4079	1/5th	137th	46th
8058	1/4th	156th	52nd	4080	1/6th	137th	46th
4034	5/6th	14th	32nd	4082	7th	33rd	11th
8059	1/7th	156th	52nd		**Suff. R.**		
4035	1/8th	Pioneer Bn.	51st	4083	2nd	76th	3rd
4036	1/9th	46th	15th	4084	4th	Pioneer Bn.	58th
4037	11th	27th	9th	4085	7th	197th	L. of C.
4038	12th	27th	9th	4086	11th	183rd	61st
4039	13th	45th	15th	4087	12th	43rd	14th
4042	17th	106th	35th	7774	15th	230th	74th
	R. Sco. Fus.			4088	1st Garr. Bn. (1 Co.)	—	L. of C.
4043	1st	8th	3rd		**E. Surr. R.**		
4044	2nd	28th	9th	8033	1st	95th	5th
8052	1/4th	155th	52nd	4089	8th	55th	18th
8053	1/5th	155th	52nd	4090	9th	72nd	24th
7766	12th	94th	31st	4091	12th	122nd	41st
7672	11th	178th	59th				

Index to Units—Infantry—*continued.*

	Unit.	Brigade.	Division.		Unit.	Brigade.	Division.
	R. W. Surr. R.				**Wilts. R.**		
4093	1st	19th	33rd	4138	1st	110th	21st
6053	2/4th	101st	34th	4139	2nd	58th	19th
4094	6th	37th	12th	4140	6th (Wilts. Yeo.)	42nd	14th
4095	7th	55th	18th	6263	7th	150th	50th
4096	8th	17th	24th		**Worc. R.**		
4097	10th	124th	41st	4141	1st	24th	8th
4098	11th	123rd	41st	4142	2nd	100th	33rd
	R. Suss. R.			4143	3rd	57th	19th
4099	2nd	2nd	1st	4144	4th	88th	29th
6054	4th	101st	34th	7840	1/8th	75th	25th
4100	7th	36th	12th	4145	2/8th	182nd	61st
4101	8th	Pioneer Bn.	18th	4147	14th	Pioneer Bn.	63rd
4102	9th	73rd	24th	7750	17th	121st	40th
6803	16th	230th	74th		**York and Lanc. R.**		
7775	17th	176th	59th	4148	2nd	16th	6th
	S. Wales Bord.			4149	1/4th	148th	49th
4105	1st	3rd	1st	4150	2/4th	187th	62nd
4106	2nd	87th	29th	4151	1/5th	148th	49th
4107	5th	Pioneer Bn.	19th	4152	6th	32nd	11th
4108	6th	Pioneer Bn.	30th	4153	7th	Pioneer Bn.	17th
4109	10th	115th	38th	4154	13th	93rd	31st
	R. War. R.			6076	18th	41st	14th
4110	1st	10th	4th		**Yorks. L.I.**		
4111	2/6th	182nd	61st	6282	1st	151st	50th
4112	2/7th	182nd	61st	4155	2nd	97th	32nd
7884	1/8th	75th	25th	4156	1/4th	148th	49th
4113	10th	57th	19th	4157	2/4th	187th	62nd
8017	14th	Pioneer Bn.	5th	4158	5th	187th	62nd
8024	16th	13th	5th	4159	9th	64th	21st
	R. W. Fus.			4160	12th	Pioneer Bn.	31st
4114	2nd	115th	38th	7752	15th	120th	40th
4115	1/4th	Pioneer Bn.	47th		16th (Garr.) Bn.		
4116	9th	58th	19th		(1 Coy.)	—	1st Army
4117	13th	113th	38th		(1 Coy.)	—	2nd Army
4118	14th	113th	38th		(1 Coy.)	—	3rd Army
4119	16th	113th	38th		(1 Coy.)	—	4th Army
4120	17th	115th	38th		**York. R.**		
7778	24th	94th	31st	4162	2nd	32nd	11th
7779	25th	231st	74th	7833	9th	74th	25th
4121	26th	176th	59th		**E. York. R.**		
	Welsh R.			4168	1st	64th	21st
4122	2nd	3rd	1st	4170	6th	Pioneer Bn.	11th
4123	1/6th	Pioneer Bn.	1st	4171	7th	50th	17th
4124	9th	58th	19th	4172	10th	92nd	31st
4125	13th	114th	38th	4173	11th	92nd	31st
4126	14th	114th	38th		**W. York. R.**		
4127	15th	114th	38th	4174	1st	18th	6th
4128	18th	47th	16th	4175	2nd	23rd	8th
4129	19th	Pioneer Bn.	38th	4176	1/5th	146th	49th
7780	24th	231st	74th	4178	1/6th	146th	49th
	W. Rid. R.			4179	1/7th	146th	49th
4130	2nd	10th	4th	4181	8th	185th	62nd
4131	1/4th	147th	49th	4182	9th (York. Hrs.)	32nd	11th
4132	2/4th	186th	62nd	4183	10th	50th	17th
4133	5th	186th	62nd	4184	15th	93rd	31st
4134	1/6th	147th	49th	4185	21st	Pioneer Bn.	4th
4135	1/7th	147th	49th	4186	No. 6 Garr.		
4137	9th	52nd	17th		Guard Co.	A.T.	4th Army.
	13th	178th	59th				

Index to Units—Infantry—continued.

	Unit.	Brigade.	Division.		Unit.	Brigade.	Division.
	NAVAL BATTALIONS.				Canadian Battalions—*continued.*		
4270	Anson Bn.	188th	63rd				
4271	Drake Bn.	189th	63rd	4367/4370	27th, 28th, 29th, 31st Cdn. Bns.	6th Cdn.	2nd Cdn.
4272	Hawke Bn.	189th	63rd	4371	P.P.C.L.I.	7th Cdn.	3rd Cdn.
4273	Hood Bn.	189th	63rd	4372	R. Cdn. Regt.	7th Cdn.	3rd Cdn.
4274/4275	1st R. Marine	188th	63rd	4373	42nd (Montreal) Highrs.	7th Cdn.	3rd Cdn.
	AUSTRALIAN BATTALIONS.			4374	49th (Edmonton) Regt.	7th Cdn.	3rd Cdn.
				4375/4378	1st, 2nd, 4th, 5th Cdn. Mtd. Rif. Bns.	8th Cdn.	3rd Cdn.
4277/4280	1st, 2nd, 3rd, 4th	1st N.S.W.	1st Aus.				
4281/4284	5th, 6th, 7th, 8th	2nd Vic.	1st Aus.	4379/4382	43rd, 52nd, 58th, 116th Cdn. Bns.	9th Cdn.	3rd Cdn.
4285/4288	9th, 10th, 11th, 12th	3rd Aus.	1st Aus.				
4289/4292	13th, 14th, 15th, 16th	4th Aus.	4th Aus.	4383/4386	44th, 46th, 47th, 50th Cdn. Bns.	10th Cdn.	4th Cdn.
4293/4296	17th, 18th, 20th	5th Aus.	2nd Aus.				
4297/4300	22nd, 23rd, 24th	6th Aus.	2nd Aus.	4387/4390	54th, 75th, 87th, 102nd Cdn. Bns.	11th Cdn.	4th Cdn.
4341, 4301/4303	26th, 27th, 28th	7th Aus.	2nd Aus.				
4304/4307	30th, 31st, 32nd	8th Aus.	5th Aus.	4391/4394	38th, 72nd, 78th, 85th Cdn. Bns.	12th Cdn.	4th Cdn.
4308/4311	33rd, 34th, 35th, 36th	9th Aus.	3rd Aus.	4397	R. Newfoundland Bn.	28th	9th
4312/4315	38th, 39th, 40th	10th Aus.	3rd Aus.	4401	No. 1 Cdn. Inf. Works Co.	...	Cdn. A.C.
4316/4319	41st, 43rd, 44th	11th Aus.	3rd Aus.	4402	No. 2 Cdn. Inf. Works Co.	...	Cdn. A.C.
4320/4323	45th, 46th, 48th	12th Aus.	4th Aus.		No. 3 Cdn. Inf. Works Co.	...	Cdn. A.C.
4324/4327	49th, 50th, 51st	13th Aus.	4th Aus.		No. 4 Cdn. Inf. Works Co.	...	Cdn. A.C.
4328/4331	53rd, 55th, 56th	14th Aus.	5th Aus.		**NEW ZEALAND BATTALIONS.**		
4332/4335	57th, 58th, 59th	15th Aus.	5th Aus.				
4336	1st Aus. Pioneer Bn.	Pioneer Bn.	1st Aus.	4409	1st Auckland	1st N.Z.	N.Z.
4337	2nd Aus. Pioneer Bn.	Pioneer Bn.	2nd Aus.	4410	2nd Auckland	1st N.Z.	N.Z.
4338	3rd Aus. Pioneer Bn.	Pioneer Bn.	3rd Aus.	4411	1st Canterbury	2nd N.Z.	N.Z.
4339	4th Aus. Pioneer Bn.	Pioneer Bn.	5th Aus.	4412	2nd Canterbury	2nd N.Z.	N.Z.
4340	5th Aus. Pioneer Bn.	Pioneer Bn.	4th Aus.	4413	1st Otago	2nd N.Z.	N.Z.
	CANADIAN BATTALIONS.			4414	2nd Otago	2nd N.Z.	N.Z.
				4415	1st Wellington	1st N.Z.	N.Z.
4347/4350	1st, 2nd, 3rd, 4th Cdn. Bns.	1st Cdn.	1st Cdn.	4416	2nd Wellington	1st N.Z.	N.Z.
4351/4354	5th, 7th, 8th, 10th Cdn. Bns.	2nd Cdn.	1st Cdn.	4417/4420	1st, 2nd, 3rd, 4th N.Z. Rif.	3rd N.Z.	N.Z.
4355/4358	13th, 14th, 15th, 16th Cdn. Bns.	3rd Cdn.	1st Cdn.	4421	N.Z. Pioneer Bn.	Pioneer Bn.	N.Z.
4359	18th (Western Ontario) Cdn. Bn.	4th Cdn.	2nd Cdn.		**SOUTH AFRICAN BATTALIONS.**		
4360	19th (Central Ontario) Cdn. Bn.	4th Cdn.	2nd Cdn.	4424	2036 1st, 2037 2nd, 2038 4th	S.A.	66th
4361	20th (Central Ontario) Cdn. Bn.	4th Cdn.	2nd Cdn.		**BRITISH WEST INDIES BATTALIONS.**		
4362	21st (Eastern Ontario) Cdn. Bn.	4th Cdn.	2nd Cdn.	4428	3rd Bn. B. W. Indies R.	...	2nd Army
				4429	4th Bn. B. W. Indies R.	...	3rd Army
4363/4366	22nd, 24th, 25th, 26th Cdn. Bns.	5th Cdn.	2nd Cdn.		6th Bn. B. W. Indies R.	...	4th Army
					7th Bn. B.W. Indies R. $\left(\frac{1}{2}\right)\left(\frac{1}{2}\right)$	...	4th Army / 5th Army
					9th Bn. B. W. Indies R.	...	1st Army

TANK CORPS.

4431	H.Q.			4435	4th Bde.	...	...	G.H.Q. Res.
4432	1st Bde.	...	...	4436	5th Bde.	...	...	
4433	2nd Bde.	...	...		6th Bde.	...	...	
4434	3rd Bde.	...	... G.H.Q. Res.					

	Battalion	Brigade		Battalion	Brigade		Battalion	Brigade
4439	No. 1	4th	4445	No. 7	1st	4451	No. 13	5th
4440	No. 2	5th	4446	No. 8	5th	269	No. 14	2nd
4441	No. 3	3rd	4447	No. 9	2nd	194	No. 15	3rd
4442	No. 4	4th	4448	No. 10	2nd	270	No. 16	6th
4443	No. 5	4th	4449	No. 11	1st	271	No. 17	4th Army
4444	No. 6	3rd	4450	No. 12	1st		No. 18	6th

CYCLIST BATTALIONS.

	Battalion	Corps		Battalion	Corps		Battalion	Corps
4454	1st	I.	4460	7th	VII.	4466	17th	XVII.
4455	2nd Cyclist Regt. (Yorks. Dns.)	II.	4461	8th	VIII.	4467	18th	1st Army
			4462	9th	IX.	4468	19th	XIX.
4457	4th	IV.	4463	10th	X.	4469	N.Z.	XXII.
4458	5th Cyclist Regt. (N. Ir. Horse)	V.	7553	11th	XI.	4470	Aus.	Aus.
			4464	13th	XIII.	4471	Cdn.	Cdn.
4459	6th	VI.	4465	15th	XV.			

Index to Units—Infantry—continued.

MOTOR MACHINE-GUN BRIGADES.

	Battery.	Allotment.		Battery.	Allotment.
2040	1st Motor Brigade, M.G. Corps	2nd Army	4480	1st Cdn. M.M.G. Bde.	... Cdn. A.C.
				2nd Cdn. M.M.G. Bde.	... Cdn. A.C.

ARMY TROOPS MACHINE-GUN BATTALIONS.

	Bn.	Company.	Allotment		Bn.	Company.	Allotment		Bn.	Company.	Allotment
7604	No. 1 (1st L.G.) Bn. Gds. M.G. Regt.	A / B / C / D	1st Army	6149	101st (Bucks & Berks Yeo.)Bn. M.G.C.	A / B / C / D	2nd Army				
6332 / 6333 / 6334 / 6335	No. 2 (2nd L.G.) Bn. Gds. M.G. Regt.	A / B / C / D	4th Army	2011 / 2012 / 6146 / 2013 / 2014	102nd (Lincs. & E. Riding Yeo.) Bn. M.G.C.	A / B / C / D	1st Army.				
7601 / 7600	No. 3 (R.H.G.) Bn. Gds. M.G. Regt.	A / B / C / D	1st Army	2015 / 2016 / 6147 / 2017 / 2018	103rd (City & 3rd Cty. of London Yeo.) Bn. M.G.C.	A / B / C / D	1st Army				
7820 / 7821 / 7819 / 7822 / 7823	100th (War. & S. Notts Yeo.)Bn. M.G.C.	A / B / C / D	4th Army	2030 / 2031 / 2039 / 2032 / 2033	104th (Westminster Dragoons) Bn. M.G.C.	A / B / C / D	2nd Army				

MACHINE-GUN BATTALIONS AND COMPANIES.

	Bn.	Company.	Division.		Bn.	Company.	Division.		Bn.	Company.	Division.
4486 / 4487 / 4488 / 4489 / 4490	No. 4 Machine Gun Guards	A / B / C / D	Guards	4521 / 4522 / 4523 / 4524 / 4525	No. 9	A / B / C / D	9th	4566 / 4567 / 4568 / 4569 / 4570	No. 20	A / B / C / D	20th
4491 / 4492 / 4493 / 4494 / 4495	No. 1	A / B / C / D	1st	4526 / 4527 / 4528 / 4529 / 4530	No. 11	A / B / C / D	11th	4571 / 4572 / 4573 / 4574 / 4575	No. 21	A / B / C / D	21st
4496 / 4497 / 4498 / 4499 / 4500	No. 2	A / B / C / D	2nd	4531 / 4532 / 4533 / 4534 / 4535	No. 12	A / B / C / D	12th	4576 / 4577 / 4578 / 4579 / 4580	No. 24	A / B / C / D	24th
4501 / 4502 / 4503 / 4504 / 4505	No. 3	A / B / C / D	3rd	6158 / 6159 / 6134 / 6160 / 6161	No. 14	A / B / C / D	14th	4581 / 4582 / 4583 / 4584 / 4585	No. 25	A / B / C / D	25th
4506 / 4507 / 4508 / 4509 / 4510	No. 4	A / B / C / D	4th	4541 / 4542 / 4543 / 4544 / 4545	No. 15	A / B / C / D	15th	4586 / 4587 / 4588 / 4589 / 4590	No. 29	A / B / C / D	29th
8037 / 8021 / 8035 / 8028 / 8045	No. 5	A / B / C / D	5th	196 / 197 / 198 / 199 / 200	No. 16	A / B / C / D	16th	4591 / 4592 / 4593 / 4594 / 4595	No. 30	A / B / C / D	30th
4511 / 4512 / 4513 / 4514 / 4515	No. 6	A / B / C / D	6th	4551 / 4552 / 4553 / 4554 / 4555	No. 17	A / B / C / D	17th	4596 / 4597 / 4598 / 4599 / 4600	No. 31	A / B / C / D	31st
4516 / 4517 / 4518 / 4519 / 4520	No. 8	A / B / C / D	8th	4556 / 4557 / 4558 / 4559 / 4560	No. 18	A / B / C / D	18th	4601 / 4602 / 4603 / 4604 / 4605	No. 32	A / B / C / D	32nd
				4561 / 4562 / 4563 / 4564 / 4565	No. 19	A / B / C / D	19th	4606 / 4607 / 4608 / 4609 / 4610	No. 33	A / B / C / D	33rd

Index to Units—Infantry—continued.

MACHINE-GUN BATTALIONS AND COMPANIES—continued.

Bn.	Company.	Division.	Bn.	Company.	Division.	Bn.	Company.	Division.
4611	{ A	}	4671	{ A	}		{ A	}
4612	B		4672	B			B	
4613	No. 34	34th	4673	No. 50	50th	6804	No. 200	59th
4614	C		4674	C			C	
4615	D		4675	D			D	
4616	{ A	}	4676	{ A	}	4726	{ A	}
4617	B		4677	B		4727	B	
4618	No. 35	35th	4678	No. 51	51st	4728	No. 1 Aus.	1st. Aus.
4619	C		4679	C		4729	C	
4620	D		4680	D		4730	D	
4621	{ A	}		{ A	}	4731	{ A	}
4622	B			B		4732	B	
4623	No. 36	36th	8089	No. 52	52nd	4733	No. 2 Aus.	2nd Aus.
4624	C			C		4734	C	
4625	D			D		4735	D	
4626	{ A	}	4681	{ A	}	4736	{ A	}
4627	B		4682	B		4737	B	
4628	No. 37	37th	4683	No. 55	55th	4738	No. 3 Aus.	3rd Aus.
4629	C		4684	C		4739	C	
4630	D		4685	D		4740	D	
4631	{ A	}	4686	{ A	}	4741	{ A	}
4632	B		4687	B		4742	B	
4633	No. 38	38th	4688	No. 56	56th	4743	No. 4 Aus.	4th Aus.
4634	C		4689	C		4744	C	
4635	D		4690	D		4745	D	
4636	{ A	}	4691	{ A	}	4746	{ A	}
4637	B	2nd	4692	B		4747	B	
4638	No. 39	Army	4693	No. 57	57th	4748	No. 5 Aus.	5th Aus.
4639	C		4694	C		4749	C	
4640	D		4695	D		4750	D	
4646	{ A	}	4696	{ A	}	4751	{ A	}
4647	B		4697	B		4752	B	
4648	No. 41	41st	4698	No. 58	58th	4753	N.Z.	N.Z.
4649	C		4699	C		4754	C	
4650	D		4700	D		4755	D	
4651	{ A	}	4706	{ A	}	4756	{ 1st	}
4652	B		4707	B		4757	2nd	
4653	No. 42	42nd	4708	No. 61	61st	4758	No. 1 Cdn.	1st Cdn.
4654	C		4709	C		4759	3rd	
4655	D		4710	D				
4656	{ A	}	4711	{ A	}	4761	{ 1st	}
4657	B		4712	B		4762	2nd	
4658	No. 46	46th	4713	No. 62	62nd	4763	No. 2 Cdn.	2nd Cdn.
4659	C		4714	C		4764	3rd	
4660	D		4715	D				
4661	{ A	}	4716	{ A	}	4766	{ 1st	}
4662	B		4717	B		4767	2nd	
4663	No. 47	47th	4718	No. 63	63rd	4768	No. 3 Cdn.	3rd Cdn.
4664	C		4719	C		4769	3rd	
4665	D		4720	D				
4666	{ A	}		{ A	}	4771	{ 1st	}
4667	B			B		4772	2nd	
4668	No. 49	49th	7797	No. 74	74th	4773	No. 4 Cdn.	4th Cdn.
4669	C			C		4774	3rd	
4670	D			D				

MILITARY POLICE.

	Unit.	Allotment.		Unit.	Allotment.
	Traffic Control Squadrons—			Traffic Control Companies—	
4805	No. 1	1st Army.	4809	No. 1 (H.Q. and 1½ platoons)	1st Army.
4806	No. 2	4th Army.		(1½ platoons) ...	5th Army.
4807	No. 3	2nd Army.	4810	No. 2	4th Army.
4808	No. 4	3rd Army.	4811	No. 3	2nd Army.
			4812	No. 4	3rd Army.

ARMY SERVICE CORPS.
RESERVE PARKS.—*See* G.H.Q. Troops.

	Company.	Allotment.		Company.	Allotment.
	4	5th Divl. Train.	4881	100	
4814	5	No. 12 Army Aux. (H.T.) Co.	4882	101	
	6	5th Divl. Train.	4883	102	14th Divl. Train.
4815	7	1st Divl. Train.	4884	103	
4816	8	33rd Divl. Train.	4885	104	
4817	9	1st Cav. Res. Park.	4886	105	
4818	10	Base Depot (Horse Transport and Supply).	4887	106	9th Divl. Train.
			4888	107	
4819	11	Guards Divl. Train.	4889	116	
4820	12	No. 11 Army Aux. (H.T.) Co.	4890	117	12th Divl. Train.
4821	13	1st Divl. Train.	4891	118	
4822	14	Advanced H.T. Depot.	4892	119	
4823	15	3rd Divl. Train.	4893	121	Guards Divl. Train.
4824	16	1st Divl. Train.	4894	125	No. 9 Army Aux. (H.T.) Co.
4825	17	6th Divl. Train.	4895	129	No. 5 Army Aux. (H.T.) Co.
4826	18	4th Divl. Train.	4896	130	No. 14 Army Aux. (H.T.) Co.
4827	19	6th Divl. Train.	4897	131	9th Divl. M.T. Co.
4828	20	No. 10 Army Aux. (H.T.) Co.	4898	133	14th Divl. M.T. Co.
4829	21	3rd Divl. Train.	4899	135	37th Divl. M.T. Co.
4830	22		4900	138	
4831	23	6th Divl. Train.	4901	139	15th Divl. Train.
4832	24		4902	140	
4833	25	4th Divl. Train.	4903	141	
4834	26	G.H.Q. Troops Train.	4904	142	
4835	27	1st Cav. Div.	4905	143	16th Divl. Train.
4836	28	2nd Divl. Train.	4906	144	
4837	29	3rd Divl. Train.	4907	145	
4838	30	No. 7 Army Aux. (H.T.) Co.	4908	146	
4839	31	2nd Divl. Train.	4909	147	17th Divl. Train.
4840	32	4th Divl. Train.	4910	148	
	33	5th Divl. Train.	4911	149	
4841	34	2nd Cav. Res. Park.	4912	150	
4842	35	2nd Divl. Train.	4913	151	18th Divl. Train.
4843	36	1st Divl. Train.	4914	152	
	37	5th Divl. Train.	4915	153	
4844	38	4th Divl. Train.	4916	154	
4845	41	8th Divl. Train.	4917	155	19th Divl. Train.
4846	44	3rd Divl. M.T. Co.	4918	156	
	45	No. 12 G.H.Q. Reserve M.T. Co.	4919	157	
4847	46	2nd Cav. Div. M.T. Co.	4920	158	
4848	48	17th Divl. M.T. Co.	4921	159	20th Divl. Train.
4849	50	6th Divl. M.T. Co.	4922	160	
4850	51	No. 3 G.H.Q. Reserve M.T. Co.	4923	161	
	53	No. 1 Base M.T. Depot.	4924	162	No. 15 Army Aux. (H.T.) Co.
	54	No. 1 Advanced M.T. Depot.	4925	165	No. 18 Army Aux. (H.T.) Co.
4851	55	G.H.Q. Troops M.T. Co.	4926	166	No. 19 Army Aux. (H.T.) Co.
4852	56	No. 2 G.H.Q. Reserve M.T. Co.	4927	167	No. 20 Army Aux. (H.T.) Co.
4853	57	1st Cav. Div. M.T. Co.	4928	168	Guards Divl. Train.
4854	59	1st Divl. M.T. Co.	4929	170	
4855	61	2nd Divl. M.T. Co.	4930	171	33rd Divl. Train.
4856	62 (6 Sec)	44th Aux. (Steam) Co.	4931	172	2nd Divl. Train.
4857	63	18th Divl. M.T. Co.	4932	173	33rd Divl. Train.
4858	65	4th Divl. M.T. Co.	4933	174	3rd Cav. Res. Park.
4859	67	38th Divl. M.T. Co.	4934	175	12th Divl. M.T. Co.
4860	68	No. 1 G.H.Q. Reserve M.T. Co.	6921	177	15th Divl. M.T. Co.
4861	69	16th Divl. M.T. Co.	4936	179	34th Divl. M.T. Co.
	71	74th Divl. M.T. Co.	4937	181	33rd Divl. M.T. Co.
4862	72	No. 4 G.H.Q. Reserve M.T. Co.	4938	182	
4863	73	3rd Cav. Div. M.T. Co.	4939	183	
4864	74	8th Divl. M.T. Co.	4940	184	21st Divl. Train.
4865	76	No. 7 G.H.Q. Reserve M.T. Co.	4941	185	
4866	77	58th Divl. M.T. Co.	4942	186	
4867	79	No. 9 G.H.Q. Reserve M.T. Co.	4943	187	30th Divl. Train.
4868	81	3rd Cav. Div.	4944	188	
4869	84	8th Divl. Train.	4945	189	
4870	85		4946	194	
4871	87	8th Divl. Train.	4947	195	24th Divl. Train.
4872	88	No. 8 Army Aux. (H.T.) Co.	4948	196	
	89	52nd Divl. M.T. Co.	4949	197	
4873	90	1st Auxiliary (Omnibus) Co.	4950	198	
4874	91	2nd Auxiliary (Omnibus) Co.	4951	199	
4875	92	50th Auxiliary (Omnibus) Co.	4952	200	25th Divl. Train.
4876	95		4953	201	
4877	96	55th Divl. Train.	4954	202	
4878	97		4955	203	
4879	98		4956	204	32nd Divl. Train.
4880	99	No. 13 Army Aux. (H.T.) Co.	4957	205	

Index to Units—Army Service Corps—continued.

	Company.	Allotment.		Company.	Allotment.
4959	213	} 56th Divl. Train.		334	No. 4 Army Aux. (H.T.) Co.
4960	214		5025	335	Attached XIII. Corps H.A.
4961	215		5026	339	51st Auxiliary (Omnibus) C.
4962	216		5027	340	50th Divl. M.T. Co.
8091	217	} 52nd Divl. Train.	5028	341	No. 8 G.H.Q. Reserve M.T. Co.
8092	218		5029	342	24th Divl. M.T. Co.
8093	219		5030	344	25th Divl. M.T. Co.
8094	220		5031	349	49th Divl. M.T. Co.
4963	221	} 31st Divl. Train.	5032	352	32nd Divl. M.T. Co.
4964	222		5033	354	55th Divl. M.T. Co.
4965	223			356 (5 secs.)	7th Aux. (Steam) Co.
	224 (4 secs.)	Aux. (Horse) Co.		358	No. 3 Heavy Repair Shop.
4966	225	} 29th Divl. Train.	5034	359	No. 10 M.A. Convoy.
4967	226			361 (3 secs.)	Aux. (Horse) Co.
4968	227		5035	363	Attached V. Corps H.A.
4969	228			364	No. 2 Base M.T. Depot.
4970	229	} 34th Divl. Train.		365	No. 2 Advanced M.T. Depot.
4971	230			366 (5 secs.)	8th Aux. (Steam) Co.
4972	231		5036	367 (5 secs.)	9th Aux. (Steam) Co.
4973	232		5037	368	6th A.C.T., M.T. Co.
4974	233	} 35th Divl. Train.	5038	370	6th Pontoon Park, 3rd Army.
4975	234		5039	371	3rd Army T.M.T., Co.
4976	235			372 (12 secs.)	Aux. (Horse) Co.
4977	236		5040	374	39th Divl. M.T. Co.
4978	251	} 36th Divl. Train.	5041	377	Attached 3rd Army H.A.
4979	252		5042	378	No. 11 M.A. Convoy.
4980	253		5043	379	36th Divl. M.T. Co.
4981	254		5044	382	7th A.C.T., M.T. Co.
	255 (10 secs.)	Aux. (Horse) Co.	5045	383	10th A.C.T., M.T. Co.
4982	256	Attached 1st Army H.A.	5046	384	1st Army T., M.T. Co.
4983	257	19th Divl. M.T. Co.		385	5th Army T., M.T. Co.
4984	259	31st Divl. M.T. Co.	5047	386	1st A.C.T., M.T. Co.
4985	261	30th Divl. M.T. Co.	5048	387	2nd A.C.T., M.T. Co.
4986	263	56th Divl. M.T. Co.	5049	388	3rd A.C.T., M.T. Co.
4987	265	51st Divl. M.T. Co.	5050	389	4th A.C.T., M.T. Co.
4988	267	20th Divl. M.T. Co.	5051	390	5th A.C.T., M.T. Co.
4989	271	46th Divl. M.T. Co.	5052	392	Cav. Corps T., M.T. Co.
4990	272	Attached Aus. Corps H.A.	5053	398	4th Army T., M.T. Co.
4991	273	21st Divl. M.T. Co.	5054	399	No. 6 G.H.Q. Reserve M.T. Co.
4992	277	47th Divl. M.T. Co.	5055	400	No. 5 G.H.Q. Reserve M.T. Co.
4993	279	31st Divl. Train.	5056	402	Attached Cdn. Corps H.A.
	280 (9 secs.)	Aux. (Horse) Co.	5057	403	Attached XXII. Corps H.A.
	281 (7 secs.)	Aux. (Horse) Co.	5058	404	2nd Mobile Repair Unit.
4994	282	Attached I. Corps H.A.	5059	405	15th Auxiliary (Omnibus) Co.
4995	283	Attached VII. Corps H.A.	5060	406	Attached II. Corps H.A.
4996	284	} 39th Divl. Train.	5061	415	1st Cdn. Divl. M.T. Co.
4997	285		5062	418	No. 1 M.A. Convoy.
4998	286		5063	419	No. 2 M.A. Convoy.
4999	287		5064	420	No. 3 M.A. Convoy.
5000	288		5065	421	No. 4 M.A. Convoy.
5001	289	} 37th Divl. Train.	5066	422	No. 1 Workshop for A.A. Guns.
5002	290		5067	423	No. 2 Workshop for A.A. Guns.
5003	291		5068	424	2nd Cav. Div.
5004	292		5069	425	No. 1 Army Aux. (H.T.) Co.
5005	293	} 40th Divl. Train.	5070	428	} 42nd Divl. Train.
5006	294		5071	429	
5007	295		5072	430	
5008	296	} 41st Divl. Train.	5073	431	
5009	297		5074	436	} Guards Divl. Train.
5010	298		5075	437	
5011	299		5076	438	
5013	302	61st Divl. M.T. Co.	5077	439	} 1st Cdn. Divl. Train.
5014	304	35th Divl. M.T. Co.	5078	440	
5015	306	Guards Divl. M.T. Co.	5079	444	No. 22 Army Aux. (H.T.) Co.
5016	310	No. 17 Army Aux. (H.T.) Co.	5080	445	No. 21 Army Aux. (H.T.) Co.
	314	No. 2 Adv. H.T. Depot.	5081	446	No. 1 Cdn. Army Aux. (H.T.) Co.
	315 (6 secs.)	3rd Aux. (Petrol) Co.	7808	447	} 74th Divl. Train.
	316 (7 secs.)	4th Aux. (Petrol) Co.	7809	448	
	317 (2 secs.)	5th Aux. (Petrol) Co.	7810	449	
	318 (7 secs.)	6th Aux. (Petrol) Co.	7811	450	
	319	No. 1 Heavy Repair Shop.	5082	451	} 46th Divl. Train.
	320	No. 2 Heavy Repair Shop.	5083	452	
	321	XI. A.C.T., M.T. Co.	5084	453	
5017	323	No. 5 M.A. Convoy.	5085	454	
5018	324	No. 6 M.A. Convoy.	5086	455	} 47th Divl. Train.
5019	326	No. 8 M.A. Convoy.	5087	456	
5020	327	No. 16 Army Aux. (H.T.) Co.	5088	457	
5021	330	} 38th Divl. Train.	5089	458	
5022	331				
5023	332				
5024	333				

Index to Units—Army Service Corps—continued.

	Company.	Allotment.		Company.	Allotment.
5090	463		5167	645	No. 24 M.A. Convoy.
5091	464	49th Divl. Train.	5168	646	No. 1 Water Tank Co.
5092	465		5169	647	10th Pontoon Pk., A.T., 1st Army.
5093	466		5170	657	No. 4 Mobile Repair Unit.
5094	467			670	5th Cav. Reserve Park.
5095	468	50th Divl. Train.	5172	672	
5096	469		5173	673	2nd Cdn. Divl. Train.
5097	470		5174	674	
5098	471		5175	675	
5099	472	51st Divl. Train.	5176	676	
5100	473		5177	677	3rd Cdn. Divl. Train.
5101	474		5178	678	
5102	479		5179	679	
5103	480	11th Divl. Train.	5180	680	No. 2 Cdn. Army Aux. (H.T.) Co.
5104	481		5181	682	12th Pontoon Pk., 5th Army.
5105	482		5183	687	XXII. A.C.T., M.T. Co.
	491	Attached XI. Corps H.A.	5184	696	15th A.C.T., M.T. Co.
5107	496	29th Divl. M.T. Co.	5185	698	No. 4 Workshop for A.A. Guns.
5106	498	41st Divl. M.T. Co.	5186	701	63rd Divl. M.T. Co.
	501 (5 secs.)	Aux. (Horse) Co.	5187	703 (8 secs.)	354th Aux. (Petrol) Co.
5108	505		5188	704	No. 30 M.A. Convoy.
5109	506	57th Divl. Train.	5189	705	No. 31 M.A. Convoy.
5110	507		5190	711	A.S.C. Workshop M.T. with Tank Corps
5111	508				
5112	509	58th Divl. Train.	5192	714	11th Divl. M.T. Co.
5113	510		5193	716	9th A.C.T., M.T. Co.
5114	511		5194	717	Attached IX. Corps H.A.
5115	512		5195	718	No. 2 Water Tank M.T. Co.
5116	513		5196	719	62nd Divl. M.T. Co.
5117	514	59th Divl. Train.	5197	721	Cdn. Corps T.M.T. Co.
5118	515		5198	722	2nd Cdn. Divl. M.T. Co.
5119	516		5199	724	3rd Cdn. Divl. M.T. Co.
5120	521		5200	726	No. 3 Workshop for A.A. Guns.
5121	522	61st Divl. Train.	5201	727	No. 5 Workshop for A.A. Guns.
5122	523		5202	731	57th Divl. M.T. Co.
5123	524			733	5th Divl. M.T. Co.
5124	525			735 (3 secs.)	39th Aux. (Petrol) Co.
5125	526	62nd Divl. Train.		736 (3 secs.)	10th Aux. (Petrol) Co.
5126	527		5211	749	
5127	528		5212	750	N.Z. Divl. Train.
5128	541		5213	751	
5129	542	66th Divl. Train.	5214	752	
5130	543		5223	761	
5131	544		5224	762	
5132	559	No. 12 M.A. Convoy.	5225	763	63rd Divl. Train.
5133	562	Attached IV. Corps H.A.	5226	764	
5134	563	16th Auxiliary (Omnibus) Co.	5227	770	Attached 4th Army H.A.
5135	564	13th A.C.T., M.T. Co.	5228	774	9th Pontoon Pk., A.T., 2nd Army.
5136	565	Attached VI. Corps H.A.	5229	775	11th Pontoon Pk., A.T., 4th Army.
5137	566	No. 13 M.A. Convoy.	5230	785	4th Cdn. Divl. M.T. Co.
5138	567	No. 14 M.A. Convoy.	5231	794	
5139	568	No. 15 M.A. Convoy.	5232	795	4th Cdn. Divl. Train.
5140	569	No. 16 M.A. Convoy.	5233	796	
5141	571	No. 3 Army Aux. (H.T.) Co.	5234	797	
5142	574	1st Cav. Div.		805 (3 secs.)	43rd Aux. (Petrol) Co.
5143	575	2nd Cav. Div.	5235	806	5th Mobile Repair Unit.
5144	576	3rd Cav. Div.		812 (69 vhls.)	41st Aux. (Amb. Car) Co.
	577	4th Cav. Div. Aux. (Horse) Co.		813 (63 vhls.)	47th Aux. (Amb. Car) Co.
	578	5th Cav. Div. Aux. (Horse) Co.		814 (66 vhls.)	48th Aux. (Amb. Car) Co.
5145	582	17th A.C.T., M.T. Co.	5237	879 (10 secs.)	Aux. (Horse) Co.
5146	583	No. 11 G.H.Q. Reserve M.T. Co.	5238	883	19th A.C.T., M.T. Co.
5147	584	No. 3 Mobile Repair Unit.	5239	884	Attached XIX. Corps H.A.
5148	585	2nd Army T.M.T. Co.	5240	885	8th A.C.T., M.T. Co.
5149	587	No. 10 G.H.Q. Reserve M.T. Co.	5241	886	Attached VIII. Corps H.A.
5150	588	18th Auxiliary (Omnibus) Co.	5242	888	66th Divl. M.T. Co.
	590 (6 secs.)	20th Auxiliary (Petrol) Co.	5243	892	59th Divl. M.T. Co.
	592 (2 secs.)	123rd Auxiliary (Petrol) Co.	5244	896	42nd Divl. M.T. Co.
5153	594	Attached X. Corps H.A.	5245	899	4th A.S.C. Repair Shop.
5155	601	Attached XV. Corps H.A.	5246	909	No. 37 M.A. Convoy.
5156	609	40th Divl. M.T. Co.	5247	912 (3 secs.)	55th Aux. (Petrol) Co.
5157	610	N.Z. Divl. M.T. Co.	5248	914 (3 secs.)	57th Aux. (Petrol) Co.
5158	611	Attached XVII. Corps H.A.	5249	915 (3 secs.)	58th Aux. (Petrol) Co.
5159	624	8th Pontoon Park, A.T., 4th Army.	5250	916 (3 secs.)	59th Aux. (Petrol) Co.
5160	625	Attached 2nd Army H.A.	5251	918 (3 secs.)	77th Aux. (Petrol) Co.
5161	627	No. 25 M.A. Convoy.	5252	929 (1 sec.)	Aux. (Horse) Co.
5162	629	No. 27 M.A. Convoy.	5253	931 (7 secs.)	60th Aux. (Steam) Co.
5163	638	No. 20 M.A. Convoy.	5254	932 (6 secs.)	61st Aux. (Petrol) Co.
5164	639	No. 21 M.A. Convoy.	5255	933 (6 secs.)	66th Aux. (Petrol) Co.
5165	640	No. 22 M.A. Convoy.	5256	934 (5 secs.)	67th Aux. (Steam) Co.
5166	641	Attached III. Corps H.A.	5257	935 (5 secs.)	68th Aux. (Petrol) Co.

Index to Units—Army Service Corps—continued.

	Company.	Allotment.		Company.	Allotment.
5258	936 (5 secs.)	69th Aux. (Steam) Co.		1085 (3 secs.)	117th Aux. (Steam) Co.
5259	937 (5 secs.)	70th Aux. (Petrol) Co.		1086	1st Tank Bde. M.T. Co.
5260	938 (4 secs.)	71st Aux. (Steam) Co.		1087	2nd Tank Bde. M.T. Co.
5261	939 (4 secs.)	75th Aux. (Petrol) Co.		1088	3rd Tank Bde. M.T. Co.
5262	940 (6 secs.)	76th Aux. (Petrol) Co.		1089	4th Tank Bde. M.T. Co.
5265	959	13th G.H.Q. Reserve M.T. Co.		1090	5th Tank Bde. M.T. Co.
5266	960	14th G.H.Q. Reserve M.T. Co.		1092 (3 secs.)	118th Aux. (Petrol) Co.
5267	974	5th A.S.C. Repair Shop.		1112	No. 6 Mobile Repair Unit.
5268	975	A.S.C. Workshop M.T. with D.G.T.		1113	Attached 5th Army H.A.
5269	979 (3 secs.)	78th Aux. (Petrol) Co. A.S.C.		1117	No. 19 G.H.Q. Res. M.T. Co.
5270	986	No. 3 Water Tank Co.		1118	No. 20 G.H.Q. Res. M.T. Co.
5271	987	No. 4 Water Tank Co.		1119	Cdn. M.M.G. M.T. Co. (C.A.S.C.)
5272	1012 (7 secs.)	No. 102 Aux. (Petrol) Co.		1120	Cdn. Eng. M.T. Co. (C.A.S.C.)
	1049	No. 42 M.A. Convoy.		1127	6th Tank Bde. M.T. Co.
5276	1051 (3 secs.)	103rd Aux. (Petrol) Co.		1128	No. 21 G.H.Q. Res. M.T. Co.
	1053 (3 secs.)	105th Aux. (Petrol) Co.		1129	No. 47 M.A. Convoy.
	1060	No. 43 M.A. Convoy.		1130	No. 48 M.A. Convoy.
	1075	No. 44 M.A. Convoy.		1131	No. 17 G.H.Q. Res. M.T. Co.
	1076	No. 15 G.H.Q. Res. M.T. Co.		1132	No. 18 G.H.Q. Res. M.T. Co.
	1077	No. 16 G.H.Q. Res. M.T. Co.		1143	No. 22 G.H.Q. Res. M.T. Co.
	1082	No. 7 Workshop for A.A. Guns.			

CORPS M.T. COLUMNS.

	No.	Allotment.		No.	Allotment.
5332	"A"	I. A.C.	5340	"N"	XIII. A.C.
5333	"B"	II. A.C.	5341	"O"	V. A.C.
5334	"C"	III. A.C.	5342	"P"	XV. A.C.
5335	"D"	IV. A.C.	5343	"R"	XVII. A.C.
5336	"E"	IX. A.C.	5345	"T"	XIX. A.C.
5337	"F"	VI. A.C.	5346	"X"	X. A.C.
5338	"G"	VII. A.C.	5347	"Y"	XXII. A.C.
5339	"H"	VIII. A.C.	5348	Australian	Australian A.C.
	"L"	XI. A.C.	5349	Canadian	Cdn. A.C.

PONTOON PARKS (M.T.).

WORKSHOPS FOR A.A. GUNS.

	No.	A.S.C. Co.	Allotment.		No.	A.S.C. Co.	Allotment.
5352	6	370	3rd Army	5358	1	422	1st Army
5353	8	624	4th Army	5359	2	423	2nd Army
5354	9	774	2nd Army	5360	3	726	3rd Army
5355	10	617	1st Army	5361	4	698	5th Army
5356	11	775	4th Army	5362	5	727	4th Army
5357	12	682	5th Army		7	1082	L. of C.

AUSTRALIAN A.S.C. UNITS.

Company.	Allotment.	Company.	Allotment.
1 Co. A.A.S.C.	No. 1 Co. 1st Australian Divl. Train.	21 Co. A.A.S.C.	No. 3 Co. 3rd Australian Divl. Train.
2 Co. "	No. 2 Co. 1st Australian Divl. Train.	25 Co. "	No. 4 Co. 3rd Australian Divl. Train.
3 Co. "	No. 3 Co. 1st Australian Divl. Train.	26 Co. "	No. 3 Co. 4th Australian Divl. Train.
4 Co. "	No. 4 Co. 1st Australian Divl. Train.	27 Co. "	No. 4 Co. 4th Australian Divl. Train.
7 Co. "	No. 2 Co. 4th Australian Divl. Train.	28 Co. "	No. 3 Co. 5th Australian Divl. Train.
10 Co. "	No. 1 Co. 5th Australian Divl. Train.	29 Co. "	No. 4 Co. 5th Australian Divl. Train.
14 Co. "	No. 1 Co. 4th Australian Divl. Train.	1 Aus. M.T. Co.	1st Australian M.T. Company.
15 Co. "	No. 2 Co. 2nd Australian Divl. Train.	2 Aus. M.T. Co.	2nd Australian M.T. Company.
16 Co. "	No. 3 Co. 2nd Australian Divl. Train.	3 Aus. M.T. Co.	3rd Australian M.T. Company.
17 Co. "	No. 4 Co. 2nd Australian Divl. Train.	4 Aus. M.T. Co.	4th Australian M.T. Company.
18 Co. "	No. 2 Co. 5th Australian Divl. Train.	5 Aus. M.T. Co.	5th Australian M.T. Company.
20 Co. "	No. 1 Co. 2nd Australian Divl. Train.	6 Aus. M.T. Co.	6th Australian M.T. Company (Corps Troops).
22 Co. "	No. 1 Co. 3rd Australian Divl. Train.		
23 Co. "	No. 2 Co. 3rd Australian Divl. Train.		

MEDICAL.

	Unit.			Division.		Unit.			Division.
	CAVALRY FIELD AMBULANCES.					**Field Ambulances**—continued.			
5364	1st	...	...	1st Cav.	5433	88th	...	...	29th
5365	2nd	...	...	2nd Cav.	5434	89th	...	...	29th
5366	3rd	...	...	1st Cav.	5435	90th	...	...	32nd
5367	4th	...	...	2nd Cav.	5436	91st	...	...	32nd
5368	5th	...	...	2nd Cav.	5437	92nd	...	...	32nd
5369	6th	...	...	3rd Cav.	5438	93rd	...	...	31st
5370	7th	...	...	3rd Cav.	5439	94th	...	...	31st
5371	9th	...	...	1st Cav.	5440	95th	...	...	31st
5372	Canadian	...	...	3rd Cav.	5441	96th	...	...	30th
	FIELD AMBULANCES.				5442	97th	...	...	30th
					5443	98th	...	...	30th
5374	1st	...	...	1st	5444	99th	...	...	33rd
5375	2nd	...	...	1st	5445	100th	...	...	2nd
5376	3rd	...	...	Guards	5446	101st	...	...	33rd
5377	4th	...	...	Guards	5447	102nd	...	...	34th
5378	5th	...	...	2nd	5448	103rd	...	...	34th
5379	6th	...	...	2nd	5449	104th	...	...	34th
5380	7th	...	...	3rd	5450	105th	...	...	35th
5381	8th	...	...	3rd	5451	106th	...	...	35th
5382	9th	...	...	Guards	5452	107th	...	...	35th
5383	10th	...	...	4th	5453	108th	...	...	36th
5384	11th	...	...	4th	5454	109th	...	...	36th
5385	12th	...	...	4th	5455	110th	...	...	36th
8041	13th	...	...	5th	5456	111th	...	...	16th
8042	14th	...	...	5th	5457	112th	...	...	16th
8043	15th	...	...	5th	5458	113th	...	...	16th
5386	16th	...	...	6th	5459	129th	...	...	38th
5387	17th	...	...	6th	5460	130th	...	...	38th
5388	18th	...	...	6th	5461	131st	...	...	38th
5389	19th	...	...	33rd	5462	132nd	...	...	39th
5390	20th	...	...	G.H.Q.	5463	133rd	...	...	39th
5391	24th	...	...	8th	5464	134th	...	...	39th
5392	25th	...	...	8th	5465	135th	...	...	40th
5393	26th	...	...	8th	5466	136th	...	...	40th
5394	27th	...	...	9th	5467	137th	...	...	40th
5395	28th	...	...	9th	5468	138th	...	...	41st
5396	33rd	...	...	11th	5469	139th	...	...	41st
5397	34th	...	...	11th	5470	140th	...	...	41st
5398	35th	...	...	11th	5471	141st	...	...	1st
5399	36th	...	...	12th	5472	142nd	...	...	3rd
5400	37th	...	...	12th	5473	148th (R.N.)	...	...	63rd
5401	38th	...	...	12th	5474	149th (R.N.)	...	...	63rd
5402	42nd	...	...	14th	5475	150th (R.N.)	...	...	63rd
5403	43rd	...	...	14th	7804	229th	...	...	74th
5404	44th	...	...	14th	7805	230th	...	...	74th
5405	45th	...	...	15th	7806	231st	...	...	74th
5406	46th	...	...	15th	5476	2/1st Highland	...	...	51st
5407	47th	...	...	15th	5477	1/2nd Highland	...	...	51st
5408	48th	...	...	87th	5478	1/3rd Highland	...	...	51st
5409	49th	...	...	87th	5479	2/1st Home Counties	...	...	58th
5410	50th	...	...	87th	5480	2/2nd Home Counties	...	...	58th
5411	51st	...	...	17th	5481	2/3rd Home Counties	...	...	58th
5412	52nd	...	...	17th	5482	1/4th London	...	...	47th
5413	53rd	...	...	17th	5483	1/5th London	...	...	47th
5414	54th	...	...	18th	5484	1/6th London	...	...	47th
5415	55th	...	...	18th	5485	2/1st London	...	...	56th
5416	56th	...	...	18th	5486	2/2nd London	...	...	56th
5417	57th	...	...	19th	5487	2/3rd London	...	...	56th
5418	58th	...	...	19th	5488	1/1st Northumbrian	...	...	50th
5419	59th	...	...	19th	5489	1/3rd Northumbrian	...	...	50th
5420	60th	...	...	20th	5490	2/2nd Northumbrian	...	...	50th
5421	61st	...	...	20th	5491	1/1st N. Midland	...	...	46th
5422	62nd	...	...	20th	5492	2/1st N. Midland	...	...	59th
5423	63rd	...	...	21st	5493	1/2nd N. Midland	...	...	46th
5424	64th	...	...	21st	5494	2/2nd N. Midland	...	...	59th
5425	65th	...	...	21st	5495	1/3rd N. Midland	...	...	46th
5426	72nd	...	...	24th	5496	2/3rd N. Midland	...	...	59th
5427	73rd	...	...	24th	5497	2/1st S. Midland	...	...	61st
5428	74th	...	...	24th	5498	2/2nd S. Midland	...	...	61st
5429	75th	...	...	25th	5499	2/3rd S. Midland	...	...	61st
5430	76th	...	...	25th	5500	1/1st W. Riding	...	...	49th
5431	77th	...	...	25th	5501	2/1st W. Riding	...	...	62nd
5432	87th	...	...	29th	5502	1/2nd W. Riding	...	...	49th

Index to Units—Medical—continued.

	Unit.	Division.		Unit.	Army.
	Field Ambulances—continued.			**Casualty Clearing Stations**—continued.	
5503	2/2nd W. Riding	62nd	5588	No. 22	1st
5504	1/3rd W. Riding	49th	5589	No. 23	1st
5505	2/3rd W. Riding	62nd	5590	No. 29	3rd
5506	2/1st Wessex	55th	5591	No. 30	1st
5507	2/2nd Wessex	57th		No. 32	5th
5508	2/3rd Wessex	57th	5593	No. 33	1st
5509	1/1st E. Lancs.	42nd		No. 34	3rd
5510	2/1st E. Lancs.	9th	5595	No. 36	2nd
5511	1/2nd E. Lancs.	42nd		No. 37	4th
5512	2/2nd E. Lancs.	66th		No. 38	3rd
5513	1/3rd E. Lancs.	42nd	5596	No. 41	4th
5514	2/3rd E. Lancs.	66th	5597	No. 42	1st
5515	1/3rd W. Lancs.	55th	5598	No. 43	3rd
5516	2/1st W. Lancs.	55th	5599	No. 44	2nd
5517	3/2nd W. Lancs.	57th	5600	No. 45	3rd
8095	1st Lowland	52nd	5601	No. 46	3rd
8096	2nd Lowland	52nd	5602	No. 47	4th
8097	3rd Lowland	52nd		No. 48	4th
5518	1st Aus.	1st Aus.	5604	No. 49	3rd
5519	2nd Aus.	1st Aus.		No. 50	4th
5520	3rd Aus.	1st Aus.	5606	No. 51	5th
5521	4th Aus.	4th Aus.	5607	No. 53	4th
5522	5th Aus.	2nd Aus.	5608	No. 54	5th
5523	6th Aus.	2nd Aus.	5609	No. 55	4th
5524	7th Aus.	2nd Aus.	5610	No. 56	3rd
5525	8th Aus.	5th Aus.	5611	No. 57	1st
5526	9th Aus.	3rd Aus.	5612	No. 58	4th
5527	10th Aus.	3rd Aus.	5613	No. 59	3rd
5528	11th Aus.	3rd Aus.	5614	No. 61	4th
5529	12th Aus.	4th Aus.	5615	No. 62	2nd
5530	13th Aus.	4th Aus.	5616	No. 63	5th
5531	14th Aus.	5th Aus.	5617	No. 64	2nd
5532	15th Aus.	5th Aus.	5619	1st Australian	5th
5533	1st Cdn.	1st Cdn.	5620	2nd Australian	5th
5534	2nd Cdn.	1st Cdn.	5621	3rd Australian	2nd
5535	3rd Cdn.	1st Cdn.	5622	1st Canadian	1st
5536	4th Cdn.	2nd Cdn.	5623	2nd Canadian	2nd
5537	5th Cdn.	2nd Cdn.	5624	3rd Canadian	3rd
5538	6th Cdn.	2nd Cdn.	5625	4th Canadian	1st
5539	8th Cdn.	3rd Cdn.		Lucknow	
5540	9th Cdn.	3rd Cdn.			
5541	10th Cdn.	3rd Cdn.		**MOBILE LABORATORIES.**	
5542	11th Cdn.	4th Cdn.			
5543	12th Cdn.	4th Cdn.	5633	No. 1	2nd
5544	13th Cdn.	4th Cdn.	5634	No. 2	1st
	14th Cdn.	4th Army	5635	No. 3	1st
5545	1st N. Zealand	N.Z.	5636	No. 4	2nd
5546	2nd N. Zealand	N.Z.	5637	No. 5 (Canadian)	4th
5547	3rd N. Zealand	N.Z.	5638	No. 6	1st
5548	4th N. Zealand	N.Z.	5639	No. 8	2nd
5549	S. African	66th	5640	No. 9	5th
			5641	No. 10	3rd
	CASUALTY CLEARING STATIONS.	Army.	5642	No. 11	2nd
			5643	No. 12	4th
5570	No. 1	1st	5644	No. 13	3rd
5571	No. 2	1st	5645	No. 16	5th
5572	No. 3	3rd	5646	No. 17	4th
5573	No. 4	3rd	5647	No. 18	3rd
5574	No. 5	4th	5648	No. 19	4th
5575	No. 6	1st	5649	No. 20	5th
5576	No. 7	1st	5650	No. 21	1st
5577	No. 8	2nd	5651	No. 22	
5578	No. 10	2nd	5652	No. 33	3rd
5579	No. 11	2nd		No. 39	5th
5580	No. 12	4th			
5581	No. 13	5th		**MOTOR AMBULANCE CONVOYS.**	
5582	No. 15	5th	5655	No. 1	G.H.Q.
5583	No. 17	2nd	5656	No. 2	2nd
5584	No. 18	3rd	5657	No. 3	4th
5585	No. 19	3rd	5658	No. 4	2nd
5586	No. 20	4th	5659	No. 5	2nd
5587	No. 21	3rd	5660	No. 6	3rd

Index to Units—Medical—continued.

	Unit.	Army.		Unit.	Army.
	Motor Ambulance Convoys— *continued.*			**SANITARY SECTIONS.**	
				1st (Ind. Force R.A.F.)	L. of C.
5661	No. 8	1st		2nd	L. of C.
5662	No. 10	4th		3rd	L. of C.
5663	No. 11	4th	5721	3A	L. of C.
5664	No. 12	5th	5722	4A	3rd
5665	No. 13	1st	5723	5A	L. of C.
5666	No. 14	2nd	5724	6A	L. of C.
5667	No. 15	3rd	5725	6th	5th
5668	No. 16	3rd	5726	8th	1st
5669	No. 20	2nd	5727	9th	4th
5670	No. 21	3rd	5728	10th	1st
5671	No. 22	5th	5729	11th	3rd
5672	No. 24	4th	5730	12th	Cav. Corps.
5673	No. 25	5th	5731	13th	2nd
5674	No. 27	3rd	5732	16th	4th
5675	No. 30	3rd	5733	17th	3rd
5676	No. 31	1st	5734	20th	3rd
5677	No. 37	4th	5735	21st	3rd
	No. 42	1st	5736	22nd	5th
	No. 43	5th	5737	23rd	4th
	No. 44	4th	5738	25th	2nd
5678	B.R.C.S. (F.A.N.Y.)	L. of C.		26th	L. of C.
				27th	L. of C.
	ADVANCED DEPOTS OF MEDICAL STORES.		5739	32nd	3rd
			5740	33rd	3rd
5681	No. 1	5th	5741	34th	5th
5682	No. 2	2nd	5742	35th	3rd
5683	No. 3	L. of C.	5743	37th	5th
5684	No. 11	2nd	5744	38th	3rd
5685	No. 12	1st	5745	40th	1st
5686	No. 13	4th	5746	41st	1st
5687	No. 14	4th	5747	42nd	2nd
5688	No. 15	3rd		44th	L. of C.
5689	No. 16	3rd	5748	45th	2nd
5691	No. 18	4th	5749	47th	2nd
5692	No. 19	1st	5750	48th	4th
5693	No. 31	5th	5751	49th	2nd
5694	No. 33	L. of C.	5752	50th	4th
5695	No. 34	3rd	5753	51st	3rd
5696	2nd Canadian	2nd	8098	52nd	5th
			5754	55th (Ind. Force R.A.F.)	L. of C.
	MOBILE X-RAY UNITS.		5755	56th	2nd
5698	No. 1	1st	6800	57th	5th
5699	No. 2	4th	5756	58th	4th
5700	No. 3	4th	5757	59th	4th
5701	No. 4	4th	5758	61st	4th
5702	No. 5	3rd	5759	62nd	3rd
5703	No. 6	1st	5760	63rd	1st
5704	No. 7	2nd	5761	66th	5th
5705	No. 8	3rd	5762	70th	3rd
	No. 13	5th	5763	71st	2nd
	No. 14	5th	5764	72nd	2nd
			5765	74th	3rd
	MOBILE DENTAL UNITS.		5766	76th	5th
5707	No. 1	3rd	5767	77th	4th
5708	No. 2	4th	5768	81st	2nd
5709	No. 3	1st	5769	82nd	2nd
5710	No. 4	2nd	5770	83rd	3rd
	No. 5	5th		87th	5th
			5771	109th	L. of C.
	STATIONARY HOSPITALS.		5772	111th	L. of C.
			5773	119th	2nd
5714	No. 1 (N. Zealand)		5774	120th	L. of C.
	No. 3 (Canadian)	2nd	5775	1st Aus.	4th
	No. 4		5776	2nd Aus.	4th
5716	No. 6		5777	3rd Aus.	4th
	No. 10	2nd	5778	4th Aus.	4th
5717	No. 12		5779	5th Aus.	4th
5718	No. 39	5th	5780	1st Cdn.	1st
7519	No. 41		5781	2nd Cdn.	1st
	B.R.C.S.		5782	3rd Cdn.	1st
			5783	4th Cdn.	1st

Index to Units—Medical—continued.

	Unit.	Army.		Unit.	Division.
	Sanitary Sections—*continued.*			**VETERINARY.**	
	5th Cdn.	1st			
5784	1st N.Z.	2nd		MOBILE VETERINARY SECTIONS.	
5785	1/1st London	L. of C.			
			5795	1st	1st Cav.
			5796	2nd	1st
	SANITARY SQUADS.		5797	3rd	2nd
	No. 1	2nd	5798	4th	4th
	No. 2	L. of C.		5th	5th
	No. 3	L. of C.	5799	6th	6th
	No. 4	L. of C.	5800	7th	2nd Cav.
	No. 5	G.H.Q.	5801	8th	2nd Cav.
	No. 6	1st	5802	9th	2nd Cav.
	No. 7	G.H.Q.	5803	10th	1st Cav.
	No. 8	1st	5804	11th	3rd
	No. 9	2nd	5805	13th	3rd Cav.
	No. 10	3rd	5806	14th	3rd Cav.
	No. 11	L. of C.	5807	15th	8th
	No. 12	L. of C.	5808	18th	29th
	No. 13	L. of C.	5809	19th	42nd
	No. 14	3rd	5811	21st	9th
	No. 15	4th	5812	22nd	11th
	No. 16	3rd	5813	23rd	12th
	No. 17	4th	5814	26th	14th
	No. 18	L. of C.	5815	27th	15th
	No. 19	L. of C.	5816	28th	37th
	No. 20	L. of C.	5817	29th	17th
	No. 21	L. of C.	5818	32nd	20th
	No. 22	L. of C.	5819	33rd	21st
	No. 23	3rd	5820	36th	24th
	No. 24	3rd	5821	37th	25th
	No. 25	L. of C.	5822	39th	1st Cav.
	No. 26	3rd	5823	40th	30th
	No. 27	3rd	5824	41st	31st
	No. 28	2nd	5825	42nd	32nd
	No. 29	2nd	5826	43rd	33rd
	No. 30	G.H.Q.	5827	44th	34th
	No. 31	L. of C.	5828	45th	35th
	No. 32	L. of C.	5829	46th	Guards
	No. 33	2nd	5830	47th	16th
	No. 34	1st	5831	48th	36th
	No. 35	5th	5832	49th	38th
	No. 36	L. of C.	5833	50th	39th
	No. 37	2nd	5834	51st	40th
	No. 38	2nd	5835	52nd	41st
	No. 39	2nd	5836	53rd	63rd
	No. 40	L. of C.	5837	57th	57th
	No. 41	2nd	5838	58th	58th
	No. 42	2nd	7812	59th	74th
	No. 43	L. of C.	5840	61st	61st
	No. 44	L. of C.	5841	1/1st London	56th
	No. 45	4th	5842	1/2nd London	47th
	No. 46	4th	5843	1/1st Highland	51st
	No. 47	4th	5844	1/1st Northumbrian	50th
	No. 48	4th	5845	1/1st N. Midland	46th
	No. 49	4th		2/1st N. Midland	59th
	No. 50	L. of C.	5846	1/1st E. Lanc.	66th
	No. 51	L. of C.	5847	1/1st W. Lanc.	55th
	No. 52	L. of C.	5848	1/1st W. Riding	49th
	No. 53	L. of C.	5849	2/1st W. Riding	62nd
	No. 54	L. of C.	8099	1/1st Lowland	52nd
	No. 55	L. of C.	5850	1st Aus.	1st Aus.
	No. 56	L. of C.	5851	2nd Aus.	2nd Aus.
	No. 57	L. of C.	5852	3rd Aus.	3rd Aus.
	No. 58	1st	5853	4th Aus.	4th Aus.
	No. 59	1st	5854	5th Aus.	5th Aus.
	No. 60	L. of C.	5855	1st Cdn.	1st Cdn.
	No. 61	L. of C.	5856	2nd Cdn.	2nd Cdn.
	No. 62	4th	5857	3rd Cdn.	3rd Cdn.
	No. 63	5th	5858	4th Cdn.	4th Cdn.
	No. 64	L. of C.	5859	"A" Cdn.	3rd Cav.
	No. 65	L. of C.	5860	1st N. Zealand	N.Z.

Index to Units—Medical—continued.

VETERINARY EVACUATING STATIONS.

	Army.
No. 1	5th
No. 2	2nd
No. 3	5th
No. 4	3rd
No. 5	3rd
No. 6	3rd
No. 7	2nd
No. 9	4th
No. 10	2nd

Veterinary Evacuating Stations—continued.

	Army.
No. 11	5th
No. 13	4th
No. 15	2nd
No. 17	3rd
No. 18	1st
No. 22	1st
Aus.	4th
Cdn.	1st

ORDNANCE.

	Unit.	Allotment.		Unit.	Allotment.
	ORDNANCE MOBILE WORKSHOPS (HEAVY).			**Ordnance Mobile Workshops (Light)**—continued.	
5868	No. 1	1st Army	5915	No. 23	XVII A.C.
5869	No. 2	5th Army	5916	No. 24	XIII A.C.
5870	No. 3	3rd Army	5917	No. 25	VI A.C.
5871	No. 4	2nd Army	5918	No. 26 Cdn. ...	Cdn. A.C.
5872	No. 5	4th Army	5919	No. 27	XVII A.C.
	ORDNANCE MOBILE WORKSHOPS (MEDIUM).		5920	No. 28	IV A.C.
			5921	No. 29	IX A.C.
5875	No. 1	IX A.C.	5922	No. 30	1st Army
5876	No. 2	IX A.C.	5923	No. 31	XI A.C.
5877	No. 3	X A.C.	5924	No. 32	VI A.C.
5878	No. 5	II A.C.	5925	No. 33	VIII A.C.
5879	No. 6	VI A.C.	5926	No. 44	VIII A.C.
5880	No. 7	IX A.C.	5927	No. 45	IV A.C.
5881	No. 8 Cdn. ...	Cdn. A.C.	5928	No. 46	V A.C.
5882	No. 9	XIX A.C.	5929	No. 47	Aus. A.C.
5883	No. 10	XIII A.C.	5930	No. 48	X A.C.
5884	No. 12	XV A.C.	5931	No. 53	IX A.C.
5885	No. 13	III A.C.	5932	No. 54	VI A.C.
5886	No. 14	V A.C.	5933	No. 55	XXII A.C.
5887	No. 15	I A.C.	5934	No. 56	XI A.C.
5888	No. 16	IV A.C.		No. 57	I A.C.
5889	No. 17	XVII A.C.		No. 62	XXII A.C.
5890	No. 18	XXII A.C.		**ORDNANCE AMMUNITION SECTIONS.**	
5891	No. 19	VIII A.C.			
5892	No. 20	XXII A.C.		Nos. 3 to 7, 12 to 16, 18, 19, 23 to 26, 57, 61, 72, 77, 78, 107, 108	1st Army
5893	No. 25	IX A.C.			
	ORDNANCE MOBILE WORKSHOPS (LIGHT).			Nos. 11, 56, 59, 60, 62 to 71, 73 to 75, 80 to 82, 84, 85, 88, 89	2nd Army
5896	No. 1	I A.C.			
5897	No. 2	XXII A.C.		Nos. 28 to 30, 32 to 54 ...	3rd Army
5898	No. 4	VIII A.C.		Nos. 31, 58, 79, 90 to 106 ...	4th Army
5899	No. 6	I A.C.		Nos. 1, 2, 8 to 10, 17, 20 to 22, 27, 55, 83, 86, 87, 109	5th Army
5900	No. 8 Cdn. ...	Cdn. A.C.			
5901	No. 9	II A.C.		No. 76	Ind.F., R.A.F.
5902	No. 10	II A.C.		**ORDNANCE GUN PARKS.**	
5903	No. 11	XIX A.C.			
5904	No. 12	XIX A.C.	5940	No. 1	1st Army
5905	No. 13	III A.C.		No. 2	2nd Army
5906	No. 14	XV A.C.	5941	No. 3	3rd Army
5907	No. 15	XIII A.C.	5942	No. 4	4th Army
5908	No. 16	XIII A.C.		No. 5	5th Army
5909	No. 17	IX A.C.		**OFFICERS' CLOTHING DEPOTS.**	
5910	No. 18	IX A.C.			
5911	No. 19	V A.C.	5945	No. 1	1st Army
5912	No. 20	IX A.C.	5946	No. 2	5th Army
5913	No. 21	XV A.C.	5947	No. 3	3rd Army
5914	No. 22	IX A.C.	5948	No. 4	2nd Army
				No. 5	4th Army

FORESTRY UNITS.

	Unit.	Allotment.		Unit.	Allotment.
	R.E. FORESTRY COS.			**R.E. Forestry Cos.**—cont.	
5951	361st	L. of C.	5957	367th	L. of C.
5952	362nd	5th Army	5958	368th	L. of C.
5953	363rd	L. of C.	5959	369th	L. of C.
5954	364th	4th Army	5960	370th	L. of C.
5955	365th	1st Army	5961	371st	L. of C.
5956	366th	L. of C.			

Index to Units—Forestry—continued.

	Unit.	Allotment.		Unit.	Allotment.
	CANADIAN FORESTRY COS.			Canadian Forestry Cos.—cont.	
	1st	L. of C.	5987	42nd	L. of C.
	2nd	1st Army.	5988	43rd	L. of C.
	9th	L. of C.	5989	44th	L. of C.
	10th	L. of C.	5990	45th	L. of C.
	11th	L. of C.	5991	46th	L. of C.
	12th	L. of C.	5992	47th	L. of C.
	13th	L. of C.	5993	48th	L. of C.
5962	14th	L. of C.	5994	49th	L. of C.
5963	15th	L. of C.	5995	50th	L. of C.
5964	19th	L. of C.	5996	51st	L. of C.
5965	20th	L. of C.	5997	52nd	L. of C.
5966	21st	L. of C.	5998	53rd	L. of C.
5967	22nd	L. of C.	5999	54th	L. of C.
5968	23rd	L. of C.	6000	55th	L. of C.
5969	24th	L. of C.	6001	56th	L. of C.
5970	25th	3rd Army.	6002	57th	L. of C.
5971	26th	L. of C.	6003	58th	L. of C.
5972	27th	L. of C.	6004	59th	L. of C.
5973	28th	L. of C.	6005	60th	L. of C.
5974	29th	3rd Army.	6006	69th	L. of C.
5975	30th	L. of C.	6007	70th	L. of C.
5976	31st	L. of C.	6008	71st	L. of C.
5977	32nd	L. of C.	6009	72nd	L. of C.
5978	33rd	L. of C.	6010	73rd	L. of C.
5979	34th	L. of C.	6011	74th	L. of C.
5980	35th	4th Army.	6012	75th	L. of C.
5981	36th	L. of C.	6013	76th	L. of C.
5982	37th	L. of C.	6014	77th	L. of C.
5983	38th	L. of C.	6015	78th	L. of C.
5984	39th	L. of C.	6016	79th	L. of C.
5985	40th	L. of C.	6017	80th	L. of C.
5986	41st	L. of C.			

LABOUR CORPS.

	Unit.	Army.		Unit.	Army.
	LABOUR GROUP HEAD-QUARTERS.			Labour Group Headquarters—cont.	
				44th	L. of C.
	1st	L. of C.		45th	3rd
	2nd	L. of C.		46th	3rd
	3rd	L. of C.		47th	4th
	4th	L. of C.		48th	3rd
6082	5th	2nd		50th Ind. Force	L. of C.
	6th	L. of C.		51st	3rd
	7th	L. of C.		52nd	3rd
	8th	4th		53rd	4th
	9th	L. of C.		55th	1st
	10th	L. of C.		57th	3rd
	11th	L. of C.		58th	5th
	12th	4th		59th	2nd
	13th	L. of C.		60th	L. of C.
	14th	L. of C.		61st	4th
	15th	L. of C.		62nd	3rd
	16th	4th		63rd	4th
	17th	3rd		64th	L. of C.
	18th	4th		65th	2nd
	19th	L. of C.		66th	2nd
	20th	L. of C.		67th	4th
	21st	1st		68th	5th
	22nd	1st		69th	5th
	23rd	1st		70th	3rd
	24th	5th		71st	1st
	25th	5th		72nd	L. of C.
	26th	3rd		73rd	L. of C.
	27th	L. of C.		74th	L. of C.
	28th	2nd		75th	2nd
	29th	1st		76th	L. of C.
	30th	2nd		78th	L. of C.
	31st	2nd		79th	L. of C.
	32nd	2nd		80th	5th
6137	33rd	2nd		81st	2nd
	34th	3rd		82nd	2nd
	35th	4th		83rd	L. of C.
	36th	5th		84th	4th
	37th	3rd		85th	4th
	38th	2nd		86th	4th
	39th	L. of C.		87th	2nd
	40th	L. of C.		88th	1st
	43rd	2nd		Canadian	1st

Index to Units—Labour Corps—continued.

LABOUR COMPANIES.

	Unit.	Army.		Unit.	Army.
	1st	5th		74th	4th
	2nd	1st		75th	3rd
6083	3rd	1st		76th	3rd
	4th	2nd		77th	5th
	5th	2nd		78th	3rd
6084	6th	2nd		79th	3rd
	7th	4th		80th	1st
	8th	2nd		81st	4th
	9th	3rd		82nd	4th
6165	10th	2nd		83rd	4th
	11th	3rd		84th	2nd
6085	12th	4th		85th	4th
6086	13th	3rd		86th	4th
	14th	4th		87th Ind. Force	L. of C.
	15th	4th		88th	4th
	16th	4th		89th	1st
6138	17th	5th		90th	4th
	18th	1st		91st	2nd
	19th	2nd	6167	92nd	2nd
6135	20th	1st		93rd	2nd
	21st	4th	6122	94th	2nd
	22nd	5th		99th	5th
	23rd	3rd		100th	5th
	24th	3rd		101st	3rd
	25th	2nd		102nd	5th
	26th	2nd		103rd	4th
	27th	3rd		104th	3rd
	28th	4th		105th	4th
	29th	5th		106th	3rd
	30th	5th		107th	4th
	31st	2nd		108th	1st
	32nd	3rd		109th	5th
	33rd	4th		110th	4th
	34th	4th	6123	111th	2nd
	35th	3rd		112th	1st
	36th	3rd		113th	3rd
	37th	1st		114th	4th
	38th	2nd		115th	3rd
	39th	1st		116th	5th
	40th	2nd		117th	3rd
	41st	3rd		118th	5th
	42nd	3rd		119th	3rd
	43rd	2nd		120th	3rd
	44th	4th		121st	2nd
	45th	1st		122nd	5th
	46th	2nd		123rd	5th
	47th	1st		124th	5th
6087	48th	2nd		125th	3rd
	49th	4th		126th	2nd
	50th	1st		127th	1st
	51st	1st		128th	3rd
	52nd	2nd	6136	129th	1st
6139	53rd	2nd		130th	2nd
	54th	1st		131st	4th
	55th	1st	6124	132nd	3rd
	56th	5th		133rd	2nd
	57th	5th		134th	2nd
	58th	2nd		135th	1st
	59th	4th	6128	136th	1st
	60th	3rd		137th	1st
6121	61st	2nd	6166	138th	3rd
	62nd	3rd		139th	2nd
	63rd	5th		140th	2nd
	64th	5th		141st	5th
	65th	4th		142nd	3rd
	66th	5th		143rd	2nd
	67th	3rd		144th	2nd
6140	68th	2nd		145th	L. of C.
	69th	3rd		146th	3rd
	70th	2nd		147th	2nd
	71st	5th		148th	3rd
	72nd	4th		149th	5th
	73rd	2nd		150th	4th

Index to Units—Labour Corps—continued.

	Unit.	Army.		Unit.	Army.
	Labour Companies—*continued.*			**Labour Companies**—*continued.*	
6127	151st	2nd		727th	4th
	152nd	1st		728th	2nd
	153rd	3rd		729th	4th
	154th	2nd		730th	L. of C.
	155th	3rd		731st	3rd
	156th	4th		732nd	L. of C.
	157th	3rd		733rd	1st
	158th	2nd		734th	L. of C.
	159th	1st		735th	1st
	160th	4th		990th	L. of C.
	161st	3rd		991st	L. of C.
	162nd	5th		1001st	1st
	163rd	1st		1002nd	2nd
6125	164th	1st		1021st	3rd
	165th	L. of C.			
	166th	3rd			
	167th	3rd			
	168th	4th		Unit.	Division.
	169th	1st			
	170th	1st		**DIVISIONAL EMPLOYMENT COMPANIES.**	
	171st	4th			
	172nd	2nd			
	173rd	4th	6355	Guards	Guards
6126	174th	2nd	6401	63rd	63rd
	175th	4th	6356	204th	1st
	176th	5th	6357	205th	2nd
	177th	4th	6358	206th	3rd
	178th	5th	6359	207th	4th
	179th	5th		208th	5th
	180th	1st	6360	209th	6th
	181st	1st	6361	211th	8th
	182nd	1st	6362	212th	9th
	183rd	1st	6363	213th	11th
	184th	2nd	6364	214th	12th
	185th	2nd	6365	215th	14th
	186th	5th	6366	216th	15th
	187th	4th	6367	217th	16th
	188th	2nd	6368	218th	17th
	189th	3rd	6369	219th	18th
	190th	3rd	6370	220th	19th
	191st	4th	6371	221st	20th
	192nd	1st	6372	222nd	21st
	193rd	4th	6373	224th	24th
	194th	5th	6374	225th	25th
	195th	1st	6375	226th	29th
	197th	2nd	6376	227th	30th
	198th	5th	6377	228th	31st
	199th	4th	6378	229th	32nd
	200th	3rd	6379	230th	33rd
	700th	3rd	6380	231st	34th
	701st	3rd	6381	232nd	35th
	702nd	3rd	6382	233rd	36th
	703rd	2nd	6383	234th	37th
	704th	1st	6384	235th	38th
	705th	4th	6385	236th	39th
	706th	4th	6386	237th	40th
	707th	3rd	6387	238th	41st
	708th	4th	6388	239th	42nd
	709th	4th	6389	240th	46th
	710th	3rd	6390	241st	47th
	712th	1st	6391	243rd	49th
	713th	4th	6392	244th	50th
	714th	4th	6393	245th	51st
	715th	5th	6394	246th	55th
	716th	L. of C.	6395	247th	56th
	717th	3rd	6396	248th	57th
	718th	1st	6397	249th	58th
	719th	2nd	6398	250th	59th
	720th	L. of C.	6399	251st	61st
	721st	5th	6400	252nd	62nd
	722nd	4th	6402	254th	66th
	723rd	1st	6403	771st	1st Cav.
	724th	4th	6404	772nd	2nd Cav.
	725th	5th	6405	773rd	3rd Cav.
	726th	L. of C.	8100	984th	52nd

Index to Units—Labour Corps—continued.

	Unit.	Allotment.		Unit.	Allotment.
	Divisional Employment Companies—continued.			**AREA EMPLOYMENT COMPANIES.**	
7813	985th	74th	6496	255th	1st Army
6406	1st Cdn.	1st Cdn.	6497	256th	1st Army
6407	2nd Cdn.	2nd Cdn.		257th	2nd Army
6408	3rd Cdn.	3rd Cdn.	6498	258th	3rd Army
6409	4th Cdn.	4th Cdn.		259th	4th Army
	AREA EMPLOYMENT (ARTIZAN) COMPANIES.		6500	260th	5th Army
			6501	261st	I A.C.
			6502	262nd	II A.C.
6421	780th	2nd Army	6503	263rd	III A.C.
6422	781st	L. of C.	6504	264th	IV A.C.
6423	782nd	5th Army	6505	265th	V A.C.
6424	828th	L. of C.	6506	266th	VI A.C.
6425	829th	L. of C.	6507	267th	XXII A.C.
6426	830th	L. of C.		268th	4th Army
6427	834th	3rd Army	6509	269th	IX A.C.
	849th	L. of C.	6510	270th	X A.C.
6428	889th	L. of C.		271st	XI A.C.
6430	927th	3rd Army	6511	272nd	XIII A.C.
6431	928th	1st Army	6512	274th	XV A.C.
6432	929th	1st Army	6513	275th	XVII A.C.
6433	936th	L. of C.	6514	276th	VIII A.C.
6434	937th	4th Army	6515	277th	XIX A.C.
6435	938th	L. of C.	6516	278th	1st Army
6436	939th	L. of C.	6517	279th	3rd Army
6437	940th	L. of C.	6518	280th	3rd Army
6438	941st	L. of C.	6519	281st	4th Army
6439	942nd	L. of C.	6520	282nd	4th Army
6440	943rd	L. of C.	6521	283rd	3rd Army
6441	944th	L. of C.	6522	284th	3rd Army
6442	945th	L. of C.	6523	285th	4th Army
			6524	286th	1st Army
	AGRICULTURAL COMPANIES.		6525	287th	3rd Army
			6526	288th	3rd Army
996		L. of C.	6527	289th	3rd Army
1037		1st Army	6528	290th	3rd Army
1038		2nd Army	6529	291st	3rd Army
1039		3rd Army	6530	292nd	4th Army
1040		5th Army	6531	293rd	3rd Army
1041		4th Army	6532	294th	3rd Army
1042		4th Army	6533	736th	5th Army
			6534	737th	1st Army
			6535	738th	2nd Army
			6536	739th	5th Army
			6537	740th	3rd Army
			6538	741st	3rd Army
			6539	742nd	2nd Army
			6540	743rd	4th Army
			6541	744th	2nd Army
			6542	745th	L. of C.
			6543	746th	2nd Army
			6544	747th	3rd Army
			6545	748th	2nd Army
			6546	749th	2nd Army
			6547	750th	2nd Army
			6548	751st	2nd Army
			6549	752nd	2nd Army
			6550	753rd	2nd Army

Index to Units—Labour Corps—continued.

	Unit.	Allotment.		Unit.	Allotment.
	Area Employment Companies— *continued.*			**Area Employment Companies—** *continued.*	
6551	754th	L. of C.	6607	847th	L. of C.
6552	755th	1st Army	6608	850th	L. of C.
6553	756th	1st Army	6609	851st	L. of C.
6554	757th	4th Army	6610	854th	L. of C.
6555	758th	4th Army	6611	855th	L. of C.
6557	759th	2nd Army	6612	856th	L. of C.
6558	760th	2nd Army	6613	857th	L. of C.
6559	761st	2nd Army	6614	858th	L. of C.
6560	762nd	5th Army	6615	859th	L. of C.
6561	763rd	2nd Army	6616	860th	L. of C.
6562	764th	2nd Army	6617	861st	L. of C.
6563	765th	G.H.Q.	6618	862nd	L. of C.
6564	766th	G.H.Q.	6619	870th	L. of C.
6565	767th	G.H.Q.	6620	871st	L. of C.
6566	768th	L. of C.	6621	876th	4th Army
6567	769th	L. of C.	6622	877th	L. of C.
6568	770th	Cav. Corps	6623	883rd	L. of C.
6569	774th	3rd Army	6624	884th	L. of C.
6570	775th	L. of C.	6625	885th	L. of C.
6571	776th	4th Army	6626	886th	L. of C.
6572	777th	5th Army	6627	887th	L. of C.
6573	778th	4th Army	6628	888th	L. of C.
6574	779th	L. of C.	6629	890th	L. of C.
6575	783rd	L. of C.	6630	891st	L. of C.
6576	784th	L. of C.	6631	892nd	L. of C.
6577	787th	L. of C.	6632	895th	L. of C.
6578	788th	L. of C.	6633	897th	L. of C.
6579	789th	L. of C.	6634	898th	L. of C.
6580	794th	L. of C.	6635	899th	L. of C.
6581	795th	L. of C.	6636	900th	L. of C.
6582	796th	L. of C.	6637	901st	L. of C.
6583	797th	L. of C.	6638	902nd	L. of C.
6584	798th	L. of C.	6639	903rd	L. of C.
6585	799th	L. of C.	6640	904th	L. of C.
6586	821st	5th Army	6641	905th	L. of C.
6587	822nd	5th Army	6642	911th	2nd Army
6588	823rd	5th Army	6643	9?0th	L. of C.
6589	824th	2nd Army	6644	916th	5th Army
6590	825th	2nd Army		917th	1st Army
6591	826th	1st Army	6645	918th	G.H.Q.
6592	827th	1st Army	6646	919th	G.H.Q.
6593	832nd	5th Army		992nd	L. of C.
6594	833rd	L. of C.		993rd	L. of C.
6595	835th	L. of C.		994th	5th Army
6596	836th	L. of C.		995th	4th Army
6597	837th	L. of C.		1013rd	G.H.Q.
6598	838th	L. of C.	6647	5th Cdn.	Cdn. A.C.
6599	839th	L. of C.	6648	6th Cdn.	Cdn. A.C.
6602	842nd	L. of C.	6649	7th Cdn.	Cdn. A.C.
6604	844th	L. of C.	6650	8th Cdn.	Cdn. A.C.
6606	846th	L. of C.		9th Cdn.	Cdn. A.C.

INDIAN LABOUR CORPS.

Unit.	Allotment.		Unit.	Allotment.
Companies—				
33rd (Bihar)	L. of C.			
55th (United Provinces)	L. of C.			
78th (Burma)	L. of C.			
79th (United Provinces)	L. of C.			
80th (Santal)	L. of C.			
82nd (United Provinces)	L. of C.			
84th (Garo)	L. of C.			
85th (Kumaon)	L. of C.			

Index to Units—Labour Corps—continued.

CHINESE LABOUR CORPS.

Unit	Allotment	Unit	Allotment
Headquarters	L. of C.	52nd	L. of C.
COMPANIES—		53rd	L. of C.
1st	2nd Army	54th	L. of C.
2nd	2nd Army	55th	4th Army
3rd	2nd Army	56th	L. of C.
4th	L. of C.	57th	L. of C.
5th	L. of C.	58th	1st Army
6th	L. of C.	59th	3rd Army
7th	3rd Army	60th	2nd Army
8th	4th Army	61st	2nd Army
9th	L. of C.	62nd	L. of C.
10th	L. of C.	63rd	L. of C.
11th	L. of C.	64th	L. of C.
12th	L. of C.	65th	L. of C.
13th	L. of C.	66th	L. of C.
14th	L. of C.	67th	2nd Army
15th	L. of C.	68th	L. of C.
16th	L. of C.	69th	L. of C.
17th	L. of C.	70th	L. of C.
18th	L. of C.	71st	L. of C.
19th	L. of C.	72nd	L. of C.
20th	L. of C.	73rd	1st Army
21st	L. of C.	74th	2nd Army
22nd	L. of C.	75th	L. of C.
23rd	3rd Army	76th	4th Army
24th	L. of C.	77th	L. of C.
25th	L. of C.	78th	2nd Army
26th	5th Army	79th	4th Army
27th	L. of C.	80th	1st Army
28th	L. of C.	81st	L. of C.
29th	L. of C.	82nd	L. of C.
30th	L. of C.	83rd	5th Army
31st	2nd Army	84th	1st Army
32nd	5th Army	85th	2nd Army
33rd	L. of C.	86th	1st Army
34th	L. of C.	87th	L. of C.
35th	L. of C.	88th	L. of C.
36th	L. of C.	89th	L. of C.
37th	L. of C.	90th	4th Army
38th	L. of C.	91st	L. of C.
39th	2nd Army	92nd	L. of C.
40th	2nd Army	93rd	L. of C.
41st	L. of C.	94th	L. of C.
42nd	1st Army	95th	L. of C.
43rd	1st Army	96th	L. of C.
44th	L. of C.	97th	L. of C.
45th	2nd Army	98th	L. of C.
46th	5th Army	99th	1st Army
47th	2nd Army	100th	L. of C.
48th	L. of C.	101st	2nd Army
49th	L. of C.	102nd	4th Army
50th	L. of C.	103rd	L. of C.
51st	L. of C.	104th	3rd Army

Index to Units—Labour Corps—continued.

CHINESE LABOUR CORPS—continued.

Unit.	Allotment.	Unit.	Allotment.
105th	L. of C.	164th	4th Army
106th	L. of C.	165th	4th Army
107th	5th Army	166th	4th Army
108th	2nd Army	167th	1st Army
109th	L. of C.	168th	L. of C.
110th	L. of C.	169th	L. of C.
111th	L. of C.	170th	L. of C.
112th	L. of C.	171st	L. of C.
113th	5th Army	172nd	2nd Army
114th	1st Army	173rd	L. of C.
115th	4th Army	174th	3rd Army
116th	4th Army	175th	L. of C.
117th	5th Army	176th	L. of C.
118th	1st Army	177th	L. of C.
119th	2nd Army	178th	L. of C.
120th	L. of C.	179th	L. of C.
121st	1st Army	180th	L. of C.
122nd	1st Army	181st	L. of C.
123rd	4th Army	182nd	4th Army
124th	L. of C.	183rd	L. of C.
125th	L. of C.	184th	L. of C.
126th	3rd Army	185th	1st Army
127th	L. of C.	186th	L. of C.
128th	L. of C.	187th	L. of C.
129th	L. of C.	188th	3rd Army
130th	2nd Army	189th	3rd Army
131st	1st Army	190th	3rd Army
132nd	L. of C.	191st	L. of C.
133rd	L. of C.	192nd	L. of C.
134th	L. of C.	193rd	3rd Army
135th	L. of C.	194th	L. of C.
136th	L. of C.	195th	L. of C.
137th	L. of C.		
138th	L. of C.		
139th	2nd Army		
140th	3rd Army		
141st	L. of C.		
142nd	L. of C.		
143rd	L. of C.		
144th	L. of C.		
145th	L. of C.		
146th	4th Army		
147th	1st Army		
148th	L. of C.		
149th	L. of C.		
150th	4th Army		
151st	L. of C.		
152nd	L. of C.		
153rd	L. of C.		
154th	L. of C.		
155th	L. of C.		
156th	L. of C.		
157th	3rd Army		
158th	L. of C.		
159th	L. of C.		
160th	L. of C.		
161st	5th Army		
162nd	1st Army		
163rd	L. of C.		

www.ingramcontent.com/pod-product-compliance
Lightning Source LLC
Chambersburg PA
CBHW082014220426
43670CB00015B/2625